A DIFFERENT CALL

A DIFFERENT CALL

Women's Ministries in the Episcopal Church, 1850–1920

MARY SUDMAN DONOVAN

MOREHOUSE-BARLOW
Wilton, CT   1986

Morehouse Barlow Co., Inc.
78 Danbury Road
Wilton, Connecticut 06897

Library of Congress Cataloging-in-Publication Data

Donovan, Mary S.
    A different call.

    Bibliography: p.
    1. Women in church work—Episcopal Church.
2. Episcopal Church—History.   3. Anglican Communion—
History.   I. Title.
BX5968.D63   1986   283'.3   86–18032
ISBN 0–8192–1396–9

Printed in the United States of America

10   9   8   7   6   5   4   3   2   1

For
MARION KIRK DONOVAN
who answers her own call to ministry
with extraordinary grace and love

Contents

Acknowledgments

Tracing the elusive women and the ministries they developed within the nineteenth century Episcopal Church has not been an easy task, partly because the church has generally failed to regard materials about women's work as worthy of preservation and partly because the women themselves saw humility and self-effacement as essential characteristics of Christian service. They sought no public approbation for their efforts and often wrote about specific projects with absolutely no mention of the women who organized and directed such works. Other writers have followed this lead. Parish historians, for example, often list the names of rectors, assistants, wardens, vestrymen and even sextons but completely exclude the names of the Woman's Auxiliary presidents or Altar Guild officers. Documents from women's organizations or the institutions founded and directed by women are rarely preserved in church archives or libraries. Churchwomen's autobiographies are very few in number when compared to the vast collection of clergymen's memoirs.

However, this very scarcity of obvious sources has forced me to discover my dependence on the marvelous company of church archivists and librarians who serve this institution with dedication and skill. Early in my research at the Bishop Sherrill Resource Center at the Episcopal Church Headquarters, I asked librarian Avis Harvey about a name that kept appearing in my research—Mrs. A.T. Twing. "Oh, yes," said Avis, "I think she was the sister of Julia Emery who directed the Woman's Auxiliary for over forty years." And with that remark,

Avis opened up a whole new phase in my understanding of the work of those two women. Again and again I have had that kind of experience and I cannot understate my gratitude for such assistance. At the Archives of the Episcopal Church, Nelle Bellamy's historical insight as well as her knowledge of Episcopal Church structures supported my work while Elinor Hearn always knew just one more place to look for a particular piece of information. Avis Harvey and Betsy Rodenmeyer, from their years as women church workers, shared both information and critical issues to consider. Judith Johnson was an amazing guide through the Archives of the Diocese of New York; as she was putting that collection into more useable order, she kept mental notes for me about unexpected sources for women's activities. Several other church archivists were particularly helpful: Phyllis Barr at Trinity Parish, New York; Scarlett S. Emerson at the Archives of the Diocese of Pennsylvania; Gertrude F. Mignery at the Jessie Ball DuPont Library in Sewanee, Tennessee; Mark J. Duffey at the Archives of the Diocese of Massachusetts and F. Garner Ranney, Historiographer of the Diocese of Maryland.

I am grateful to several sisterhoods for allowing me to visit their libraries and for the assistance of Sister Mary Jean, Sister Mary Angela and Sister Kiara of the Community of St. Mary; Mother Margaret Helena at the Convent of St. John Baptist; Mother Anne Marie of the Society of St. Margaret in Boston; and the Reverend Columba Gilliss of the Order of St. Helena. Ruth S. Leonard, Archivist of the Society of the Companions of the Holy Cross, shared freely her wealth of experience and knowledge about the Companions. The painstaking work of Madeline Dunlap, Sandra H. Boyd and Kathryn Piccard in the Episcopal Deaconess History Research Project has made my study of the deaconess movement much easier.

Walter P. Metzger, my teacher and adviser at Columbia University, helped me shape the research data into a coherent presentation with his penetrating questions and demand for intellectual accuracy. The interest in women's history from such church historians as Fredrica Harris Thompsett, John Booty, Roland Foster, Frank Sugeno and John Woolverton has been an important source of encouragement for me and I am grateful for their advice and counsel. And from my colleagues in the formation of the Episcopal Women's History Project—Joanna B. Gillespie, Margaret R. Woolverton, Miriam Anne Bourne, Salome Breck, Catherine McFarland, Betty Gray, Hilah F. Thomas, Joyce M. Howard and Cynthia McLean—I have drawn strength in the joy of our shared conviction that the history of women in the Episcopal Church must be recovered. This list would be incomplete without reference to my conversations with Dorothy Lyford and Violet Emery, nieces of Mary Abbot and Julia Emery, who introduced me to the astounding talents of the Emery family. Although both Dorothy and Violet died before this book appeared, their spirit is alive in the story it conveys.

Above all, I have depended upon the support and encouragement of my husband, Herbert. His interest in the stories of women church workers was inbred; his mother, Marion, served as a missionary nurse in Liberia where she met the young clergyman who later became his father. But Herbert's deep love for this imprecise institution, the Episcopal Church, and his astounding recall of the men and women who have served and are serving in Christ's name, have provided me with both inspiration and information. Our children, Mary Ellen, Herbert Alcorn, and Jane Elizabeth, have added spice and reality to the story, for they demand that the church and its history be relevant to their world.

A DIFFERENT CALL

CHAPTER ONE

The Woman's Sphere

> The Woman's Work of the Church is womanly work. It asks no great things for itself—no place, no power, no temporal rewards, nor honors; only the opportunity to do more and better work each year, sheltered by the Church's protecting care, governed by the Church's laws, ministered to by the Church's sacraments and teaching.
>
> It asks of the Board of Missions, as the Church's representative in missionary work, to point out its mistakes in the present, and to direct its labors in the future; and to help it in time to come, as in time gone by, to keep steadfast upon those Churchly lines on which, through the wisdom of the Board, it has been founded, and to which it will be the wisdom of the Board to see that it remains forever true.[1]

With these words, Mary Abbot Twing outlined her concept of women's work in the Episcopal Church of 1895. Twing's rhetoric is typical of that of her generation of churchwomen—humble, pious, subservient, asking no rewards for self, and content in all areas to follow the directives of the Board of Missions (a body made up of bishops, clergymen, and laymen—no women). In many ways, Twing herself was the quintessential Episcopal churchwoman. Daughter of a New England sea captain and a pious mother of Puritan ancestry, she was raised in a family that exalted the virtues of piety, dedication, self-sacrifice, discipline, and hard work. Because economic necessity dictated that the daughters (she had seven sisters and only three brothers) contribute to the family income, Mary Abbot and her sisters followed the traditional pursuits of teaching and writing, producing bland children's stories of virtue rewarded and vice punished. As a young woman, she worked primarily from the family home in Boston, and throughout her life she retained close ties and regular correspondence with each family member. Mary Abbot worked briefly for the Episcopal Church's Board of Missions in New York City but dutifully resigned when she married a coworker, the Reverend Doctor A.T. Twing. As the wife of a prominent clergyman, she entered the elaborate social world of New York City's upper class, her days occupied with visiting and entertainment, charitable work, and church services and meetings. When Dr. Twing died, she donned widow's weeds, moved back with her sisters, and continued to lead the life of a New York City matron. Pious, soft-spoken, courteous, Mary Abbot Emery Twing appeared to be the epitome of the Victorian lady.[2]

And yet, Twing's gentle exterior belied a perceptive, analytical mind, and her orderly and disciplined habits enabled her to become an extraordinary administrator. Her piety produced a steadfast devotion to a cause—that of extending the gospel of Jesus Christ to all people, everywhere. Her reading of the Bible diminished in her view the importance of class distinctions and enabled her to relate to, and work with, people from diverse social and economic classes. And her daring and love of adventure (perhaps acquired from her seafaring father) enabled her to traverse the world, learning from and teaching people of many nations.

During the period from 1872 to 1876, when she worked for the Board of Missions of the Episcopal Church, Twing established and served as national secretary for the Woman's Auxiliary to the board. She set up the organizational patterns that would be followed for the next fifty years. She traveled and spoke and encouraged local parishes to organize chapters of the Woman's Auxiliary. She met with women working in all phases of Church work and inspired others to seek it. Consulting with bishops and clergy, she arranged inspirational and educational conferences for auxiliary members. And when she relinquished her job as secretary, she continued to function in an advisory capacity, using her new-found freedom to become *the* major theoretician of women's work in the Church, lobbying for ecclesiastical legislation that would authenticate such work and pressing for better methods of education and recruitment of women workers. She traveled twice around the world, meeting with women workers in remote mission stations as well as in the cities, and made seven journeys through the American West. Friend of bishops, priests, and lay leaders, welcome in the parlors of the Vanderbilts and the Astors in New York, the Saltonstalls in Massachusetts, and the Biddles in Pennsylvania, and also remembered with affection by Sioux Indians in South Dakota and Chinese Bible Women in Hankow, Mary Abbot Emery Twing led an extraordinary life.

Although Twing was an unusual churchwoman, her life expressed the contradictions common to most of the early women workers in the Episcopal Church. Though their mien was self-effacing and subservient, their actions were courageous and innovative. While deferring to authority, they generally managed to get their way. They claimed no credit for institutional change, yet because of their activities the Church in 1920 was a very different institution than that of 1850. Partly because they claimed no credit and partly because Church leaders have rarely sought to analyze the process of change, the effect of women's work on the Church's ministry has generally been overlooked by Episcopal historians.

DENOMINATIONAL HISTORIES

Historians have only recently begun to study the history of women's work in religious denominations. Though some general themes emerge, the present work indicates there were important differences between the experiences of women in various denominations. For example, Rosemary Ruether and Eleanor McLaughlin, in their analysis of the circumstances that favor women's religious leadership, contended that women have claimed religious leadership on the basis of charisma or spiritual gifts and have tended to be closed out of power when institutionalization takes place.[3] But Theressa Hoover, in her inquiry into the role of women in the United Methodist Church, found that though the United Methodist Women became a powerful organization in the Church, its leaders rarely based their leadership on "gifts of the Spirit" or a unique vision of the gospel. "Instead they were inspired to meet the combined evangelical, physical, and social needs of marginal people—especially women and children, who could not be reached by male missionaries abroad and who were ignored by church and society at home," wrote Hoover, pointing to a pattern very similar to that which I have found in the Episcopal Church.[4] In the Methodist Church, however, the women from the beginning established a separate missionary organization over which they maintained political control—an organization that continues today. But the

Episcopal women's group was organized as an auxiliary to the all-male Board of Missions that exercised political control over the auxiliary's work.

Still another pattern emerged in the Presbyterian Church, U.S.A. A separate women's group, which controlled its own finances and recruited and deployed women missionaries, was merged with the existing denominational mission program in 1922. Though Elizabeth Howell Verdesi contended that the primary reason for the merger was the need "to eliminate overlapping programs, to streamline projects, and to manage resources efficiently," she did not question whether abolishing the women's organization was the best way to accomplish those goals. Her evidence—of the resulting drop in women's missionary giving—seems to point toward another conclusion.[5]

In her study of the Southern Baptist Church, Helen Emery Falls described the significant mission-support work done by the Women's Missionary Union, which also retained control of its own missionary program.[6] Harry Leon McBeth has analyzed the process through which women finally were accorded the right to serve as delegates to the Southern Baptist Convention in 1918. He contended that in the denomination women "helped shape Baptist patterns of Sunday School, higher education, stewardship, local church programs, and church staff patterns." Not until 1964, however, was a woman ordained to ministry in a Southern Baptist Church. Since then, there has been considerable internal controversy about the role of women, many women as well as men advocating a submissive role.[7]

One area that has been virtually ignored by historians is the role of women in the Roman Catholic Church in the United States. Aside from official histories of various religious orders and biographies of a few outstanding individuals, little work has been done.[8] One of the few exceptions is Mary J. Oates's study of Catholic sisters in Massachusetts. It outlined the extent to which the sisters' labor subsidized the parochial-school structure and detailed the general disregard of the sisters' welfare that characterized Church policy.[9] Her conclusions are important and suggest areas for further study. Why was it, for example, that the sisters did not protest as their working conditions gradually deteriorated? How do women ever obtain power from a traditional masculine hierarchy? The latter question is particularly important for Episcopal women, for they too have had to deal with an entrenched male hierarchy. In an intriguing article, James Kenneally suggested the pervasive power of the images of women as

"Mary" (Virgin Mother) or "Eve" (evil seductress) in shaping both the Catholic hierarchy's attitude toward women and the women's views of themselves.[10] His analysis points to a significant distinction between Catholic and Episcopal women, for in the Episcopal Church the image of Mary never received the veneration it had in the Roman Catholic Church. Thus, Episcopal women were free to choose from a wide variety of role models and were not as locked into the "domestic motherhood" image as were their Catholic sisters.

The history of women's work within the Episcopal Church is unique because it encompasses both Protestant and Catholic traditions and practices. Some Episcopal women exercised their call to ministry by founding religious orders like those in the Roman Catholic Church; others founded Bible and missionary societies based on Baptist or Methodist models. They even invented some forms—the Protestant sisterhoods, for example—that combined both traditions. For these reasons, individual Episcopal churchwomen could choose from a broader range of activities than in most other denominations. This latitude, however, did tend to diffuse energy, making it impossible for one single organization or form of ministry to be identified as "the women's voice" within the Episcopal Church. Furthermore, the Church's insistence on a sacramental ministry and the fact that (except in rare cases) women were not allowed to administer the sacraments made their status within the Church more similar to that of Roman Catholic than Protestant women.

This study focuses on the history of women's work in the Episcopal Church from 1850 to 1920, outlining its various phases and indicating how women shaped the Church's development. I chose the 1850s as the starting point because they marked the beginning of Episcopal women's conscious efforts to claim for themselves a share in the Church's ministry. Though featuring women who found their careers in some form of Church work, this book also surveys the formation of the Woman's Auxiliary—the Church's voluntary organization for women—which provided the support system necessary to recruit and maintain women missionary workers throughout the world. Crucial to this history was the evolution of various models for women's ministries: the sisterhood, the order of deaconesses, the missionary worker, and the institutional warden or headmistress. This study ends with 1919, for in that year the national Church drastically reorganized itself and in the process definitively excluded women from the ecclesiastical political structure. The issues involved in the subsequent reordering of women's work (after the 1919 General Convention) are complex enough to require a separate study.[11]

My contention is that in the period between 1850 and 1920 women transformed the Episcopal Church by providing the labor force and the moral initiative to establish social-service ministries (schools, hospitals, orphanages, neighborhood centers, etc.), by structuring the support system necessary to enable missionary expansion, and by developing a communications network that fostered a diocesan rather than a parochial identity for individual Church members. By the 1910s some churchwomen were beginning to sense their role in this transformation, but most clergy and laymen were unaware of their influence. Hence, when the opportunity came, in 1919, to adapt the ecclesiastical political structures to this new reality by giving women representation in the decision-making councils, churchmen refused to do so, choosing instead to perpetuate the nineteenth-century understanding of separate spheres for men and women.

In one sense, the decision was the direct result of the strategy the women had used to develop and support their work. From the beginning they had assumed the role of humble servants. Mary Abbot Twing's statement that women's work asked nothing for itself, "no place, no power, no temporal rewards, nor honors," defined women's view of their ministry. Such a stance was an effective means to begin to establish roles for women in an institution generally very suspicious of such roles. But the women's failure to move beyond the "humble servant" role, to claim for themselves the initiating and policy-making roles they were indeed fulfilling, was a significant factor in the 1919 decision. The "woman's sphere," which the General Convention endorsed by limiting its membership to male deputies, had been designed, in part, by the women themselves.

CHAPTER TWO

Enlarging the Scope of the Church's Ministry

In 1902 St. George's Episcopal Church, Stuyvesant Square, New York City, celebrated the twentieth anniversary of the rectorship of Dr. William S. Rainsford. The occasion prompted a review of the state of the parish. A staff of seven men and seven women—the rector, four assistant ministers, three deaconesses, four women workers, an organist, and a secretary—ministered to a congregation of over eight thousand. Covering an entire city block, the parish facilities included the stone Gothic church and a six-story parish house with classrooms, offices, meeting rooms, and a fully equipped gymnasium. Across the street was a four-story deaconess house with residential quarters and on the top floor an infirmary for convalescents. Sunday morning and evening services included a Sunday school for over three thousand pupils and teachers; morning and evening prayer services were held each day. In addition, the daily schedule included meetings for such groups as the Girls' Friendly Society, the King's Daughters, Mothers' Meetings, Young Married Women's Society, the Dramatic and Literary Society, St. Andrew's Brotherhood, Men's Club, and the Battalion. The parish sponsored a sewing school for girls and an evening trade school for boys. Weeklong visits for women and children during the summer at the parish cottage in Rockaway and daily excursions had refreshed over twelve thousand people the previous summer. The Employment Society, the Helping Hand, and the Clothing Department offered relief to destitute families. Contributions to foreign and domestic missionary programs totaled over eight thousand dollars, and the Women's Auxiliary packed and sent boxes of supplies to missionaries in many parts of the world. The parish also supported, with funds and voluntary assistance, mission chapels on Stanton Street and on Avenue A.[1]

The wide scope and great variety of activities offered by this parish at the turn of the century contrasted starkly with its program fifty years earlier. In 1850 St. George's parish was made up of fewer than five hundred communicants ministered to by one priest, Dr. Stephen H. Tyng. Sunday church services included a Sunday school, with 42 teachers and 455 children, that had been begun three years before. The only other parish organization was a Dorcas Society, made up of women who met to sew garments for the poor. The church members were bitterly divided over the issue of moving the church to a growing residential area uptown or continuing at the present location. There were no parish visitation or neighborhood outreach programs, no evident concern for the economic or social needs of those in the neighborhood. Contributions to the Domestic and Foreign Missionary Society totaled less than a thousand dollars.[2]

The drastic change that took place between 1850 and 1900 in the concept of parish ministry was evident at St. George's Church. Although that church was clearly one of the leaders in the social-action ministry, it was by no means an isolated example. By 1900 Episcopal churches throughout the country had similar programs. The Church of the Epiphany in Washington, D.C., maintained Epiphany Old Ladies' Home and the Lenthall Home for Widows as well as providing a schedule of guilds, club meetings, and vocational instruction. St. Mark's Church, Philadelphia, had pioneered in a neighborhood visitation program and a workingmen's association. Trinity Cathedral, Davenport, Iowa, supported boarding schools for boys and girls and a hospital with a school for nurses. St. Paul's Chapel, Lawrenceville, Virginia, maintained a Normal School and an extensive neighborhood-development program in the black community. Neighborhood outreach and social-service ministries had become standard features of parish life in the Episcopal Church.[3]

DEVELOPMENT OF CHURCH-SPONSORED INSTITUTIONS

Coinciding with the expansion of parish ministries was the burgeoning development of Church-sponsored institutions to serve the community. In Manhattan, for example, there were in 1850 fifty Episcopal churches, most of which held Sunday services and administered the sacraments but had minimal contact with non-Episcopalians in the neighborhood. Although a few of them reached out to the unchurched through Sunday-school classes for children, they were the exception rather than the rule.[4] Coordinated diocesan charitable endeavors were also rare. The City Mission Society, organized in 1832, had expanded rapidly for a brief period, then foundered for lack of funds. Though to retain its charter it continued to hold annual meetings, the society was inactive after 1844, except for providing support for St. Barnabas' House, a temporary shelter for women and children, established in 1833. Only two other charitable institutions in the city received support from the Episcopal Church in 1850: the Missionary Society for Seamen in the Port of New York, organized in 1844, and the Leake and Watts Orphan House, founded in 1831 as a "free home for orphans of respectable parentage."[5]

By 1900, however, the Church's posture toward the city had changed dramatically. The Charity Organization Society's *New York Charities Directory, 1900*, listed sixty-two charitable agencies sponsored by the Episcopal Church, including such institutions as St. Luke's Hospital, the Midnight Mission, St. Bartholomew's Medical and Surgical Clinic, The Sheltering Arms, and Church Settlement House. In addition to these specialized institutions, thirty-three pages of the directory are filled with listings of charitable, educational, and social-action programs sponsored by Episcopal parishes.[6] Virtually all these institutions were heavily dependent on women staff members and volunteers. Clearly, a change had taken place in the Church's concept of its mission.

Nor was this change limited to New York City. In cities and towns throughout the United States, Episcopal Churches had developed programs and institutions to serve the sick, the elderly, the poor, and the handicapped. *Whittaker's Church Almanac* for 1899 devotes fifty pages to listing such educational and benevolent institutions and organizations throughout the United States.[7] Paralleling this move into social-action programs at home was an extensive expansion of the Church's missionary program abroad, which also included the establishment of educational and health-care institutions. Hospitals, orphanages, clinics, and schools were assumed to be essential parts of the Church's mission, wherever the Church was to be found.

IMPACT OF THE SOCIAL GOSPEL

Historians have attributed this change in the Church's understanding of the parameters of its ministry to the rise of the social gospel in that institution. Defined by one of its leaders as "the application of the teaching of Jesus and the total message of the Christian salvation to society, the economic life, and social institutions . . . as well as to individuals,"[8] the social gospel involved both a critique of conventional Protestantism and an active program of reform. In his classic work *The Rise of the Social Gospel in American Protestantism,* Charles Howard Hopkins traced the movement from its beginnings in the preaching and teaching of a few isolated churchmen in the 1870s to its climax in the optimistic period just preceding the First World War.[9] He contended that four currents of thought in the Gilded Age combined to yield the social gospel: (1) the complacency of conventional, institutionalized, orthodox Protestantism, (2) the attempt to reconcile the truths of Christianity with the new science, (3) the evangelical hope and fervor that had inspired the previous generation's crusade against slavery, and (4) the Unitarian school that challenged both the presuppositions and the ethics of conservatism.[10] Amid the unsettled economic conditions and industrial strife of the 1880s, these factors combined to produce a growing emphasis on the Church's responsibility to the social order—the call to work for the coming of the kingdom of heaven on earth. According to Hopkins, this sense of responsibility led to the development of a wide variety of institutions designed to meet urban needs—churches, social settlements, child-saving agencies, municipal centers.[11] From the experience of ministering in these agencies, a new social theology was forged, a theology that "exerted a definitely ethical influence upon the conceptions of God, man, sin, salvation, and other doctrines" and "proposed a new and realistic view of sin in terms of the implications of a solidaristic society." By enlarging the concept of sin to include not only mere heresy or personal vice but the collective forces of evil, the theology emphasized society's responsibility for its corporate sins.[12] This new theological stance was a permanent revolution in the Protestant attitude toward sin and was perhaps the most significant effect of the social-gospel movement.

RELATIONSHIP OF WOMEN'S MINISTRIES
TO THE SOCIAL GOSPEL

The importance of churchwomen's role in promulgating the social gospel is the one area that has been virtually ignored by Hopkins and the later historians who have elaborated on his work.[13] The work of only one woman, Wellesley professor Vida Scudder, has been cited with any regularity by social-gospel historians, and the significance of organized women's groups in the Church has been totally overlooked. This oversight is due in part to these historians' dependence on literary sources—sermons, lectures, and books—for with the exception of Vida Scudder, who wrote extensively on Christian socialism, women were not prominent as writers and preachers. When one moves from the written material—the sources of inspiration and motivation—to an examination of the work accomplished, however, one cannot miss the significance of the women's activities. In the Episcopal Church, and probably in most other denominations, the labor force that implemented the social gospel—providing health care, education, and economic assistance to the disabled and the disadvantaged—was composed overwhelmingly of women. And the reason the Church was able to offer so many programs to ameliorate social evils was that churchwomen were willing to work for long periods of time either as volunteers or at extremely low wages. The women accomplished the social gospel with their actions, not their words.

Furthermore, an examination of women's work in these areas leads one to amend the chronology Hopkins established, for the Episcopal churchwomen's movement into institutional ministries began in the 1850s and was well established by the 1870s—*before* the clergy began to preach the social gospel. Clergy learned from the women already at work, examples of which are many. On arriving at Grace Church, New York City, in 1868, Henry Codman Potter found that an industrial school had already been established by the previous rector's wife.[14] When he wanted to found a monastic order for men in the Episcopal Church, one that would work among the urban poor, Father James O.S. Huntington turned to the sisters of St. John Baptist to learn about their mission work among German immigrants on the Lower East Side of New York City. The Order of the Holy Cross, which Huntington subsequently established, took its name from that mission, and Huntington was professed as the first member of the order in the sisters' chapel at St. John the Baptist House.[15] A visit to

Toynbee Hall, London, inspired Dr. Morgan Dix, rector of Trinity Parish, Wall Street, to open a similar center in New York. He, too, found that sisterhoods were already engaged in such work and asked Sister Edna, C.S.J.B., to establish the program of Trinity Mission House.[16]

THE PATTERN FOR MINISTRY EXPANSION

The extension of the Church's ministry from the local parish to the neighborhood around it followed a similar pattern in most cities. Each step in the process depended heavily on women volunteers. The parish began with a Sunday school for parishioners, taught primarily by women, who soon opened classes for nonmember children and a sewing school on Saturdays for members and nonmembers alike. Among their responsibilities as teachers, the women visited their pupils at home. Discovering there the effects of poverty and disease on the children, they sought ways to ameliorate them. They organized mothers' meetings and sewing and employment societies. As the extent of the need became apparent, Church-sponsored institutions—hospitals, homes for the aged, schools, orphanages, houses of refuge—were founded.

This development of neighborhood outreach, which had begun in the 1850s, was well established in many cities by the end of the Civil War. By 1865, for example, eight Manhattan parishes held industrial or sewing schools, fourteen parishes had day schools, and the Ladies' Mission to Public Institutions made regular visits to Randall's Island, the Emigrants' Hospital at Ward's Island, the Leake and Watts Orphan Home, the Infant Asylum, the Sheltering Arms, and the House of Mercy.[17] The founding of Church-sponsored institutions began slightly later but was accelerating nationwide long before the heyday of social-gospel preaching. St. Luke's Hospital, New York City, was opened in 1858, followed by: Christ Church Hospital, Philadelphia (1864); St. Luke's Hospital, Chicago (1864); Children's Hospital, Boston (1869); Trinity Hospital, Wilmington (1871); St. Luke's Hospital, San Francisco (1871); St. Luke's Hospital, Denver (1881); St. Mary's Cottage Hospital, Memphis (1887); and many others.[18]

THE SOCIAL GOSPEL IN EPISCOPAL CHURCH HISTORIES

None of the standard Episcopal Church histories indicates the extent to which the parishes' sense of ministry broadened during this period, nor do they recognize how widespread was the founding of Church-sponsored institutions.[19] Episcopal historians have scarcely analyzed the causes of the social gospel's rise in the Church. Though they note the broadened concept of ministry in a few "institutional parishes," they credit it to the leadership of certain innovative clergymen—William Augustus Muhlenberg, William S. Rainsford, Henry Codman Potter, Frederick Dan Huntington, R. Heber Newton, and James O.S. Huntington. Addison attributes the transformation at St. George's Church, for example, to "the abounding energy of Rainsford's personality, the unwavering support of his vestry and the exceptional quality of the curates whose loyalty he enlisted through many years," making no mention of the women who ran most of the social-action projects.[20] Though most accounts classify such groups as the Church Association for the Advancement of the Interests of Labor (C.A.I.L.), the Society for Christian Socialists, and the Christian Social Union as advocates for social justice, the organizations' work is attributed also to a few notable spokes*men*.

By combining in one chapter "Social Action and the Rise of the Orders," Raymond Albright in his book implicitly recognized a connection between the ministries exercised by sisterhoods and deaconesses and the social gospel. He did not elaborate on it, however, except to say that the monastic orders were begun "largely to supply the need for such persons in the Christian social work of the church."[21] Monastic orders as initiators of policy or as innovators in social-action ministries were not discussed. Albright did refer, however, in passing, to a very significant example of the way in which women were leading the Church to a new understanding of its responsibility to society:

> In phrases suggested to the House of Bishops by the Society of the Companions of the Holy Cross, a society of women promoting intercession, thanksgiving, and simplicity of life, the convention declared three years later "that the service of the community and the welfare of the workers, not primarily private profit, should be the aim of every industry and its justification."[22]

Why was it that a group of women dictated to the bishops about the relationship between labor and capital? Was this an aberration or a consistent pattern? Albright does not address these issues. Actually, by the early 1900s the Society of the Companions of the Holy Cross had become one of the most effective advocates of social justice and reform in the Episcopal Church. Its work is considered in chapter 10.

Albright's comment is noteworthy, for otherwise he, like most Episcopal Church historians, includes almost no information about women in his history. Generally such books contain two paragraphs on the Woman's Auxiliary and one paragraph on sisterhoods and deaconesses, ignoring the roles women played in founding parishes and social institutions and in Christian education and missionary work. Even the organization of Episcopal sisterhoods is credited to the men: "Six years earlier [William Augustus] Muhlenberg had completed the organization of 'the Sisterhood of the Holy Communion'," wrote Addison, thus ignoring Anne Ayres, first sister and head of the order for the next fifty years.[23] Albright described "the Sisterhood of the Holy Nativity, organized in Wisconsin by Charles C. Grafton," making no mention of the founding sisters.[24]

Of course, both these books were written before the current interest in women's history and social history had sensitized scholars to gender issues. But even a much more modern work, sponsored by the national Church as a part of its adult-education program, John Booty's *The Church in History* (in which the author made a conscious effort to include information about women), overlooked women's relation to the social gospel. Booty listed three factors as crucial to the development of that movement: "the American religious ferment of revivalism, voluntary societies for the alleviation of the sufferings of the poor and other victims of society, and liberalism in theology."[25] Yet he never mentioned the primacy of women in the voluntary societies. Indeed, Booty even eliminated them from membership in the Church Association for the Advancement of the Interests of Labor with these words: "The society was formed of men of various church groups and parties . . . ," thus ignoring the many women who were members and active officers of C.A.I.L.[26]

Discussions of C.A.I.L. are an interesting example of the extent to which women have been omitted from Church history. Virtually every historian points to that organization as one of the earliest and most effective manifestations of the social gospel. Hopkins labeled C.A.I.L. "the most remarkable organization in the half century of social Christianity."[27] Henry F. May claimed it "far more vigorously than any other major church organization, stressed action and practical solidarity with the labor movement."[28] Hopkins and Ronald C. White, Jr., laud the work of its "remarkable quarterly" *Hammer and Pen.*[29] Yet the name of Harriette Keyser, the quarterly's editor, never appears in these accounts. Keyser became national secretary of

C.A.I.L. in 1896 and served in that position until the society disbanded in 1926. By 1907 she was also editing its newsletter. Correspondence from the C.A.I.L. office regarding the newsletter clearly indicates that Keyser was the driving force behind its publication; she badgered and bullied bishops and priests to provide her with information and articles on topics she chose. She was particularly close to Bishop Henry Codman Potter and could generally get his endorsement for whatever cause she wanted.[30] Most of C.A.I.L.'s pronouncements were based on investigations of industry and labor that Keyser and her assistant, Margaret Lawrance, conducted.[31] In addition, Keyser's biography of Bishop Potter revealed the names of several other women who played responsible roles in C.A.I.L.'s activities: Miss Mary Leute, who helped organize the Working Women's Society; Miss Alice Woodbridge, who served as secretary of that society; Dr. Annie S. Daniel, a physician (for the New York Infirmary for Women and Children) who chaired the tenement house committee; and Miss Lily F. Foster, a deputy state factory inspector, who chaired the legislative committee that worked for the passage of an anti-child-labor bill in the New York State Assembly.[32] Yet all these women are missing from the historical accounts of C.A.I.L.

THE LEADERSHIP ROLE OF THE EPISCOPAL CHURCH IN THE SOCIAL GOSPEL

Social-gospel historians generally have agreed with Henry May's observation that the Episcopal Church "was the first major denomination to receive the new doctrines with any general welcome,"[33] but they have ventured few conjectures as to why this should be so. Among the reasons given are the effect of Anglican social reformers like F.D. Maurice and Charles Kingsley, the editorial policy of *The Living Church*, which insisted on "the importance of the church as a teacher of public virtue," and the perception that the church was losing the membership of "the laboring class."[34] It is my contention that these historians have overlooked the most important reason for the Episcopal Church's primacy in the social-gospel movement—the activities of its women. I am convinced that the women who moved into social-action ministries shaped a climate of Church opinion that was receptive to sermons emphasizing Christian responsibility to the poor and the laboring classes. It was precisely because these women were at the opposite end of the socioeconomic scale from the people with whom they worked that they were able to initiate such ministries. Rigid social conventions kept upper-class Episcopal women from gainful employment but encouraged benevolent and charitable activities. Their lofty economic status enabled the women to hire domestic help, thus freeing their time for volunteer work. Their affluence also made possible for them a level of education higher than that of the surrounding population, thus enhancing their effectiveness in creating and administering new programs. Some of them had been active in the Sanitary Commission during the Civil War and could use the organizational and administrative skills they had acquired there. That the Episcopal Church could tap such a large force of capable volunteer labor was key to its primacy in the social-gospel movement.

To be sure, the women of other denominations also moved into social-action ministries, but the blend of the Catholic and the Protestant traditions in the Episcopal Church produced among its women a unique attitude toward social service. For though the Church's Protestant tradition insisted that the gospel was for everyone and that believers must share the "good news" with others, the Catholic stress on an ordained ministry severely limited the "preaching" the layperson was allowed to do. Issues of theology and dogma were left to the priests. Hence, the Episcopal women who moved into social service did not focus on evangelism as the reason for their activities. One nursed the sick, aided the poor, and visited captives in prison because Christ had mandated such practices for his disciples—not to add members to the Episcopal Church.

Clearly this is an oversimplified rationale for a complex pattern of motivation. Some Episcopal women did indeed use the social-service programs primarily as a means of evangelism. Many women of other Protestant denominations engaged in social service for its own sake. The concept of "noblesse oblige" was the prime motivation of many Episcopal women, who saw social service as a class responsibility rather than a religious one. But the fact remains that the social-service programs and institutions begun and maintained by Episcopal women, both at home and in the mission field, placed far less stress on the conversion of clients than did those of other Protestant denominations.[35] Education rather than evangelism was the primary focus. A key reason for this emphasis was that the Episcopal women did not feel qualified to evangelize; the Church gave them no authority to do so. The process of becoming a member of an Episcopal Church involved learning and assenting to a series of theological tenets reflected in the catechism, a process that in 1850 was almost universally guided by a priest.

Between 1850 and 1920, the women's expectations about their work would change. As they gained experience in social-service programs, they also gained confidence about their abilities to administer. In their work, they began to see they had opportunities for religious teaching the priests would never have. They began to insist on theological as well as domestic training for women workers. But the pattern of social service as a response to the gospel imperative had already been set. The work of its women had enabled the Episcopal Church to claim the social gospel as its own, to ally itself with the poor, the laboring classes, and the victims of discrimination. Although the majority of the women who established the social-service ministries never sought credit for their labors, their work had a lasting effect on the Church they served.

CHAPTER THREE

The Episcopal Church in 1850

In his description of the Reverend Jonathan M. Wainwright, who was elected bishop of the diocese of New York in 1852, Elliott Lindsley actually says more about the common perception of the Episcopal Church in that period than about the bishop:

> New York in the 1840s was rampantly Anglophilic. The Gothic revival was firmly rooted and coming into full flower. Why should a man of Wainwright's taste and ability not be urged into the city's various literary clubs and groups? Most of them were "Federalist and Episcopalian and all but abjectly respectful of the mother-country." His companions at such meetings would be from old New York families, or rising notables gravitating to them; men, in short, "who survived either by their own wits, or by husbanding inherited wealth, dined at four in the afternoon, told good stories, dressed well, and managed, despite the muck of New York's streets, to act as though Gotham were London."[1]

Amidst the renewed veneration of all things English that characterized Victorian America, the Episcopal Church was *the Church* of social status. A combination of circumstances accounted for its prestige. Having been the established Church in New York and all the southern colonies, the Anglican tradition was deeply embedded there. The Episcopal Church survived a period of disarray and anti-English sentiment just after the Revolutionary War and gradually began to recapture its position as the religious home of the ruling gentry. Family tradition had kept many leaders within the Anglican fold. Others joined the Church in response to the emotional excesses of the Second Great Awakening, turning to the Episcopal Church for the order and dignity of its worship services and the conservative tradition of its intellectual life.

By midcentury, the Episcopal Church was the sixth largest Church in the United States, claiming a membership of 89,359 communicants, who were ministered to by 1,595 clergymen. Though it ranked sixth in membership, the Church ranked third in the value of its property, an indication of the socioeconomic status of its members. It required of its clergy a high level of education; by the 1850s a university degree and three years at a theological seminary were becoming standard.[2] Episcopal clergy generally came from at least moderately wealthy families that could provide the education necessary for ordination. Parishes supported their clergy well. In a study of southern clergy, for example, E. Brooks Holifield found that though the average wealth of free adult males in the United States in 1860 was $2500, the average for urban Episcopal clergy was $19,000. (Presbyterian clergy ranked next but significantly lower with an average wealth of $12,000.)[3] Noting that "Episcopal congregations are generally composed of highly intelligent and respectable people, many of whom have received an excellent education," one English clergyman serving in the United States lamented that the Church "exerts at present but little influence on the population at large. Although many of the first families in the United States are enrolled among its members and friends, its field of usefulness is generally limited to the cities and towns."[4] Episcopalians in those cities and towns enjoyed a high social status. Describing the church in Natchez to a prospective rector, M.R. Babcock assured him that it would offer "the pleasantest possible associations" and "the consequent advantages (by no means small) of such society."[5]

For the Church's women, the "society" was very traditional. Women held no sacramental positions in the Church. Only men could be ordained as clergy, preach, or administer the sacrament. Only men could serve on vestries, administering the local parish's temporal affairs. The deputies who represented local congregations at the annual diocesan conventions and those elected by the diocese to meet every three years at the Church's General Convention were men. In most parishes, even the power to vote at congregational meetings was denied to women.

Barred from institutional roles, the Episcopal woman found her highest calling in the family. Her ministry was to her husband, her children, and those in her extended family. Because Sunday schools did not become a standard feature of Episcopal Church life until well into the nineteenth century, she bore the primary responsibility for her children's Christian education.[6] In the southern states, religious instruction of the slaves often fell also within her province.[7] During the antebellum period, many religious services—baptisms, weddings, and funerals—were held in homes rather than churches. Although clergymen officiated at them, all the social arrangements were the special province of the women of the household. As Carroll Smith-Rosenberg has so aptly demonstrated, women surrounded these events with a complex of rituals that served both to define their own lives and to pass those definitions on to their daughters.[8]

Essentially, then, the Episcopal woman's religious life, like her secular life, was exercised in two spheres—the home, in which she was the controlling agent, and the church, in which she participated primarily as a respondent. Reinforcing the religious-spectator role was the Anglican theological stance that stressed grace rather than works and emphasized redemption rather than conversion. Religion was a given, a gift of God that parents passed on to their children through infant baptism, and the proper response to it was not to search one's soul for the evidence of worthiness but to "obediently keep God's holy will and commandments," as they were conveyed through the Bible and *The Book of Common Prayer*.[9] When most Protestant Churches in America held conversion to be necessary for baptism and thus refused to baptize infants, the Episcopal Church's emphasis on grace rather than works was distinctive.

It was this theological position that attracted Catharine Beecher to the Episcopal Church. As she worked on her treatise *Religious Training of Children*, she decided she preferred the way the Episcopalians treated children, "for they, by baptism, *do* [erase] the evil done by Adam's sin, so that the child can be successfully *trained* by a *religious growth*."[10]

Beecher's conversion to the Episcopal Church was not an isolated incident. A surprisingly large number of nationally known women writers and educators converted to the Episcopal Church in the mid-nineteenth century. Among them were Catharine and her sister, Harriet Beecher Stowe, and the founder of the Troy Female Seminary, Emma Willard, along with her sister, Almira Hart Lincoln Phelps, who served for many years as superintendent of the Patapsco Female

Institute of the Episcopal Diocese of Maryland. Sarah Josepha Hale, the influential editor of *Godey's Lady's Book,* also chose the Episcopal Church, as did millworker and writer Lucy Larcom and two of the most popular novelists, Mrs. E.D.E.N. Southworth and Lydia Sigourney.[11]

THE FEMINIZATION OF RELIGION

What was it that attracted such women to the Episcopal Church? The Church's high social status and its traditional ritual were doubtless of importance in the decision. I suspect, however, that women were attracted to the Church precisely because it had proved less susceptible to what historian Barbara Welter has termed the "feminization" of religion. In her analysis of American religious life from 1800 to 1860, Welter noted that established Churches became "more genteel and less rigid," citing as examples women's increased involvement in voluntary and missionary societies, the growing use of female images for God, the sharp rise in the percentage of women attending church, and the increasing focus on Christ's love and God's mercy in the hymnody of the period.[12]

Several other historians have documented this theme. Nancy Cott, in her analysis of women's diaries and preachers' sermons from New England in the period from 1780 to 1835, found ample evidence of feminization. Through the diaries she traced the high esteem in which women held their religious activities and the satisfaction they derived from participating in the women's voluntary religious associations. Turning to the sermons, however, she found the clergy responded with an ambivalent message, needing "both to elevate women as religion's supporters and yet (in order to sustain social stability, as they saw it) to reaffirm women's subordination to men."[13] Ann Douglas extended the analysis by suggesting that the disestablishment experienced by both clergy and women at the beginning of the nineteenth century produced between them a kind of unwritten alliance that "feminized" not only religion but the national culture.[14] Her failure, however, to take into account the importance of denominational differences is an important weakness in her thesis. For although she mentions that one-third of the women writers she studied converted to the Episcopal Church, she never speculates why women claiming clerical prerogatives as their own would move into the one Church in which women had so little power. Her explanation is that these women "converted to Episcopalianism in part to demonstrate that they had attained status and to insure its possession; they sought in religious affluence a respite from the very real if unexamined struggles they had fought, not a continuation of them."[15] Moreover, that she only included one Episcopal clergyman among the thirty she studied, and never quotes him directly, implies that she, too, found few examples of the shift toward sentimentality in Episcopal sermons.

These and other historians have clearly established a pattern of increasing female involvement in religious concerns, and they have documented its general effect on the nation's Churches.[16] It is my contention, however, that owing to several factors, the feminization process moved more slowly in the Episcopal Church. Sunday church services used the proscribed liturgy of *The Book of Common Prayer,* which was replete with masculine, hierarchical, and authoritarian language and images. Because Episcopal theology did not require conversion as a prerequisite for Church membership, sermons tended to be aimed at educating rather than converting; hence the preacher was not quite as dependent on a favorable reception from his hearers. Episcopalians' traditional attitude discouraged innovation. To be used in the Sunday service, hymns had to be officially approved. Many of the sentimental favorites sung in other Churches were never approved. Of those cited by Welter, "Just as I Am, Without One Plea" and "Nearer My God to Thee" were not included in the Episcopal hymnal until 1874; "O Perfect Love" and "I Need Thee Every Hour" were first included in 1892. The other hymns she mentions do not appear in Episcopal hymnals.[17] Thus, without extemporaneous prayers or the freedom to select biblical passages or hymns, modification of the worship service to accommodate a more feminine tone was difficult.

Whether Episcopal congregations in the antebellum period were made up of a growing percentage of women is difficult to say; research on the topic remains to be done. In the course of my research, however, I have not come across any complaints about the lack of men in the Sunday congregations or comments on the growing number of women in attendance. It may well be that the change in the proportion of men and women attending the services came about so gradually that it did not attract clerical attention until well into the century.[18]

Separate societies for women also do not seem to have been as widespread in the antebellum Episcopal Church as they were in other denominations. Although early records show several small, local women's associations forming, the level of organization, sophistication, and strength remained low in comparison to that of the Methodists and the Presbyterians. These local associations were either educational and tract societies[19] or auxiliaries to the Domestic and Foreign Missionary Society of the Protestant Episcopal Church (founded in 1821). By 1830 the annual report of the society listed only fifty-one member organizations, of which sixteen were specifically titled "Ladies Associations."[20] Such ladies' groups remained local and limited in objectives and do not appear to have been important facets of parish life.[21]

Thus the traditional style of worship, the political structure in which only men held positions of authority, and the lack of an extensive development of women's organizations in the Church all point to the conclusion that the process of "feminization" had less effect on the Episcopal Church than it had on other Protestant denominations. Perhaps more than any other factor, the essential conservatism of the Anglican character prevented contemporary trends, regardless of how popular they were, from overwhelming the Church.

POLITICAL ACTIVITY IN THE EPISCOPAL CHURCH

Another arena for women's activities in many Protestant Churches during the antebellum period was the emancipation crusade. Female antislavery societies proved to be many women's first venture into the realm of political activity, as they distributed pamphlets and collected signatures on petitions to the U.S. Congress.[22] But the antislavery campaign was virtually absent from the Episcopal Church, which generally remained aloof from the political questions of the day. As the House of Bishops stated in an 1856 resolution in response to the antislavery agitation in Kansas, "the constituted rulers of the Church . . . are the ministry. With party politics, with sectional disputes, with earthly distinctions, with the wealth, the splendor, and the ambition of the world, they have nothing to do."[23] Some clergymen, such as Boston's Reverend E. M. P. Wells, who served as vice-president of the American Antislavery Society, and Bishop Alonzo Potter of Pennsylvania, denounced slavery, but equally prominent clergy defended the system. Few southern clergy challenged the system; many were slaveholders themselves.[24]

Although southern dioceses united in the Protestant Episcopal Church in the Confederate States of America in 1862, at the war's end they returned to the national Church, which exemplified its spirit of reconciliation by recognizing as valid the consecration of Bishop Richard Hooker Wilmer of Alabama and the admission of Arkansas as a diocese.[25] Though hostile feelings persisted, the general ease with which reunification took place was evidence that Episcopal leaders saw the Church as transcendent to the affairs of the world.

Also indicative of this attitude was that the Church was often able to continue to insist on a ministry to the Negroes while remaining silent on the slavery question. "Let care be taken to provide in our churches, good accommodations for such colored persons as are disposed to attend," urged Bishop Alfred Lee of Delaware in 1849. "I should feel it to be a sinful failure of duty, if we considered ourselves released from all responsibility for their spiritual welfare; and in the hope that the church may thus prove a blessing, to souls for whom Christ died, would urge that the doors of our Sanctuaries should be always open to them: and that a place should be always reserved for such as are disposed to worship with us."[26] Even during the war, the southern bishops in a pastoral letter reminded Church members of their responsibility toward the Negroes, saying, "Slaves of the South are not merely so much property, but are a sacred trust committed to us, as a people, to be prepared for the work which God may have for them to do." By 1865 the church of South Carolina consisted of 3,404 white and 2,142 black adult members; during the previous three years twice as many blacks as whites had been baptized.[27]

THE OXFORD MOVEMENT

Of far more interest to mid-century Episcopal leaders were theological and liturgical questions. From its beginning, the Episcopal Church had been divided between High Church and Low Church. (The High Churchmen emphasized the Church's institutional life, stressing the sacraments as the means of conveying God's grace and the Church, with its threefold ministry of bishops, priests, and deacons, as the institution Christ created for salvation. The Low Churchmen took a more evangelical approach, believing in salvation by faith, confirmed by works, and stressing the necessity for the individual's conscious acceptance of Christ.[28] The spread of the Oxford Movement from England to America fostered greater interest in forms of worship and ecclesiastical tradition. Reading the English tracts, American High Churchmen were affirmed and strengthened in their determination to promote traditional theological scholarship emphasizing the importance of the three orders of ordained ministry, whereas the evangelical wing of the Church became more militant in its emphasis on lay ministry. Bishop Charles P. McIlvaine of Ohio began the evangelical attack in 1840, in *Oxford Divinity Compared with That of the Romish and Anglican Churches*. He charged that the movement was "thoroughly Popish in principle," for it had surrendered the truths of the gospel and the doctrine of justification by faith. He charged that the only logical recourse for the Tractarians would be to move as a body into the Roman Church.[29] Many other bishops, particularly Manton Eastburn of Massachusetts and William Meade of Virginia, supported his position, whereas Bishops Doane of New Jersey, DeLancey of Western New York, and Benjamin T. Onderdonk of New York enthusiastically supported the Tractarians. With battle lines thus drawn, the debate raged over the next twenty years, focusing variously on such areas as the educational requirements for ordination, the nature of ecclesiastical authority, the design of liturgical rites, and the proper use of *The Book of Common Prayer.*

Of particular importance to the subsequent development of women's work in the Church was the conversion of several of the Tractarians to the Roman Catholic faith. In 1852 Church leaders were stunned when Bishop Levi Silliman Ives of North Carolina announced his decision to become a Roman Catholic. Although several clergymen had preceded him, Bishop Ives was considered the most prominent defector, and the Low Churchmen were quick to use his decision as a warning against the Oxford Movement's pernicious influence. Much of the controversy that later surrounded the beginnings of religious orders for women was rooted in the fear that the sisterhoods would lead to further defections to Rome.[30]

Although the controversy and the debate continued for many years, neither party eventually triumphed. Gradually the Church developed the capacity to tolerate diversity and to allow a range of theological opinion and interpretation of the Scriptures and the requirements of *The Book of Common Prayer.* Tractarian liturgical reforms, such as the use of clerical vestments, the increased frequency of celebrations of the Eucharist, and greater attention to Church music and vested choirs, gradually made their way into congregations across the country. The renewed emphasis on service to the poor and the alleviation of their suffering was to be especially important in terms of women's ministries and is discussed in greater detail later. The Evangelicals' heightened consciousness of mission set the stage for the missionary expansion of the next four decades.

FOREIGN AND DOMESTIC MISSIONARY ORGANIZATION

During the first decades of the nineteenth century, Episcopal leaders sought to establish an effective missionary program for the Church. Following the English pattern of separate missionary societies, some parishes founded local societies and diocesan organizations were formed in New York, Pennsylvania, New Jersey, South Carolina, Vermont, North Carolina, Ohio and Virginia. In 1821 The Domestic and Foreign Missionary Society of the Protestant Episcopal Church in the United States of America was established as a national organization which recruited individual members. But churchpeople were slow to enroll in the Society and many bishops refused to support its work, feeling that it diverted funds from cherished diocesan projects. Critics contended that mission ought to be central rather than peripheral to each Christian's life—that to channel mission work through a society was both redundant and ineffective. Finally, in 1835, the General Convention decided that the work of Christian missions was the responsibility of the entire Church and the duty of each communicant. Hence the convention assumed control of the Domestic and Foreign Missionary Society and became responsible for the entire mission program. To oversee the work, a thirty-member Board of Missions was chosen. It, in turn, appointed two committees, one for domestic and one for foreign missions, each of which would oversee the work of an executive secretary for that area. The secretaries were to raise funds and recruit and deploy missionaries. Although its composition changed several times, the Board of Missions continued to be elected by, and responsible to, the General Convention until the major administrative reorganization of 1919.

The House of Bishops was authorized to establish missionary districts and to elect missionary bishops who would administer the work in those districts. At the 1835 meeting, two such bishops were elected: Francis L. Hawks, for the area including Arkansas, Louisiana, and Florida, and Jackson Kemper, for Missouri and Indiana. Hawks declined the honor, but Kemper accepted and on September 25, 1835, was consecrated the first missionary bishop for the Protestant Episcopal Church.[31] Domestic and foreign missionary districts continued to be created by the House of Bishops, which then chose bishops to administer those districts. A missionary district could become a diocese (which had the power to elect its own bishop) once the churches within it were financially self-supporting and could continue their work without funds from the national Church.[32] Staff members were located initially in Philadelphia and New York City, until 1840 when the national office was moved permanently to the latter city. Domestic and foreign work continued to be administered by separate heads until the 1885 reorganization, which united all the work under one general secretary, the Reverend William S. Langford.[33]

The problem that constantly faced the Board of Missions was that of financial support. Although the General Convention declared, when it assumed responsibility for the mission program in 1835, that the giving would be "systematic," no system for the collection or distribution of the funds was established and the newly appointed executive officers had to begin immediately raising funds for their own office expenses. Throughout the nineteenth century, no effective system of fund raising was ever established; the board depended on voluntary annual donations from individuals, churches, and dioceses, and on the income from legacies. It was in this area—financial support for missions—that the activities of women became vital to the program's continuation. The women's work is discussed more fully in chapter 6. Suffice it to say here that for the remainder of the century, without the persistent financial support of the Woman's Auxiliary, the Church's missionary program would have been drastically curtailed.

By 1850 Episcopal dioceses were established in every state east of the Mississippi River; west of the river were the dioceses of Missouri and Texas and three missionary districts: Iowa, Wisconsin, and Minnesota (1849); Arkansas and Indian Territory (1838); and California (1850). Foreign missionary districts had been organized in China (1844), Constantinople (1844), and West Africa (1850), and missionaries were also at work in Greece. But neither domestic nor foreign missionary districts were more than skeletal organizations; most were staffed only by the bishop (with assistance from his wife) and perhaps one other missionary couple. By 1850 the Church was supporting ninety-six domestic missionaries and nineteen missionaries (of whom nine were women) in foreign countries.[34] In terms of communicant strength, the Church was overwhelmingly centered in the eastern United States; less than 3 percent of the communicants lived west of the Mississippi or in one of the foreign missionary districts.[35] Essentially, then, the Episcopal Church of 1850 was an insular, parochial institution, divided between High Church and Low Church positions and generally unresponsive to the need for missionary work.

The next half century would see a drastic change in the Episcopal Church. Membership patterns shifted. Several missionary districts became self-sufficient, and new districts were added both at home and abroad. Within the United States, the Church's involvement in social-service ministries increased dramatically, as did the number of Church-sponsored institutions. In all these changes Episcopal church-women would play an important part. The following chapters outline the various ways in which women organized to develop their ministries in the Episcopal Church.

CHAPTER FOUR

Episcopal Sisterhoods, 1850–1920

By 1850 a few Episcopal churchwomen began to balk at the restrictive roles society imposed on them. Having taken seriously the Christian injunction to feed the hungry and care for the poor, they began to assume personal responsibility for it, seeking ways to carry on those ministries that were yet in the realm of "proper" behavior. This search led several women to consider religious sisterhoods, because a group of women, committed to a common ideal, might venture into areas that otherwise would be considered unsuitable for a lone woman. As Anne Ayres, the founder of the first Episcopal sisterhood, stated:

> Look at the quantity of work waiting for some of us to do, among the miserable young vagrants in our streets, in the thousand wretched houses within view of our own comfortable dwellings, in our prisons, our penitentiaries, our hospitals, and other asylums. . . . Then picture . . . a household united by their mutual love to Christ, led by that love to count as especially their neighbors and brethren all whom they can save or serve, see them combining amongst them all the talent necessary for ministering effectually to each several case of suffering or need; ready, submissively and without partiality, to use their respective talents where it will most avail, . . . and see whether the true Christian sisterhood is not adapted, as no other form of charity could be, to reclaim the long neglected wastes of misery and degradation.[1]

Though many Episcopalians viewed ordered communities of

women with great suspicion, Ayres imagined the sisterhood would serve primarily as a structure through which churchwomen could accomplish tasks society needed done. In several cities, between 1850 and 1875, Episcopal women founded sisterhoods that became the forefront of their movement into social-service ministries.

The development of orders for women in the United States was greatly influenced by the Oxford Movement in England. Americans claimed that their countrywoman Anne Ayres was the first Anglican sister since the Reformation, for she made her profession early in 1845.[2] Actually, an English woman, Marion Hughes, had made a similar profession before Dr. Edward Pusey in 1841, and a community first known as the Park Village Sisterhood had formed under Pusey's tutelage in 1845. The recovery of the monastic tradition by the English Tractarians led to the establishment of several sisterhoods in England: the Community of St. Thomas the Martyr (1847) initiated by the Rev. Thomas Chamberlain; the Community of St. Mary the Virgin at Wantage (1848) begun under the influence of the Rev. W.J. Butler; Priscilla Lydia Sellon's Sisters of Mercy of Devonport and Plymouth (1848); the Society of the Holy Trinity (1849) founded by Marian Hughes; the Community of St. John Baptist at Clewer (1852) with Harriet Monsell as mother superior and the Rev. T.T. Carter as spiritual director; the Society of St. Margaret (1855) founded by the Rev. John Mason Neale and Ann Gream; and the Society of the All Saints Sisters of the Poor (1856) begun by Harriet Brownlow Byron and the Rev. W. Upton Richards.[3]

A similar period, in which several women's orders were founded, followed in the United States with the establishment of the Sisterhood of the Good Shepherd in Baltimore (1863), the Order of Deaconesses of the Diocese of Alabama (1864), the Community of St. Mary (1865), the Sisterhood of the Good Shepherd in New York (1869), the Sisterhood of St. John the Evangelist in Brooklyn (1872), and the Sisterhood of the Holy Child of Jesus in Albany (1872). In addition, three English orders—All Saints Sisters of the Poor, the Society of St. Margaret, and the Community of St. John the Baptist—began work in Baltimore, Boston, and New York City during the 1870s.[4]

Tracing the origin of these orders is an intriguing task. Clergymen are generally credited with founding each of the English orders except the Sisters of Mercy and the Society of the Holy Trinity. Studying the origins of the sisterhoods, however, with a sensitivity to the unwritten roles that women played, one discovers that in each instance one of the first sisters quickly became the director of the order and remained in that position for many years. Often the order was founded in direct response to a call which she experienced. My hunch is that further research would indicate that the English sisters themselves were far more active in organizing the orders, writing the constitutions and rules, and establishing community patterns than has hitherto been credited. Such a discovery would not discount the important contributions of the English clergy in the administration of the sisterhoods and in writing apologetics for the recovery of religious orders in the Anglican Church.

In the United States, clergymen were less involved in the establishment of sisterhoods. Only two of the American orders—the Sisterhood of the Holy Communion and the Sisters of the Holy Nativity—were identified with a particular priest. Instead, the primary impetus for forming the orders seems to have come from the women themselves, and their principal motivation was social service rather than religious reform. Most of the American orders were founded within a decade after the Civil War. Not only did the social upheaval of the war provide an atmosphere in which such a break with the Protestant tradition might be attempted but the high casualty figures left many women bereft of economic support. That the death of thousands of young men had greatly diminished women's opportunities for marriage sanctioned the development of an alternative lifestyle for women. Nevertheless, the formation of sisterhoods was still considered a radical step by most Church members, and the early communities met with substantial opposition, as the following review of their origins will show.

THE SISTERHOOD OF THE HOLY COMMUNION

With the profession of Sister Anne in 1845, the Sisterhood of the Holy Communion began. Since this sisterhood lacked a structured religious life, it could not be strictly defined as a religious order. In the United States, however, it played a significant transitional role by introducing the possibility of a church-related community for women and demonstrating the impressive work such a group might accomplish. Though the founding of the order coincides chronologically with the Oxford Movement's revival of sisterhoods in England, its model came not from England but from the order of nursing deaconesses founded by Pastor Theodore Fliedner and his wife in Kaiserswerth,

Germany, in 1836. The Reverend William Augustus Muhlenberg had read of the Lutheran deaconesses' work and was convinced that a similar corps of nursing sisters would be the key to his dream of establishing a Church-sponsored hospital in New York City. Famous as the educator who had founded the Flushing Institute and St. Paul's College, Dr. Muhlenberg had come to Manhattan in 1845 to create a new model for urban ministry at the Church of the Holy Communion. He envisioned a Church both evangelical and catholic—a ministry that began with the sacraments at the altar and went forth to meet both the spiritual and the physical needs of the local people. Breaking with standard Church practices by abolishing pew rents and instituting a weekly Sunday Eucharist as the chief service of the day, Muhlenberg reached into the neighborhood with a ministry of education, healing, and poverty relief.

Attracted by Muhlenberg's vision, Anne Ayres joined the Church of the Holy Communion and soon began to seek ways to express her unique sense of calling. A young woman in her late twenties who had immigrated to the United States from England a decade earlier, Ayres had supported herself by teaching the daughters of well-to-do families. She first met Muhlenberg when she accompanied his niece (one of her pupils) to church. She later described the event as a lightning conversion: "The arrow from the bow thus drawn . . . was guided by a Higher Power, straight to the heart of at least one of his hearers."[5] The meeting was propitious for both Ayres and Muhlenberg, for the two would continue to work closely together on a variety of projects over the next half century, until Muhlenberg's death in 1877. Sharing his vision of the Church's servant ministry, Ayres was willing to dedicate herself totally to its attainment, working with great competence yet crediting all her accomplishments to his inspiration.

Aware of the Church's hostility to monastic orders for women, Ayres and Muhlenberg proceeded slowly with the organization of the sisterhood. Sister Anne made her initial commitment in an empty church, with only Muhlenberg and the sexton "waiting to put out the lights" as witnesses.[6] Secrecy was essential, she wrote, because the Church was alarmed by "the secession of Mr. Newman and others of the Oxford School to Rome. . . . The very name 'Sister' would have been obnoxious."[7] For the next few years she worked with Muhlenberg, providing "the womanly element essential to the domestic administration of the various charities . . . clustering around the Church." Her rhetoric is significant; throughout her life, Ayres de-

scribed herself as a "domestic administrator," using the skills of a
housewife to manage first the infirmary, then St. Luke's Hospital, and
finally St. Johnsland with both efficiency and loving care.[8] Together
she and Muhlenberg initiated a number of programs that would later
become standard offerings in churches throughout the country—a
Fresh Air Fund, a weekly offering for the relief of the poor, an Employment Society, a Thanksgiving distribution of food, a dispensary,
an infirmary, and church schools.[9] While involved in these various
parish activities, Ayres also served as principal of the Church School
for Young Ladies, a secondary school quartered in the church buildings.[10] Although she characterized the women who worked with her
as "sisters," the next formal profession was that of Meta Brevoort, in
1853, followed by those of Sister Catharine, in 1854, and Sister Harriet, in 1857.[11]

The sisterhood itself was formally organized in 1852 with the adop-
tion of the principles of association. At the same time, Ayres prepared
a pamphlet that defined evangelical sisterhoods, clearly delineating
how the Sisterhood of the Holy Communion differed from the Roman
Catholic model.[12] The sisterhood was to be a community of Christian
women devoted to works of charity but held together only by unity
of purpose. There were no lifetime vows, only a simple statement of
commitment, usually to a three-year term, with the provision that,
whenever she wanted, a woman might leave the sisterhood simply by
making her intention known to the pastor. Sisters were clothed in a
plain adaptation of "the ordinary attire of a gentlewoman." Community life revolved not around a schedule of religious devotions but
around the sisters' charitable acts and services. Within the society,
however, each sister was expected to work for "an advancement in
personal holiness" through Bible reading, private prayer, and corporate worship. To disassociate the evangelical sisterhood clearly from
the Roman Catholic model, Muhlenberg wrote in his introduction to
Ayres's pamphlet:

> At once, then, let it be said, that while we do not underrate the
> good that is done by such orders as the Sisters of Charity in the Roman
> Communion, we desire to attempt no copying of them among our-
> selves. They are essentially Roman. To say nothing of their corruptions
> and errors of faith, their perpetual vows, their constrained celibacy,
> their unreserved submission to ecclesiastical rule, their subjection of
> the conscience to priestly guidance, their onerous rounds of cere-
> monies and devotions, the whole tenor of their exterior religious life

make them a homogeneous part of the system of that Church. . . .
There can be no imitations of them in a Protestant Church.[13]

Ayres herself, however, was more interested in establishing a rationale for women's ministries in the Episcopal Church than in discrediting the Roman orders. As she explained:

> It is customary to urge men to the work of the ministry, missions,
> etc., and why should not kindred argument be addressed to us also,
> to stir us up to something in the Christian life more distinct and
> impressive than is now common to us? Yet when do we hear a word
> from the pulpit to this effect? We women have a little faith; we have
> warm affections and pure impulses; we have heads and hands. Why
> not show that too many of us are not living up to our vocation; not
> turning to account the powers we are indued with; that . . . we are
> frittering away our lives . . . dwarfed and cramped into the niches of
> custom and worldly conformity, when we might be growing . . . toward perfect stature in Christ?[14]

With few women responding to this plea, the order grew slowly. Because there is almost no biographical information about these first sisters, it is impossible to assess their motives for choosing their new lifestyle.[15] Their seriousness of purpose, however, can be inferred from the fact that most of them remained nursing sisters for the rest of their lives.

The Sisterhood of the Holy Communion was inextricably linked with Muhlenberg's plan for founding a Church-sponsored hospital. While Muhlenberg promoted the cause of St. Luke's Hospital through his sermons and writings, the sisters expanded their nursing activities. In 1853 they opened a seventeen-bed infirmary with an outpatient clinic and a dispensary. Three sisters, two probationers, and one non-resident associate staffed the infirmary, caring for outpatients and serving as visiting nurses who dispensed clothing as well as medication to the needy. At the same time they ran a parish day school for seventy children. Though the sisters had no training as nurses, during their years of operating the infirmary they gained experience and established basic nursing procedures. In doing so, they were among the pioneers of the nursing profession in the United States.

NURSING SISTERHOODS

The importance of the early sisterhoods in establishing nursing as a career for women should not be underestimated. As Lavinia Dock, the nurse-historian of the first generation of trained American nurses, has written:

> The influence of the Anglican nursing orders was very great, because the women who entered them were of admirable culture, refinement, and capacity. They set a high standard wherever they went, and began the work of rescuing nursing from the depths into which it had fallen.[16]

The Sisterhood of the Holy Communion extended this tradition to America. In the 1850s most nursing care in the United States took place in homes; hospitals were generally seen as places of last resort—to be avoided if at all possible. With the exception of a few established by Roman Catholic sisterhoods with strong nursing traditions, most hospitals offered minimal nursing care, generally by poorly paid and untrained men and women.[17]

The Sisters of the Holy Communion were indeed pioneers, for they opened their infirmary at the same time Florence Nightingale (with members of at least two Anglican sisterhoods) was nursing the sick and wounded soldiers of the Crimean War. Although Nightingale's work was highly publicized in the English newspapers, it was not until 1860, when she established the nurses' training school at St. Thomas' Hospital in London, that the nursing practices and training techniques she developed received widespread publicity. By that time St. Luke's Hospital had already been in operation for two years and the Holy Communion sisters had established their own nursing procedures based on the need for cleanliness and loving care.[18] There is no evidence that the earliest sisters had any previous nursing training, though Anne Ayres is known to have read widely and was doubtless familiar with the current nursing literature. Once the hospital was opened, however, the sisters trained other women as nurses and, in 1888, opened the St. Luke's Hospital Training School for Nurses.[19]

Two other Anglican sisterhoods played crucial roles in bringing nursing education to America. Both the Society of St. Margaret and the Society of All Saints had begun as nursing communities in England and were among those with which Florence Nightingale worked as she developed her plans for nursing education. In 1872 three All Saints sisters came to America to work in Baltimore. Among them was Sister Helen, who had been trained at University College Hospital, London. The following year, she heard of the plan to establish a training school for nurses at Bellevue Hospital and volunteered to move to New York City to direct the program. As superintendent of nurses, Sister Helen modeled the training program after the Nightingale system used at St. Thomas' Hospital, London (which in America came to be known as the Bellevue system and was widely copied by hospital nursing schools).[20] After the Bellevue school was functioning effectively, Sister Helen returned to the order and was sent to South Africa to begin nursing there. The Society of St. Margaret, which moved to Boston in 1873 at the request of the organizers of the Boston Children's Hospital, brought English nursing methods to that city and, in 1907, established a highly respected training school at that hospital, under the direction of Sister Amy.[21]

SAINT LUKE'S HOSPITAL

Even before the first wing of St. Luke's Hospital was completed, the Board of Managers requested that the Sisterhood of the Holy Communion be prepared to take charge of the wards. The task of equipping the hospital was left to the Ladies' Furnishing Committee—women Dr. Muhlenberg had appointed from several parishes. They decided how the wards should be furnished, raised the funds, tested the furnishings for utility and durability, and procured the necessary items. Combining supply work with social service, they employed several women left destitute in the panic of 1857 to sew the necessary sheets, dressings, and garments from fabrics donated by cotton merchants.[22]

When the hospital opened in 1858, Sister Anne served as house mother or chief administrator of the institution, and Muhlenberg left the Church of the Holy Communion to become house father, attending to the spiritual needs of the patients. Ultimate fiscal responsibility remained with the Board of Trustees, whereas the lady managers continued to share with the sisterhood the overseeing of housekeeping details. The hospital included living quarters for the sisters, who not only served without pay but were expected to provide from their own means for personal expenses other than food. Eventually the sisters had to hire and train lay assistants. Each ward, however, remained under the direction of a nun, and not until 1888, when St. Luke's Training School for Nurses was established at the hospital, was anyone other than a sister given supervisory powers.[23]

The relationship between the Sisterhood of the Holy Communion and St. Luke's Hospital vividly demonstrates the importance of such women's orders to the development of Church-sponsored institutions, for the sisters constituted an unpaid hospital nursing staff for at least fifty years. Ayres herself remained as house mother until 1877—nineteen years. In 1876, recognizing that she was exercising almost complete control of the hospital, the trustees voted her the title of "Sister Superintendent," conferring on her powers commensurate with those of Dr. Muhlenberg.[24] Sisters continued to supervise most of the hospital's departments until after the turn of the century, although after 1890 the drop in vocations forced the hospital to hire additional nurses. Many of those hired, however, had been trained at the St. Luke's School for Nurses. The service the sisters provided went far beyond the working hours; because they lived at the hospital, they were on twenty-four-hour call and spent hours after work visiting the patients, reading the Bible with them, or helping them write letters or contact their families.

Nor was the work of the Sisterhood of the Holy Communion limited to St. Luke's Hospital. Some of the members continued to be associated with the parish, staffing an industrial school and an employment society, a babies' shelter, and a home for the aged. Another woman, Sister Catharine, who entered the order in 1854, founded in 1872 the Shelter for Respectable Girls and administered it for the next thirty-three years. Still others worked at St. Johnland, a community founded by Muhlenberg in 1870 and incorporating several social-service institutions—an orphanage, a home for the aged, an industrial school, and workers' cottages—in one place, with shared staff and facilities. Ayres herself moved to St. Johnland in 1877 and did most of her work collecting and editing Dr. Muhlenberg's papers from there.[25]

THE COMMUNITY OF ST. MARY

A rift within the Sisterhood of the Holy Communion resulted in the formation of a second order, the Community of St. Mary. In 1863 three of the sisters, dissatisfied with Anne Ayres's domineering control of the sisterhood and desiring a more intensive devotional routine combined with a lifetime rather than a three-year commitment, withdrew to found a more traditional order. The Community of St. Mary dedicated itself to "the performance of all the corporeal and spiritual works of mercy of which a woman is capable, . . . particularly the care of the sick and needy, the orphan and the fallen, and the education of the young."[26] Harriet Starr Cannon, who became the order's superior, stressed the equal importance of prayer and service in what she called the "mixed" life of the sisterhood. With a prescribed habit, a return to the ancient daily offices from prime to compline, and the three perpetual vows of poverty, chastity, and obedience, the Community of St. Mary was similar to Roman Catholic orders and thus became the first traditional religious order in the Episcopal Church. It was, therefore, destined to receive far more public opposition than had the Sisterhood of the Holy Communion.

Aware of the strong anti-Catholic prejudice they faced, the founding sisters carefully enlisted the support of three powerful New York clergymen: Thomas McClure Peters, rector of St. Michael's Church; Morgan Dix, rector of Trinity Parish; and the diocesan bishop, Horatio Potter. Peters was enthusiastic about the women's plans and arranged for them to take control of the House of Mercy, a refuge (for former prostitutes and homeless women) established a few years earlier by Mary Richmond.[27] With living quarters and an occupation assured, the women approached Dr. Dix, asking him to compose a rule they might follow. He did so, and also served as chaplain to the order for the next ten years, providing wise counsel and public support throughout a difficult period.

In the formation of the Community of St. Mary the sisters had come to terms with the essential problem of religious community life—the question of obedience. The Holy Communion sisters had tried to avoid this question, for though their rule included a section on the first sister, "to whom the others are expected to yield a cheerful obedience in all things pertaining to the ordering of the community, and the work given it to do," their rather informal organization and pattern of life did not reinforce the ideal of discipline with meditations or discussion.[28] And the sisters found they had underestimated how difficult it was to live under strict discipline.

In contrast, when the Community of St. Mary was formed, the women organized around an ordered religious life, with worship services scheduled throughout the day. To deal with the crucial problem of intention, of ordering one's will to a spirit of obedience, the instructions Dr. Dix prepared on the religious life began with the premise that the community must be based on "the subordination of the individual to the Order."[29] The first chapter of the rule concerned intention. It read:

1. Do all to the glory of God.

2. Let the love of our Lord Jesus Christ be the constraining motive of all your actions.
3. Lay aside, as far as possible, all self-will and selfishness, seek for entire conformity to the Will of God.
4. Do nothing because you prefer it, or to please yourself, or to advance your own reputation, interests or advantage.[30]

Obviously what would be required of the woman who entered the order was a life-changing commitment. Retreats, meditations, regular self-examinations, and a far more extensive program of education for novices were established to reinforce the ideal of obedience. This requirement—that the novice completely reorient her personality, learning to consider others first and herself last—was difficult to fulfill. Some women failed at the attempt and left the order, but those who stayed built a vital community. Fortunately, Harriet Starr Cannon, who served as Reverend Mother from the beginning of the sisterhood until 1896, was a woman of great wisdom and spiritual depth, so that loving obedience to her rule was generally joyful rather than onerous. But the sisters found that obedience, even to such a wise taskmistress, required rigorous spiritual discipline.

Seeking Episcopal approval for their community, the women approached Bishop Potter. He proceeded warily, appointing a committee of priests to consider the formation of a sisterhood and writing to Bishop William Rollinson Whittingham of Maryland to ask about his experiences with the Sisterhood of the Good Shepherd in Baltimore. He drew up a list of necessary provisions, which included the stipulation that the bishop have the "power to impose an Episcopal check on all their proceedings."[31] Eager to proceed with their work, the women gladly assented to the bishop's conditions, and on February 2, 1865, Bishop Potter received five candidates into the Community of St. Mary. But even after all his precautions, the bishop feared an antagonistic response to the formation of the sisterhood and "desired it to be kept very quiet—he felt he was taking a great step and expected to be taken to task for it."[32]

His fears were well founded. Criticism of the move was so widespread he was compelled to defend his actions at the next diocesan convention, stressing particularly that "there are no irrevocable vows, no engagements which could interfere to prevent their return to ordinary positions in life."[33] (Though the bylaws expressly stated that no sister should be required to take irrevocable vows, the earliest sisters made lifetime vows privately to their confessor.)[34] Antagonistic clergy, not satisfied with the bishop's statements, plotted to rid the diocese of the sisterhood.[35]

Despite criticism, the order began to attract new members. As it expanded, it assumed charge of two new institutions—The Sheltering Arms, a children's home, and St. Barnabas' House, a rescue center for women and children—supported by the City Mission Society of the Diocese of New York. The sisterhood's stay at St. Barnabas' House was short-lived, for the Low Church party in the diocese had finally found a lever to use against it. On a visit to the house they were horrified to discover an oratory (a small chapel the sisters used for daily prayers) in the building. Objecting to the "mawkish Mariolatry" of the communal devotional life and the "Roman extravagance" of the chapel, these critics threatened to cut off funds for the City Mission Society unless the sisters abandoned this "ritualism."[36] Unwilling to let financial considerations dictate their devotional life, the Community of St. Mary withdrew from St. Barnabas' House in June 1867. (It left the house in the care of Ellen Hulme, a laywoman, who waited until the furor died down and then organized a "protestant" sisterhood, the Sisterhood of the Good Shepherd, which operated St. Barnabas' House for the next fifteen years.)[37]

Opposition to the sisterhood erupted with renewed intensity in 1870, in the events surrounding The Sheltering Arms's move to a larger building designed especially as a children's home. The parishioners of St. Michael's Church planned a fund-raising bazaar to furnish the new home. As the publicity for the bazaar increased, evangelistic Church papers began to warn their readers about the "Catholic" rituals practiced by the sisters. Opposition culminated in a letter from the rectors of five prominent city parishes to St. Michael's rector, Thomas McClure Peters, demanding a full investigation to determine whether the sisterhood was disloyal to the doctrines and usages of the Episcopal Church. Faced with such powerful opposition, Dr. Peters quietly made plans for some other women to take charge of The Sheltering Arms and asked the sisterhood to leave.[38]

Feeling betrayed by Dr. Peters and intensely disappointed about leaving the children for whom they had cared, the sisters of Community of St. Mary moved back to the House of Mercy, determined to establish a home for themselves, free of outside control. These two episodes indicate both the intensity of the opposition to the early sisterhoods and the orders' vulnerability to such attacks. The Community of St. Mary had learned that support, even from priests and bishops, was undependable. If their community was to survive, it would have to control and manage its own resources. Henceforth, the order financed its own institutions. Funding was channeled through The Friends of the Sisters of Saint Mary, organized by a laywoman, Miss Ellen Kemble, whose financial acumen and staunch support proved an invaluable asset. Her work and the financial contributions of several wealthy women were critical to the sisterhood's survival. Eventually they raised funds sufficient not only to support the present work but to begin several new ventures—the St. Mary's Free Hospital for Children, St. Mary's School in Manhattan, and St. Mary's Convent, Peekskill. Once the convent was opened, the community expanded rapidly and received invitations to work in several other cities.[39] Other sisterhoods, subsequently formed in the United States, learned from the experience of the Community of St. Mary to retain financial control of the institutions they administered. Such economic independence enabled them to have far more control over their development than they might have had were they beholden to a diocese or a parish for financial support.

The sisters' dedicated work at these institutions gradually eroded public disapproval of such religious orders. One final, heroic episode won for the Community of St. Mary the respect of its most severe critics and signaled a decisive change in Church members' attitude toward monastic orders for women. During the yellow-fever epidemic that struck Memphis, Tennessee, in 1878, sisters in the branch house there remained in the city despite the highly contagious disease, continuing to care for the victims. They moved from house to house, nursing the sick and receiving the most desperately ill into their convent. They took over an orphanage for Negro children, making it a refuge for black and white children orphaned by the fever. Additional nuns came from the Peekskill convent and from the Society of St. Margaret in Boston to assist with the work. Nursing even as they took sick themselves, the sisters persisted; four of the seven Memphis sisters—Constance, Thecla, Ruth, and Frances—and their associate sister, Mrs. Bullock, perished, along with over five thousand Memphis residents. In the face of such heroism, the shopworn theological disputes about popery seemed hollow. Although this story of self-sacrifice was unique in the number of sisters who perished, such self-sacrifice stood at the center of each sister's commitment. The national publicity given to the Memphis crisis produced a decided change in public acceptance of sisterhoods in the Episcopal Church.[40]

The Community of St. Mary continued to proliferate, establishing houses in Chicago, Kenosha (Wisconsin), and Sewanee (Tennessee) and expanding its work in New York City to include the Laura Franklin Hospital and the Trinity Mission House. From the convent in Peekskill, Mother Harriet administered her widespread community with wisdom and vision until her death in 1896. Her own willing attitude of service inspired her sisters' confidence and emulation, and the annual meetings of the General Chapter rarely decided matters contrary to her advice.[41] Her community remained the largest of the Episcopal sisterhoods, serving as the model for several smaller local orders, among them: the Sisterhood of the Holy Child Jesus (founded in 1870 in Albany, New York), the Sisterhood of St. John the Evangelist (1888, Brooklyn), the Community of the Transfiguration (1898, Cincinnati), the Community of St. Saviour (1901, San Francisco), and the Order of St. Anne (1910, Massachusetts).[42]

ENGLISH SISTERHOODS IN THE UNITED STATES

In addition to those that developed in the United States, three major orders that had originated in England opened houses in the United States. They were the All Saints' Sisters of the Poor, the Society of St. Margaret, and the Community of St. John Baptist (CSJB). Unique circumstances accounted for the immigration of each group. The All Saints' Sisters had responded to the Reverend Joseph Richey's invitation to "help him in his difficult work" at Mount Calvary Church, Baltimore. In 1872 they established All Saints' Mission Home, which included a school for girls, a neighborhood visitation and outreach program, and mission work in the Negro community.[43] Well known as an order of nursing sisters, the Society of St. Margaret came to Boston in 1873 at the request of the board of directors of the newly founded Children's Hospital, to assume the direction of that institution. It later developed a school of nursing at Children's Hospital, St. Margaret's Infirmary, an orphanage, a school for girls, and a school of ecclesiastical embroidery.[44] A wealthy New York City resident, Helen Folsom, who was serving her novitiate in the English convent of the Community of St. John Baptist, urged the sisterhood to begin work in the United States, offering her home and considerable financial support for the venture. It began work (particularly among German immigrants) on the Lower East Side in 1874 and gradually added to its care several schools and mission work at Trinity Parish, Wall Street.[45]

Like the Community of St. Mary, these three English orders required the traditional vows of poverty, chastity, and obedience, wore distinctive habits, and followed a daily rule of regular worship services. The Society of St. Margaret began their work in Boston with a branch house that could elect its own sisters and control its own finances but was bound by the same rules and wore the same habit as the mother house.[46] The other two orders continued to be directed from England, requiring their novices to be trained in England and accepting the discipline of the English superiors. This English connection enforced conservatism and a rigid adherence to the rule. Affiliated status, with power to elect a superior, to choose their own visitor, and to have a separate novitiate, was eventually granted to the Community of St. John Baptist in 1881 and to the All Saints' Sisters in 1890.[47]

PERIOD OF EXPANSION

Thus, by 1880 six major sisterhoods were at work in the Episcopal Church. For the next two decades, they grew slowly but steadily and gradually acquired responsibility for many institutions. New projects were begun in a variety of ways, sometimes by clerical initiation, as in 1869 when the Reverend Milo Mahan asked the CSJB to establish St. Paul's Orphanage in Baltimore.[48] In other cases, the nuns themselves developed new work. Having witnessed the dearth of pediatric medical services in New York City when they worked at The Sheltering Arms, the sisters, in 1870, founded St. Mary's Hospital for Children.[49] Often the orders were asked to staff existing institutions, as was the case in 1884 when Deaconess Louise G. Hall invited the CSJB to run the House of the Holy Comforter, which she had founded to care for chronically ill women and children.[50] The sisterhoods grew and spread geographically, so that by 1900 they were responsible for the following institutions:

EPISCOPAL RELIGIOUS ORDERS FOR WOMEN, 1900, WITH INSTITUTIONS COMMITTED TO THEIR CARE[51]

All Saints' Sisters of the Poor, Baltimore, MD   **1872**

All Saints' Home for Children, Baltimore, MD
St. Katherine's Mission (school and mission to blacks)

St. Clement's Mission, Philadelphia, PA
Summer Sea Shore House, Point Pleasant, NJ
Boarding School for Young Ladies, Germantown, PA
Mission House and Care for Poor, All Saints', Orange Valley, NJ
The Chase Home for Aged and Infirm Women, Annapolis, MD

Community of All Angels, Wilmington, DE   1895

St. Michael's Hospital for Babies, Wilmington, DE
St. Matthew's Colored Mission, Wilmington, DE

Community of St. John Baptist, New York, NY   1874

Church Work Room (Ecclesiastical Embroidery), NYC
St. John Baptist School, NYC
St. Hilda's Industrial School for Girls, Morristown, NJ
St. Andrew's Hospital for Convalescent Women, NYC
Mission Work and Girls' School among Germans, NYC
St. Anna's Cottage Summer Home for Women and Girls
St. Michael's Reformatory, Mamaroneck, NY
Christ Church Home for Children, South Amboy, NJ

Community of St. Mary, New York, NY   1865

St. Mary's School (boarding and day), NYC
St. Gabriel's School (boarding and day), Peekskill, NY
St. Mary's School (boarding and day), Memphis, TN
Kemper Hall (boarding and day school), Kenosha, WS
The House of Mercy (reformation of fallen women), NYC
St. Agnes House, Inwood-on-Hudson, NY
St. Saviour's Sanitarium, Inwood-on-Hudson, NY
St. Mary's Free Hospital for Children, NYC
Convalescent Summer House for Children, Norwalk, CT
Noyes' Memorial Home, Peekskill, NY
Trinity Hospital, NYC
Summer Seaside Home for Poor Children, Great River, NY
Trinity Mission, NYC
Laura Franklin Hospital, NYC
St. Mary's Orphans Home, Memphis, TN
St. Mary's Mission and Home for Children, Chicago, IL
St. Mary's Mission on the Mountain, Sewanee, TN

Community of the Transfiguration, Glendale, OH   1898

Mother House and Children's Home, Glendale, OH
Bethany Mission House, Mothers' Meeting, Sewing School and Neighborhood Visitation, Cincinnati, OH

Diaconal Community of St. Martha, Louisville, KY   1875

Boys' Orphanage of the Good Shepherd, Louisville, KY
Home of the Innocents, Louisville, KY

Order of Deaconesses of the Diocese of Alabama   1864

Orphanages for Girls and Boys, Mobile, AL

Order of the Holy Resurrection, Georgia   1894

Charitable and Educational Work

Saint Monica Sisters, Springfield, IL

Association of Widows for Intercessory Prayer

Sisterhood of the Good Shepherd, New York, NY   1869

School of the Good Shepherd (boarding), Asbury Park, NJ
Summer Home for Church Workers, Asbury Park, NJ
Buttercup Cottage (summer for working girls), Philadelphia, PA
Clothing Bureau, New York, NY

Sisterhood of the Good Shepherd, St. Louis, MO

Bishop Robertson Hall (school for girls), St. Louis, MO

Sisterhood of the Holy Child Jesus, Albany, NY   1873

St. Agnes' School, the Cathedral and St. Peter's Parish, Albany, NY
St. Paul's Parish, Troy, NY
Summer Hospital and Industrial School, Saratoga Springs, NY
Orphan House of the Holy Saviour, Cooperstown, NY
The Church Home, Troy, NY

Sisterhood of the Holy Communion, New York, NY   1852

St. Luke's Hospital, New York, NY
Home for Aged Women, New York, NY
House of Reception for Society of St. Johnland, Long Island, NY

Sisterhood of the Holy Nativity, Providence, RI   1882

> Training House for Parish and Spiritual Work, Providence, RI
> Mission work in the west, Fond du Lac, WI
> Indian work on the Oneida Reservation, WI

Sisterhood of St. John the Evangelist, Brooklyn, NY   1888

> School for Girls, Brooklyn, NY
> Orphan Home, Brooklyn, NY
> Home for the Aged, Brooklyn, NY
> St. John's Hospital, Brooklyn, NY
> Summer School, Holderness, NH
> Cottage by the Sea, Belmar, NJ

Sisterhood of Saint Joseph of Nazareth, Bronxville, NY   1892

> St. Martha's Training Home for Girls, Bronxville, NY

Sisters of the Annunciation B.V.M., New York, NY   1893

> House of the Annunciation (care for crippled children)
> St. Elisabeth's House (summer retreat), Riverbank, CT

Sisters of Bethany, New Orleans, LA

> Children's Home, New Orleans, LA

Sisters of the Church, New York, NY   1870

> Boarding and Day School For Girls, New York, NY
> Clothing Bureau, New York, NY

Sisters of the Resurrection, St. Augustine, FL   1891

> House of the Resurrection (spiritual retreat)
> Trinity Home for Girls (industrial training)

Sisters of Saint Mary and All Saints, Baltimore, MD (colored women)

> St. Mary's Home for Colored Orphans, Baltimore, MD
> Visitation and Teaching from Mount Calvary Chapel, Baltimore, MD

Society of the Epiphany, Washington, DC   1897

> Caring for the fallen, protecting and training young girls
> Retreat House, Washington, DC

Society of St. Margaret, Boston, MA 1873

Two infirmaries, Boston, MA
School of Embroidery, Boston, MA
Home for Girls, Brighton, MA
Mission work at St. Augustine's Church for Colored People
St. Monica's Hospital for Colored People
Children's Hospital, Boston, MA
St. Barnabas' Hospital for Crippled Children, Philadelphia, PA
Parish work: St. Mark's, Philadelphia; House of Prayer and St. Philip's
    Church, Newark; St. John's, Montreal
Home for Incurables, Montreal
Several Summer Seaside Cottages

Although founded for various purposes, these institutions followed a general pattern. All were administered, and most were completely staffed, by women who lived in the building and were on twenty-four-hour call. The sisters served without pay, and lay assistants received meager wages.[52] Overall finances were generally raised and controlled by the sisterhoods themselves; a few of the larger institutions vested these responsibilities in a board of managers.[53] Crucial to the work was a volunteer auxiliary of women who dedicated hours to visiting within the agency and fund raising without. These women were the early case-workers, investigating prospective adoptive parents for an orphanage or accompanying a young female offender to the court-room.[54] They were the institution's link to the world, procuring supplies, publicizing events, and negotiating with city and state authorities when difficulties arose. With the training they received under the sisters' supervision, the volunteers often went on to develop similar programs in their own parishes.

For the sisters, the work was never-ending; except for a month's vacation each year and a period of free time for receiving visitors on Sunday afternoon, most of them were always on call. Periods of service were exceedingly long: Sister Catharine began the Shelter for Respectable Girls in 1874 and served there for thirty-three years; Sisters Annette and Elsa moved to the House of Prayer in Newark in 1889 and worked there for the next half century; Sister Catharine administered St. Mary's Hospital for over fifty years; Harriet Starr Cannon served as superior of the Sisterhood of St. Mary from 1865 until 1896—thirty-one years.[55]

Only through such lengthy periods of service could the sisterhoods have been as influential as they were, for they were remarkably few. The Community of St. John Baptist initiated forty sisters in the period between 1867 and 1900 in the United States.[56] By 1900 the Community of St. Mary consisted of seventy-four sisters living in twelve houses across the country.[57] In 1880 there were ten All Saints' Sisters and one lay sister at work in the United States; in the next two decades four choir and six lay sisters were professed and three sisters came from England to make their homes in the United States community.[58] The Society of St. Margaret was larger, but its sisters' movement among houses in Canada, South Africa, England, and the United States makes it difficult to ascertain the number of them at work in the United States in a given period. By 1877 the Sisterhood of the Holy Communion had divided into two communities—one that remained at the founding parish and another that worked at St. Luke's Hospital and St. Johnland. The parish community listed three sisters and thirty-five associates in 1901; figures on the other branch are unavailable.[59] By 1900 most of the other orders had fewer than ten professed sisters.

Information about the economic or social backgrounds of those who became sisters is difficult to find. The Register of the Community of St. John Baptist, for example, lists each enrolled sister's full name along with her chosen name but records no other personal information—e.g., residence, family, etc. Even biographical information about the social and economic backgrounds of the heads of the order is scanty. Anne Ayres was an immigrant from England, wealthy enough to have had some education but poor enough to have to support herself as a tutor. Harriet Starr Cannon, Sister Superior of the Community of St. Mary, had been orphaned at an early age and was raised by an aunt and uncle in Connecticut. She, too, was supporting herself (in Brooklyn, as a music teacher) when she entered the order. Helen Folsom and Frances Constance of the Community of St. John Baptist were of wealthy, aristocratic backgrounds and used their wealth to finance the sisterhood's activities.

As for the rank-and-file sisters, very little is known. References, such as that of Dr. Dix to the sisters of St. Mary as "ladies of refinement, education, and high social position," abound in the literature and indicate that many of the women were from the upper social strata.[60] The first woman initiated into the Community of St. Mary who originally had not been one of the Sisters of the Holy Communion was "little Katie Hassett," an orphan (suffering from a hip disease) who had been left at St. Luke's Hospital. Although never explicitly stated, the impression that she was of lower social status than the other sisters is unmistakable in the writings. Whether her profession was unusual or became the general pattern for the sisterhood is not clear.[61] That so many of the sisters were responsible for running institutions or for teaching and that several were involved in a bilingual ministry indicate a higher-than-average level of education.

One factor, however, is important: Although never explicitly stated, the orders generally followed the Roman canon requiring that the candidate be a virgin or, if widowed, that she have been the faithful wife of one husband. Thus, the wayward women with whom many of the sisterhoods worked might become gray sisters or stay and work in the convents as domestics, but they might never aspire to full sisterhood. A woman's purity rather than her economic or social status became the determining factor for sisterhood—a fact that established a marked social gap between the sisters and many of the women with whom they worked. Thus, in a sense, the ordered life was the highest manifestation of what Barbara Welter has called the "cult of true womanhood," the public emphasis on purity and virtue as women's most precious attributes.[62] That the nuns were able to transform this ideal into a full life of caring for others is significant, for they discovered the sisterhood could free them from the trap the ideal of true womanhood represented. The nun's habit was the testimony of her purity; wearing it, she was free to plunge into the dirty work of the world without having to worry about society's pressure to keep her on a pedestal.

The order was also a pathway to a wider and more diverse life than many of the women might otherwise have found. As Sister Ursula, S.H.N., testified:

> For my part, I have never lived so full a life as I am living now. In the world, I went every morning to an office and came back at night too tired to want to go anywhere but to bed. There was nothing at all in my life but the office routine and an occasional evening's amusement. We were all tired at home all the time, and didn't even talk very much. Father read the paper, and mother and I sewed, and then we went to bed early because we had to get up early. And what have I deserted that wide and useful life for? I make anywhere from twenty to fifty calls a week. I talk with all sorts of people on all sorts of things. I am looked upon as a sort of oracle who can give an opinion worth listening to on any subject, from How to feed the baby to How to manage "him." Then I have a Sunday School class of sixty infants— dears! They alone are a wider world than any I ever expected to touch before I came here.[63]

How, then, does one assess the work of these sisterhoods? Essentially, theirs was a ground-breaking role—opening new occupational possibilities to women. Crucial to it was the ordered community; the sisters drew from one another and from the steady sustenance of their worship life the strength to break custom, to walk where it was unacceptable for a lone woman to walk, to accept a task society felt a genteel lady ought to shun. As pioneer women professionals, the nuns were generalists—specialists would follow later—but they proved that women could manage large institutions, supervise employees, and develop educational and rehabilitative programs.[64] At the same time, however, their tendency toward self-effacement, their threefold vows of poverty, chastity, and obedience, and their dedication to service tended to obscure their accomplishments, so that they did not serve as role models for a secular generation of women. Clearly the stress on anonymity was partly the result of many Church members' antagonistic attitude toward the formation of monastic communities, but became so ingrained that even after the orders had gained public approval, the sisters were reluctant to claim any credit for their work or to suggest publicly that others might follow their examples. The sisterhoods remained submissive and thus, in a sense, out of step with a Church population growing increasingly assertive and publicity conscious.

In the Episcopal Church, however, the sisterhoods were the radical edge of ministry in the 1870s and 1880s. As conduits of the Church's charity, they became the means through which the alms collected in innumerable offering plates were dispensed to "deserving" and "undeserving" poor. As teachers in secondary schools for upper-class girls, the sisters fostered a social conscience in many young women who aspired to higher education and a profession. They brought into the Church many members with sufficient education in its rituals and worship to take pride in their membership. This evangelism markedly broadened the population base of the Episcopal Church by adding communicants from the lowest socioeconomic classes to what had been a Church of middle- and upper-class members.

While accomplishing their missions of charity and evangelism, the nuns were also transforming the institution in which they worked. A list of the groups to whom they ministered is significant: aged men and women, hospital patients, prostitutes, crippled and handicapped children, orphans, battered wives, homeless and drunken women, the blind and the deaf—a catalog of society's least-esteemed members.

In caring for these groups, the sisters had assumed a task no one else wanted; powerless themselves, they ministered to those even less powerful. Their acceptance by the Church depended on the low status of their chosen ministry and on the humility with which they performed it. Though Church leaders rarely recognized it, their own ministries were gradually being changed by the sisterhoods, for the nuns both pinpointed new areas of ministry to be developed and trained volunteers to work in them.[65] The seventeen-bed infirmary begun by three sisters of the Holy Communion developed into the huge complex that is St. Luke's Hospital on Amsterdam Avenue, New York City, today. Many other people and organizations played a part in the development of St. Luke's Hospital, too, but the sisterhood's initiating and sustaining roles during the early years were crucial to it. And those roles were repeated in institutions all across the United States: Children's Hospital, Boston; St. Barnabas Hospital, Newark; St. Mary's School, Memphis, Tennessee; St. Barnabas' Hospital, Salina, Kansas; St. Monica's Home, Roxbury, Massachusetts; St. Helen's Hall, Portland, Oregon; and many others.

For Episcopal churchwomen, the sisterhoods played a transitional role. Very few of the Church's women became nuns; a few more took on the commitment of being lay sisters or associates to the orders. But the sisters' ministries authenticated similar ministries for laywomen, made a career in "Church work" a possibility for a later generation of women who rejected the rigid requirements of the ordered life but accepted the ideal of a life of commitment. The latter women would develop Church work as a profession, forging standards of education and training and working for recognition and certification by the national Church. But they learned from, and built on, the first sisterhoods' experiences.

CHAPTER FIVE

The Church's First Hired Women Workers, 1865–1879

Ellie's tact, sense, good-nature, and energy conquered the U.S.A. surgeon in charge, Dr. Page, at once, and coerced all his official dignity . . . into hearty, grateful cooperation in the care of his cargo of 500 "cases." . . . She had the great satisfaction of producing . . . while amputations were going on—the bandages and the stimulants of which the surgeon really believed he had not any on board. The little woman has come out amazingly strong during these two months. Have never given her credit for a tithe of the enterprise, pluck, discretion, and force of character she has shown.[1]

Thus did George Templeton Strong describe his new-found appreciation for his wife's abilities after he had witnessed her work as a volunteer for the U.S. Sanitary Commission during the Civil War. He also remarked on the effect the work had on Ellie—she returned "in the best of spirits and good health. . . . [She] has had a jolly time of hard work and useful work."[2]

Strong's comments reflect the changing attitude—brought on by the wartime experience—toward women's work. Whether nursing on the battlefield or gathering supplies and raising funds at home, women had proved to be competent and creative managers, fully able to complete the tasks before them. And in doing so, they had gained confidence and experience, and many, like Ellie, had found they enjoyed the work.

As a result of such wartime experiences, the next ten years saw a tremendous change in churchwomen's activities. Every major Protestant Church in the United States organized a national women's association.[3] What became probably the most effective interdenominational body ever assembled, the Woman's Christian Temperance Union, was founded.[4] Several Episcopal sisterhoods began to develop institutional ministries. Women across the United States were restive, seeking new forms of ministry, new ways to respond to the physical and spiritual needs of the world around them.

The decade following the Civil War was a period of experimentation for Episcopal women, a time for testing possible Church-related vocations and establishing employment patterns. The founding of sisterhoods was one manifestation of this ferment. Two other programs were significant: the establishment of freedom schools in the South and the development of a training school (the Bishop Potter Memorial House) for women Church workers.

THE FREEDOM SCHOOLS

As the Civil War ended, concern over the plight of the former slaves had led to the organization of the Freedmen's Commission of the Protestant Episcopal Church, responsible for a loosely organized coalition of local freedmen's-aid societies.[5] The Reverend J. Brinton Smith, hired as the commission's general agent, pushed for the organization of women's auxiliaries to the aid societies, for "ladies have more influence than gentlemen in works of benevolence and mercy, and they can do more than any agency to awaken and sustain an interest."[6] By November, women's auxiliaries from Pennsylvania, New Jersey, and Delaware had united to form the Pennsylvania branch of the Freedmen's Commission. This network of women was dedicated to establishing schools among the newly freed blacks. Persuading one parish after another to pledge support for one teacher, the Pennsylvania branch had thirteen teachers in the field by summer 1867; the following fall twenty-four teachers were sent out.[7]

The driving force behind this organization was Mrs. Isabella Batchelder James, an abolitionist who had worked with the Sanitary Commission during the Civil War. As president of the Pennsylvania branch, she organized local auxiliaries, raised money, recruited teachers, and kept up a steady correspondence with the latter once they were placed. She badgered General Oliver Otis Howard for more assistance from the Freedmen's Bureau, insisting that the bureau should pay for renting or repairing school buildings and should transport books and supplies to the new schools, and then writing to complain when the supplies did not arrive promptly.[8] She was a relentless fundraiser; even after the Avery estate had given $25,000 to build a normal school in southern Virginia, she pursued the family for additional funds.[9] She recruited both black and white teachers and was even willing to accept a non-Episcopalian "who was an excellent worker" as long as the latter would subscribe to the Episcopal form of worship.[10] Under Mrs. James's leadership, the Pennsylvania branch was the only organization in the Episcopal Church that provided effective support for freedmen's programs.

Not only were women the chief fundraisers for the work, but they made up most of the teaching force—thirty-one of the thirty-eight teachers sent the first year, forty-eight of the fifty-eight sent the second.[11] Determining how many women served as teachers is difficult; at least seventy-three are mentioned by name in either the minutes of the Freedmen's Commission or in *The Spirit of Missions*, but the list is probably not exhaustive. Local women were employed in some of the schools, whereas other teachers were sent and completely supported by their home parishes in the North and thus may have been omitted from the official Church publications. They served in schools in Florida, Georgia, Kentucky, Mississippi, North Carolina, South Carolina, Tennessee, Virginia, and the District of Columbia. Although some taught in schools established by existing black churches, the majority set up schools in buildings provided by the Freedmen's Bureau and gradually gathered Episcopal congregations around them.[12] By 1873 twenty-four such schools were operating under the sponsorship of the Freedmen's Commission.[13]

The women assumed their duties with evangelistic fervor. "If I can be instrumental in saving one soul, or guiding one erring foot into the narrow path, I shall feel happy and content," wrote Miss Hammond from Charleston.[14] Boston native Matilda Hicks, teaching in Newbern, North Carolina, testified that "it is God's work we are doing, and unless it receives the blessing of the Holy Spirit's influence, it cannot prosper."[15] Others were urged to join the cause. "I earnestly hope our friends at the North will do what they can to assist us," wrote Mrs. Simons, a Charleston woman who found herself teaching several of the children of her former slaves, one of whom brought his daughter to her and said, "Take her and teach her, my dear mistress; I know if she can get an education at all, you will give it to her."[16]

No easy task confronted these women. Classes were large, facilities primitive. "My class was so large that it had to be divided; and fifty-four of my boys were given to another teacher," wrote one woman.[17] Miss E.R. Ancrum noted that her Charleston High School class had increased to sixty—thirty-four girls and twenty-six boys.[18] Irene Smith had *ninety* children in her class.[19] Enrollment changed constantly. "Quite a large number of new scholars have taken the places of those who have left," wrote Miss Swetland from North Carolina. "Consequently the old road is to be travelled again with its wearying amount of drudgery and repetition; . . . it is drill, drill, drill."[20] Mrs. Dawson in Charleston echoed her complaint, "It is rather rough work sometimes, when new pupils fresh from the islands enter, just about as wild as 'tis possible to be, and requiring to be watched so closely that one is sorely tried at times, for so many are found ready to follow the example of the newcomer."[21] There were also, however, students of diligence and perseverance, such as the six students who had been in Mrs. Hall's class for five years and "have not been absent more than a day or two at a time. . . . They began the alphabet then, and now are studying history, grammar, and geography," she boasted.[22]

Many of the teachers taught children during the day, then held classes for adults in the evening and church-school classes for all on Sundays. "I quite surprise my friends here because I go out in all kinds of weather and work so regularly, and never appear fatigued," noted Miss Hicks, "but I have ever been deeply impressed with the usefulness of a cheerful, happy face, and I try not to look weary when I really am very tired."[23] Money was certainly not the incentive for such labor, for salaries were low. Most of the female teachers were paid twenty dollars a month plus room and board, whereas clergymen working under the same conditions generally made forty dollars a month with room and board.[24] Some, like Mrs. Virgil Hillyer of Grace Church, Jersey City, teaching in Camden County, Georgia, served without pay at their own request.[25] Conditions of employment were uncertain. Schools were generally open from October through May, although some continued throughout the entire year. The commission's desperate financial plight forced it in 1868 to suspend payment of salaries to teachers after April, cutting the school year short by a month.[26]

Despite these difficulties, the women persisted. Many returned year after year to the same schools. Although scarce documentation makes exact information impossible, at least ten women who started teaching in 1866 or early 1867 were still at their posts in 1872.[27]

Several other women served for at least four years. An 1889 Board of Missions report lists twenty-two women who continued to work in schools for colored people throughout the South. Some of them were among those who had been first sent out in the late sixties.[28]

Back home, the national Church's enthusiasm for the work among former slaves was short-lived. General agents consistently complained about the lack of support. "Why did the Church establish a Freedmen's Commission at all, and why did it authorize the appointment of an Executive Committee to conduct its work, if it was not prepared to supply the necessary means for prosecuting it to the fullest extent?" questioned J. Brinton Smith just before he left the position of general agent to become the principal of the Protestant Episcopal Normal School at Raleigh, North Carolina.[29] Even Mrs. James's untiring efforts could not keep the Pennsylvania branch afloat, and in 1870 it discontinued operations, Mrs. James having borrowed (on her own note) twelve hundred dollars to pay the final salaries of the teachers the branch still supported.[30]

Dismayed at the lack of support for their work, teachers attempted to rekindle public enthusiasm. "I have little courage in making a re-statement of the character of this work and yet, year by year, I realize more fully its importance. I think the Church, as a body, feels but a slight interest, comparatively, in this Department of Missions. It has been very feebly sustained, and I only wonder that, with all the drawbacks, it has not ceased to exist," wrote Miss Swetland in 1872.[31] "Time only will show the good that has been done among these poor people, and let me assure you, that all has not been in vain," wrote Miss Hesketh, as she pleaded for continued supplies of money, books, and clothing. Revealing her sense of isolation, she also admitted that "the laborers in the field need from many a 'God bless you,' and to be told, 'Go on; we will take care of you.'"[32] "I trust God will open the hearts of all earnest people to aid us in continuing this Christian work," said Kate Savage from Charleston.[33]

Major support was not forthcoming, however, and gradually the Freedmen's Commission dismantled the program. When the general agent, the Reverend Charles Gillette, died suddenly in 1869, his position was not re-filled; instead, several New York clergy voluntarily shared the duties. Fewer and fewer teachers were sent out. In 1877 the commission voted itself out of existence. Several of the schools remained in operation, receiving some funds from the domestic missionary budget and miscellaneous voluntary contributions. The Board of Missions continued to oversee the department, but its financial resources were spent on sending clergymen rather than teachers to the South. Some of these men went to parishes that had grown up around the schools, such as St. Augustine's and St. Cyprian's Churches in Newbern, North Carolina, and St. Stephen's Church in Petersburg, Virginia, or to existing churches that had been strengthened by the addition of a school program, such as the Church of Our Merciful Saviour in Louisville, Kentucky, or St. John's Church, Fayetteville, North Carolina.[34]

As the first extensive use of women workers in the mission field, however, the work among the southern Negroes was significant. The women proved to be a dedicated and self-motivated labor force, willing to work long hours for meager salaries—and with few complaints. Many tactfully reached out to the white southerners. "These southern pastors treated me with perfect courtesy, manifesting much interest in the work," wrote Ada Smith. "They both expressed a desire to assist in the work, and promised all assistance in their power."[35] Often the teachers developed a broad view of their task; recognizing that education alone was no panacea for the Negro's plight, they encouraged the development of black-run parishes that would serve as community centers for young and old alike. Although they often felt themselves isolated and unsupported, they persevered with a strong sense of the righteousness of their cause. Local women's groups, such as the Hartford guild that supported Almira Hesketh, gained a sense of participation in the noble work by frequently corresponding with teachers who described their activities and the needs of the people they served. The groups' experience in raising funds and collecting and distributing clothing and supplies for the freedmen's schools would be used very effectively later, in providing for other missionaries at home and abroad.

In dealing with these first women workers, the Church established a pattern that would prove to be its general method of dealing with women workers over the next half century: The women were recruited, sent to the mission field, and forgotten. No provisions were made for their economic security. School years were cut short on a month's notice if funds were not available. Such items as pension, disability pay, and tenure were not even considered. The women were an expendable labor force.[36]

They were also a labor force to be used for work among disadvantaged populations. Work with the former slaves was still well within the nineteenth-century ideal of domesticity; the women were sent to enlighten and uplift and civilize a population viewed as ignorant, downtrodden, and barbaric. By defining the work in these categories, churchmen were able to move it into the "woman's sphere," thus ignoring the gospel imperative, which theoretically fell equally on men and women. The fact is that women were hired for these positions because men did not apply for them.

Although the overall school program was relatively small, it nevertheless was the first Episcopal Church-sponsored missionary operation not primarily focused on establishing new churches. The freedom schools were founded in response to the black community's need for education. The teachers quickly found that their ministry involved feeding, clothing, and tending the sick as well as teaching. In a real sense, the work was a social-gospel ministry, the first such ministry sponsored on a national level. And the Church's women were crucial both to its development and its execution.

It is difficult to measure the long-term effect of the work of these early women teachers. As missionaries, they brought many black members into the Episcopal Church, thus broadening its population base. Particularly important was their success in inspiring a number of black men to seek ordination. Both the Reverend Thomas W. Cain, who served in Virginia and Texas, and the Reverend Peter Andrew Morgan, who worked in Pennsylvania, New York, and Louisiana, were educated and inspired by Amanda Aiken and Sallie Coombs in the Freedman's School at St. Stephens Church in Petersburg, Virginia. The Reverend James Solomon Russell, who served as the archdeacon of "Colored Work" for the diocese of Southern Virginia for over thirty years, often acknowledged his debt to Mrs. Pattie Buford of Brunswick, Virginia, for her teaching and inspiration. [37] Prior to 1865 only fourteen Negroes had been ordained to the priesthood, none of them from a diocese south of Maryland. Between 1865 and 1880 twenty-seven Negroes were ordained, seventeen from the South. The next decade saw an even greater rise in the number of southern blacks who were ordained. [38] Although the numbers are small, they indicate the significance of the freedom schools in educating a large percentage of the first black clergymen.

Most of the church congregations associated with the freedom schools have continued to prosper, and the latter's graduates have organized many other Episcopal congregations throughout the South. [39] The number of rural schools continued to increase—as late as 1920, there were over fifty in the Fourth Province. After the influx of northern teachers declined, these academies were often run and generally staffed by local women. Three notable women—Mrs. Pattie Buford, Julia Clarkson, and Deaconess Mary Amanda Bechtler—devoted their lives to them. In the 1880s Mrs. Buford, "a cultivated Southern lady of refinement," founded a school, a hospital, and an infirmary for blacks in Brunswick County, Virginia. Because of her zealous efforts, most of the members, including the clergy, of a small independent church called the Zion Union Apostolic Church joined the Episcopal Church at once.[40] Julia Clarkson took over the Middleburg, South Carolina, school her parents had founded in 1879, taught industrial classes in her home, and made the schoolhouse the center of community life. One contemporary observer noted that though the Reverend J.C. Perry baptized the babies and administered the Holy Communion, "Miss Clarkson [was] the tireless day-by-day minister to all needs of the needy."[41] Deaconess Bechtler was a North Carolinian who began work under the supervision of the Negro priest Reverend Oscar L. Mitchell at St. Mary's Chapel in Washington, D.C., and remained there from 1901 until her death in 1918. She nursed the sick, taught children and adults, and supervised a host of voluntary organizations.[42] The efforts of these and many other southern women broadened the Church's ministry in the South to include education and social service in the black community.

By the turn of the century two Church-sponsored colleges, St. Paul's College in Lawrenceville, Virginia, and St. Augustine's College in Raleigh, North Carolina, had developed directly from the early freedom schools. Modeled after Booker T. Washington's famous Tuskegee Institute, both offered teacher training and agricultural and industrial education for black students. St. Agnes Hospital, founded on the St. Augustine grounds in 1896, offered a nurses' training program. On the same campus the Bishop Tuttle School for training Negro women church workers operated from 1925 until 1940, educating women to work in those rural congregations too small to support a priest's salary. In 1906 the Episcopal Church organized the American Church Institute for Negroes, which eventually supervised eleven institutions of higher learning: the three mentioned above, along with the Bishop Payne Divinity School (Virginia), the Calhoun School (Alabama), the Voorhees Normal and Industrial School (South Carolina), the Okalona Normal and Industrial School (Mississippi), Fort Valley College (Georgia), the Gaudet Normal and Industrial

School (Louisiana), St. Mary's College (Tennessee), and St. Mark's Industrial School (Alabama).[43] All these schools built on the educational tradition established by the freedom schools, depending heavily on women teachers and administrators and, for financial support, on contributions from the Woman's Auxiliary and individual donors.

THE BISHOP POTTER MEMORIAL HOUSE

Though the work among former slaves was noteworthy as the Church's first deployment of women workers, the schools employed the women as teachers, as members of a profession that already had been established as suitable for women. During the same period, an experimental program evolved in Philadelphia around the Bishop Potter Memorial House. It sought to train women to serve as church workers—assistants in busy urban parishes or lonely mission outposts. The women who developed it were pioneers, defining the roles they would fill and shaping the necessary training system.

It is not surprising that this program originated in Philadelphia, for that city had long had a tradition of female leadership, especially among the Quakers.[44] Episcopal women also exhibited this spirit of independence. As early as 1834 they had organized the Female Protestant Episcopal Prayer Book Society, which raised funds to distribute *The Book of Common Prayer* "to destitute Parishes, institutions, and to all places where it will be acceptable and do good."[45] Pennsylvania women were also among the most active promoters of the freedom schools (described above). The diocesan bishop, the Right Reverend Alonzo Potter, was committed to an active lay ministry by both men and women. In his address to the Diocesan Convention in 1862, he urged the delegates to work to enlist female energies:

> We have but to remember what a vast amount of talent and hearty zeal among women wants to be employed, we have but to contrast the homes of our poor . . . our prisons, our asylums, our reformatories, our almshouses, our hospitals, *as they were, with what they might be if pervaded with a higher feminine and religious influence,* and we shall perceive that nothing but organization and a wise directing spirit is needed to achieve this mighty and beneficent revolution.[46]

Under Bishop Potter's leadership, a variety of programs to involve laywomen in social-service ministries were begun. The most notable was that of St. Mark's Church, Frankford, in which members of the parish (men and women) would call on the unchurched people in the neighborhood (primarily a working-class area), minister to their needs, and attempt to involve them in Church life. Two women headed the program—"a lady of cultivation and refinement" and "an ardent Christian woman from the working class." Together they organized an intensive schedule of mothers' meetings, boys' and girls' clubs, sewing and industrial classes, and morning and evening worship services. Women not only ran many of these programs but served on the governing councils. Although historians often cite St. Mark's Church as one of the first parishes to implement social-gospel ideals, they neglect the important role women played in designing and implementing those activities.[47]

Deeply committed to St. Mark's Church was an extraordinary couple, Mr. and Mrs. William Welsh. Welsh was a wealthy Philadelphia merchant and philanthropist. A devout Episcopalian, he had served as a deputy to both the Diocesan and the General Conventions for many years and was an active member of the national Board of Missions. In Philadelphia he was a director of Girard College, a trustee of the Wills Eye Hospital, and president of the Board of City Trusts. During the Civil War, Welsh had worked with the Episcopal Freedmen's Commission and with the United States Sanitary Commission; after the war President Grant had appointed him to the Board of Indian Commissioners, of which he was the first president. In addition, he was the primary architect of the Episcopal Church's Indian mission work.[48]

Mrs. Welsh shared her husband's religious concerns. She and her daughters founded the Bible classes at St. Mark's Church. She traveled with her husband to Board of Missions' meetings and to the Indian reservations. Missionary bishops found she was a responsible ally in their work. In 1869, when Bishop Morris founded a school for girls in Portland, Oregon, he asked her to raise funds to furnish the school. Her success at this enterprise brought her another job—Bishop Tuttle enlisted her aid for a similar school in Salt Lake City.[49]

Owing to William Welsh's active promotion, several parishes copied St. Mark's neighborhood-outreach scheme. The proliferation of clinics, youth clubs, and Bible and industrial classes created a demand for administrators and a school to train them. Quarters for the school became available in 1866, when the Episcopal Hospital vacated the Leamy Mansion for its new buildings. A committee led by the

Welshes converted the mansion to a residence and training house for women workers, naming it the Bishop Potter Memorial House in honor of the late bishop. With Mrs. William Jackson as principal, the house opened in 1867 with courses—in nursing, mission work, and parish schools—taught by women already active in those fields. Thus began the first training school for women workers in the Episcopal Church.[50]

The house served as a residence both for students in training and for the women already responsible for social-service ministries in Philadelphia. The residents formed a sisterhood, taking care, however, to stress its Protestant aspects. There would be "no private oratories, no extraordinary services . . . no graduated orders of novice and devotee for life; no needless bar to departure or to reasonable interchange with family or friends." Above all, the sisters would not "mimic the worn-out costume of the Roman nunnery . . . its black and grey sisterhoods, its hideous head-dress, its knotted cords and pendant crosses." Instead, each woman chose her own dress, provided it was "characterized by Christian simplicity and inexpensiveness, avoiding needless singularity."[51] Basically, the sisterhood was an association of those who lived at the house and of its graduates. One became a full sister after a six-month probationary period and could leave the sisterhood at any time. Local Philadelphia women could become associate sisters by supporting the work and giving time to Christian service. The associate sisters could also participate in the training programs. Some of Philadelphia's most prominent women, including Elizabeth and Catharine Biddle, Louisa Claxton, Lilla S. Pechin, and Mrs. William Welsh, became associate sisters.[52]

As word of the school spread, it attracted students from several northern states. The course work was divided into three departments—nursing, mission work, and parish schools—and involved theological and biblical studies along with a heavy component of practical training in nearby institutions. The students began an extensive neighborhood-visitation project centered around the Episcopal Hospital Chapel, which was located in a working-class area not served by any other church. By 1870 they were teaching Bible classes of over 400 men and women, a Sunday school of 350 children, and night and industrial classes attended by over 150 pupils. In-service training at the hospital included patient visitation and the operation of an out-patient dispensary.[53]

Admission was controlled by the lady principal and was generally open to single women, between the ages of twenty-five and forty, who were recommended by their parishes. Those who were able were expected to contribute toward their support; a parish could sponsor one of its members for three hundred dollars per year. Women who wanted extensive hospital training were sent to St. Luke's Hospital in New York City because "St. Luke's being under the entire charge of Sisters, affords better facilities for such instruction than the Episcopal Hospital."[54]

By 1872 thirty-seven women had been trained at the Bishop Potter House. One woman was in charge of a hospital in Detroit, another of a city mission house, and several had returned to work in their own parishes. Those in training included one nurse specializing in pediatric medicine, a missionary returned from Africa and seeking more medical training, and one woman who intended to serve in China. Welsh was particularly interested in using the school to train women for work among the Indians; by 1875 seven of the school's graduates were serving among the Dakotah and Santee Indians in the Niobrara Diocese.[55]

The school was hampered, however, by the fact that it was widely perceived in the diocese as "a private enterprise governed by a few of its principal supporters," notably the Welshes and the Biddle sisters. Although Bishop William Bacon Stevens urged diocesan leaders to "enlarge, endow, and sustain" the Memorial House's work, few heeded his call and William Welsh remained its primary financial supporter.[56] In 1877 the governing board was reorganized and placed under diocesan management. The name was changed to the Bishop Potter Memorial House for Deaconesses in an attempt to capitalize on a growing movement to authenticate women's ministries with the biblically sanctioned title of "deaconess."[57] The reorganization came too late, however, for William Welsh died in 1878, and without his guiding spirit the institution floundered. After Mrs. Jackson died, the new board was unable to find anyone to replace her as principal and refused to continue the training programs without a head. The house appears to have remained as a residence for a few women, who continued the hospital mission work until 1891, when the board was dissolved and the remaining funds turned over to the diocese.[58]

Despite its short life, the Bishop Potter Memorial Training House had demonstrated that there were women who would avail themselves of the opportunity for such training and that many dioceses and churches were eager to hire them. Its graduates served not only in

Pennsylvania but in New York, Nebraska, Minnesota, Colorado, Virginia, and South Dakota, working as teachers, parish assistants, rescue workers, and administrators of hospitals and orphanages.[59] Many remained at their posts for lengthy terms. Sister Eliza Barton, for example, served as a mission worker in Colorado for over twenty-seven years, helping found at least three Denver churches and maintaining the ministry to the county hospital.[60] Sister Hannah Austin did city mission work in Philadelphia, then went west to begin a school at Red Cloud, Nebraska. Later she joined Sister Eliza in Colorado, working at St. Luke's Hospital and St. Mark's Church in Denver until her death in 1917.[61] Sister Annette Relf headed the Cottage Hospital in Minneapolis and later directed the Old Ladies Home and a children's home called The Sheltering Arms.[62] In 1872 Sister Hannah Elizabeth Stiteler began teaching at the Crow Creek Reservation in South Dakota. She married the Reverend William J. Cleveland and raised their four children while living at various mission stations among the Dakotah Sioux.[63] The examples of these women (and of many other Memorial House graduates) undoubtedly inspired others to consider similar careers.[64]

The closing of the Bishop Potter Memorial House, however, demonstrated a problem that was to continue to plague the Church. Though many leaders were eager to enlist the services of women workers, they were not realistically prepared to pay for them. Women were viewed as angels of mercy, whose natural qualities of gentleness and tact would appeal to the most downtrodden of souls, proving that:

> Down in the human heart, crushed by the Tempter,
>   Feelings lie buried, which Grace can restore:
> Touched by a loving hand, wakened by kindness,
>   Chords that were broken, will vibrate once more.[65]

That such angels would need to be fed, clothed, and cared for in sickness and old age scarcely entered the minds of many of the most enthusiastic supporters of women workers. The possibility that feminine "natural inclinations" would be inadequate to meet the tasks set before the woman worker, that her skills might need to be developed through education and training, was equally beyond the romanticized ideal. Consistently throughout this period, the most vociferous advocates of financial support for women workers and of educational programs for them were the women themselves. In a Church in which women had no access to the decision-making councils and no members on the budget committees, however, garnering support for such proposals was difficult. The women eventually realized that if they were to provide adequately for women workers, they would have to develop their own financial-support system.[66] Clearly this came not as an instantaneous realization but as a conclusion drawn from many experiences, such as those of the freedmen's teachers and of the graduates of the Bishop Potter Memorial House. The Woman's Auxiliary to the Board of Missions eventually became the organization to provide that support. The following chapter traces the history of this national organization of Episcopal churchwomen.

CHAPTER SIX

The Woman's Auxiliary to the Board of Missions, 1872–1900

> What we want every woman to do . . . is to think seriously whether she really cares anything for the Missionary work which is being done by the Church or whether she confines her sympathy and her labors to her own country, her own parish, or her own family. What we want every member of the Association to do is to think and to read much about Missions, to keep herself constantly informed upon the subject, and to be ready to present it frequently to others in such a way as shall win their interest in the work and create a desire to share in it.[1]

Thus Mary Abbot Emery outlined her hopes for a new organization, the Woman's Auxiliary to the Board of Missions of the Protestant Episcopal Church. In January 1872 Emery had been appointed general secretary and charged with the dual task of organizing women for mission and of encouraging female vocations in the Church.[2]

Although first proposed in 1862, it was not until nine years later that the General Convention approved a vaguely worded statement allowing "the formation of such Christian organizations as may consist with the government and rules of the Church."[3] With that lukewarm endorsement, the Board of Missions hired Mary Abbot Emery and assigned her to the task of organizing a voluntary association of churchwomen.

In the next twenty-five years, the Woman's Auxiliary became the primary support for the Board of Missions. As the first Church-sponsored organization for all Episcopal women, the auxiliary raised money and recruited workers for the mission field. Its members wrote and published mission education programs and trained the teachers who spread this knowledge throughout the Church. For many lay-women, work in the auxiliary was their first step into the world outside the home. Though pious motives generally led them into the work, their associations with other women in the parish and later with similar groups in other parishes provided a supportive female network that enhanced and broadened their lives.

Technically the auxiliary had no autonomy. Its activities were directed, and its goals set, by the Board of Missions. Though the Board of Missions had no women members, the auxiliary eventually began to play a role in shaping the Church's mission strategy. Gradually the women became not *auxiliary* but *essential* to the Board of Missions. By the turn of the century, the Church's missionary program was heavily dependent on its women. The evolution of the Woman's Auxiliary is the subject of this chapter.

THE EMERY FAMILY

Perhaps the most remarkable aspect of the development of the Woman's Auxiliary was the extent to which it was indebted to the Emery family. Mary Abbot Emery served as its national secretary from 1872 until 1876; she was succeeded by her sister, Julia Chester Emery, who held the position until 1916—forty years. Though she left the salaried position, Mary Abbot continued to be closely involved in the work. After her husband's death, she was appointed honorary secretary and served in that position until she died in 1901. A third sister, Susan Lavinia Emery, edited *The Young Christian Soldier* briefly, followed in 1876 by Margaret Theresa Emery (yet another sister), who continued to work in the national office as coordinator of the "box work" until 1919—forty-three years. In addition, two of Mary Abbot's brothers were Episcopal clergymen and supported the auxiliaries in their respective dioceses. Children of a New England ship captain and a pious, well-educated mother, the Emery sisters were models of nineteenth-century virtue—devout, disciplined, hard-working, frugal, modest, and devoted to family and friends. Their extraordinary ability to work together and to recognize and support each other's talents without envy or jealousy was crucial to their success at establishing a woman's sphere within the masculine hierarchy of the Episcopal Church.[4]

The national missions staff, which Mary Abbot Emery joined in 1872, consisted of the Reverend A.T. Twing (domestic missions), the Reverend W.H. Hare (foreign missions), their assistants, secretaries for the Freedmen's Commission and the Indian Commission, and Susan Emery, who edited *The Young Christian Soldier*. The overseeing of all the mission work, including decisions regarding the Woman's Auxiliary, rested with the Board of Missions, made up of all the members of the General Convention and delegates from the missionary jurisdictions. Its large membership made the body unwieldy, so practical control was exercised by specially appointed committees.[5] No women served on the board or any of its committees. Because the entire missions office consisted of only eight people, however, Emery and the other secretaries had substantial freedom to enact their own policies.

DESIGNING A NATIONAL STRUCTURE

Because Mary Abbot Emery took office at the behest of the General Convention and not in response to church women's request for a national structure, her first task was to win the acceptance of the existing women's groups. As has been indicated earlier, several churches had women's missionary or tract societies. In the 1860s some of these societies began to band together to work for specific missionary goals. For example, the Hartford Bureau of Relief (organized in 1865) aided poorly paid missionaries, and the Dakota League of Massachusetts (1864) and the Indians' Hope of Philadelphia (1868) sent missionaries to work among the American Indians.[6] The largest of these associations was the Ladies' Domestic Missionary Relief Association, which had chapters in several prominent New York City parishes.[7]

To create the Woman's Auxiliary to the Board of Missions, Emery devised a plan to unify the diverse women's groups. The rector of every Episcopal church would be asked to appoint a secretary who would correspond with the national secretary about the women's work in that parish. Women in the parishes might organize any way they chose; recommended models were available on request from the national secretary, but groups already at work on specific objectives were welcome under the Woman's Auxiliary umbrella.

One by one, the existing female missionary associations declared themselves part of the Woman's Auxiliary: the Niobrara League of

New York and the Dakota League of Massachusetts in 1872, the Providence Indian Aid of Rhode Island, the Fairfield County Indian Aid Association of Connecticut, the Indian Aid Association of Baltimore, and the Indians' Hope of Philadelphia in 1873. Finally, in 1874 the Ladies Domestic Missionary Relief Association also voted to discontinue independent operation and to work through the auxiliary.[8]

Paralleling these associations' enrollment in the national body was the organization of the diocesan branches. Bishop Abram Newkirk Littlejohn (of Long Island), an enthusiastic supporter of women's ministries, invited a clergyman and a female representative from each parish to meet in December 1872. After presentations by Dr. Twing and Mary Abbot Emery, the assembled convention adopted an organizational plan for the first diocesan branch of the Woman's Auxiliary. It elected officers and established a diocesan board consisting of committees on the five phases of mission work—foreign, domestic, diocesan, Indian, and Colored missions. A yearly meeting of delegates from each church was planned.[9]

Similar diocesan branches were organized in Ohio, western Michigan, Milwaukee, and central New York in 1875; southern Ohio, Newark, and New Jersey in 1876; Massachusetts in 1877; Rhode Island in 1878; and Vermont, Maine, New Hampshire, and Florida in 1879.[10] Gradually branches were formed in each diocese and even in the missionary districts themselves. By working through an administrative structure that paralleled that of the national Church, the Woman's Auxiliary eventually came to be seen as an integral part of the Church's administrative structure rather than as an isolated and extraneous organization. And many of the women who worked in these organizations came to view their own ministries from a diocesan or a national rather than a parochial point of view.

ORGANIZATIONAL DEVELOPMENT

Though other Protestant women's organizations of this period established their own publications, Emery simply inserted the "Woman's Work" section in the Church's national periodical, *The Spirit of Missions,* thus maintaining the auxiliary's image as an integral part of the overall mission program.[11] She published letters from women already serving in the mission field: Miss Savery, who ran an orphanage in Liberia; Marion Muir, who continued the educational work begun by Dr. and Mrs. Hill in Greece; and Mrs. Elliott Thomson, who had served in China since 1854. "I want a lady helper badly," wrote Mrs. Stanforth from the Ponca Indian Camp on the Missouri River, "but would rather not have help unless it could be given with the whole heart, nay, heart, soul and body."[12] Lydia M. Fay described her recent visit to Cha-ka-pang, China, convinced that "day schools in these little hamlets are really the only efficient means of teaching the truths of our holy religion to the people. They interest the mothers as well as the children, and the mothers are the real teachers and keepers of idolatry among the Chinese. I would like so much to open a girls' day school in this hamlet, if some generous friends would be responsible for the expenses of such a school."[13] Along with pleas for assistance, Emery included letters of gratitude. "It would have done you and your Society good to have seen us all around the boxes, with bright and joyous faces, as the things were taken out," or, "The young ladies of the school requested me to thank you a thousand times. . . . These are the first library books the school has been able to get."[14] Women who were inspired by these letters to further action found articles suggesting ways to organize a local auxiliary or to plan a fund-raising event. Over the next twenty-five years, Mary Abbot and Julia Emery skillfully used the pages of *The Spirit of Missions* to inspire, inform, and build a strong sense of community among churchwomen throughout the world.

As the number of local branches grew, the need to systematize their missionary contributions became apparent. In 1875 Mary Abbot Emery centralized the distribution of missionary boxes by establishing in the national office a central clearinghouse to which missionaries could send their lists of needed articles, which would then be conveyed to the local auxiliaries willing to pack the boxes. The box contained needed supplies for the mission family—clothing, books, furniture—and equipment for the mission—hospital supplies, medicines, church-school materials, needles, fabric—whatever was necessary for the work. Generally the auxiliary from a church worked with the same missionary year after year, becoming acquainted with members of the mission family, the type of clothing needed in that particular climate, and the mission's work. As they filled the boxes, the women grew to share a sense of partnership in the work of their mission. The educational advantage of this sense of connectedness with mission should not be underestimated. The monetary value of the fully stocked boxes increased dramatically: The total worth of boxes sent in 1875 was $61,000; ten years later it was $127,000; and in 1900, $191,000.[15] An added benefit was that the women's work of amassing the supplies, clothing, and educational materials freed the missionary for the Lord's work. Essentially the Woman's Auxiliary became the Quartermaster Corps of the mission field—an organization of workers who marshaled and moved equipment and supplies to a far-flung complex of mission stations.

Fund raising was the other key function of local auxiliaries. The Board of Missions was perpetually in need of additional money and found the women a ready source of financial support. Mary Abbot and, later, Julia Emery began by suggesting specific needs a local or diocesan group might address. Sister Eliza Barton, for example, in 1877 was the first woman the Board of Missions appointed to serve as a domestic missionary; her salary was supplied by the auxiliaries of the dioceses of Central New York, Southern Ohio, Northern New Jersey, and Massachusetts.[16] Rhode Island supported Miss Eddy in Japan, whereas one young New York woman met the salary of Miss Thomas in Africa.[17] The auxiliary consistently funded two programs—fringe benefits for mission clergy and secondary schools for women. Included under the former were the Foreign Insurance Fund, which provided life insurance for foreign missionaries, scholarships for missionary children to boarding schools and colleges, and special benefits to missionary widows.[18] In terms of women's education, the Episcopal Church established in almost every major city in the western United States a secondary school for girls that depended heavily on funds from eastern women. Among them were Wolfe Hall in Denver, Ivinson Hall in Laramie, Irving Institute in San Francisco, St. Paul's School in Walla Walla, St. Helen's Hall in Portland, and St. Mary's School in Dallas. *Whittaker's Church Almanac* for 1899 lists eighty Church-sponsored schools for girls and sixty-seven for boys.[19] Without the auxiliary's steady, continual support for education for women, many of these schools might never have been built. (Also crucial to the continued existence of these schools were the headmistresses and teachers, many of whom were recruited and sent by the auxiliary.)

The growth of the Woman's Auxiliary paralleled the enlargement of the mission field. When Mary Abbot Emery became secretary, there were seventeen missionary bishops; ten years later there were twenty-nine—seven foreign and twenty-two domestic bishops.[20] As the new bishops began to recruit workers and build churches, schools, and hospitals, they found the Woman's Auxiliary a ready source of funds. Not only was it easier for a bishop to ask a laywoman or a group to contribute the funds to build a new school than to go through the complex process of requesting funds from the Board of Managers but the process gave him greater control over financial allocations in his diocese. These direct contributions to particular bishops were known as "specials." The Board of Managers generally felt the "specials" interrupted the orderly planning of missionary strategy and served as a constant source of contention between the board and the Woman's Auxiliary.

Possibly as significant as its financial support of the missionary bishops was the *psychological* support the auxiliary provided. The Emery sisters' correspondence is filled with examples of it; women working in the churches probably also filled the same roles. Work in mission outposts was lonely and demanding, and bishops especially had few people to whom they might turn for psychological support. The Emerys knew from correspondence and personal visits what each diocese was like; they shared the bishops' sense of purpose and high calling, and they responded immediately to correspondence. "Dear Mrs. Twing, surely I may write freely to *you*? I have put a bit upon my pen when writing to others, and say no more of the shadows of missionary work, but if I can't write to *somebody* I shall explode," wrote a Mississippi clergyman beseiged because of his work with black Episcopalians.[21] Bishop Henry B. Whipple shared his grief at the death of his son: "Few men could feel it as I do. . . . I leave Zack with God, but it is a sore heart I shall carry to the grave. . . . I had to write to somebody and you won't blame me."[22] From Alaska, Bishop Peter Trimble Rowe wrote, "The trip in this year was exhausting on mind, body, nerves, etc., and I could not always overcome the spells of depression which seize me. But your helpful letters . . . have been effectual in charming these 'spells' away. . . . What we owe to you and your sisters, your thought, untiring interest and labors, is more than I can estimate or ever repay in gratitude."[23]

Mary Abbot Emery served as national secretary for just four years; she resigned in 1876 to marry Dr. Twing, the domestic secretary. During her administration, over three hundred and fifty local secretaries had been appointed and diocesan groups formed in nine dioceses.[24] Organizational patterns continued to vary. Some dioceses were led by women appointed by the bishops; others developed legislative assemblies. Both kept in touch with the national office through the corresponding secretary and the constant demands of the box work. National auxiliary meetings began in 1874 with a gathering of those women present for the General Convention in New York City and continued at each succeeding convention. Inspirational, these triennial meetings featured addresses by prominent missionary bishops and women who worked in the mission field, giving delegates the opportunity to exchange programmatic and administrative ideas. A monthly meeting of diocesan officers at the New York office became an informal cabinet meeting open to Woman's Auxiliary members from throughout the country, to discuss matters of national program and policy.

In reviewing this early history, one is struck by the organizational informality and inclusive spirit. One of the Emery sisters' great virtues was their ability to allow for diversity and to encourage others to contribute their own abilities, talents, and ideas. But they were plowing a fertile field, for there were literally hundreds of churchwomen who sought an occupation both socially respectable and spiritually challenging and who found that ideal in the auxiliary. Ida Soule was one such person. As a young woman, she volunteered to take her rector's wife to the Woman's Auxiliary at the 1877 General Convention, "little dreaming what it would mean to me all my life." She died in 1944, having served as an officer or organized auxiliary chapters in Boston, Frankfort (New York), Pittsburgh, Englewood (New Jersey), and Roanoke (Virginia); attended several General Conventions; worked with domestic missionary Deaconess Alice J. Knight in eastern Oregon; and visited the Church's mission stations in Japan.[25] In one sense, she was a traditional housewife; because her husband was a railroad builder, they lived in many places. But her use of auxiliary work as a means to establish herself in a new community, and the way she expanded that work (by serving as a missionary in Oregon) after her husband's death illustrate how it had broadened her horizons. For innumerable women, work with the Woman's Auxiliary was the first step from the home into a wider sphere of activity.

Julia Chester Emery was appointed to succeed her sister as national secretary in 1876. Though she was just twenty-four years old, she accepted the position with the knowledge that Mary Abbot would remain nearby for advice.[26] "Miss Julia," as she would affectionately become known to women around the world, was a small woman with a merry sense of humor. Less assertive than her sister Mary, she was nevertheless a sternly disciplined individual with a strong sense of her mission to win the world for Christ. Although her manner was consistently quiet, soft-spoken, and gentle, through hard work and persistence she generally managed to achieve her aims. She traveled often, using her speaking engagements as excuses to visit other auxiliaries or workers *en route*. By the time she retired she had visited every diocese and missionary district in the United States, made two trips to England and one world tour in which she visited almost every mission station except those in Africa and Alaska.[27] When Julia became secretary, her sister Margaret Theresa joined the staff to edit *The Young Christian Soldier* and superintend the growing box work. Another sister, Helen Winthrop, eventually also moved to New York to keep house for the others and to help entertain the steady succession of missionary workers who made the Emery household on East 24th Street their "home away from home."[28]

As a married woman, Mary Abbot Twing continued to be closely involved with the auxiliary. Traveling with her husband to promote domestic missions, she met churchwomen and spoke to their fledgling societies. She familiarized herself with women's work in charitable institutions and schools. Her elevated social status as the wife of a prominent New York clergyman gave her entry to the parlors of the city's social elite, and she used those contacts to encourage wealthy women to increase their philanthropic gifts. She was particularly close to Mrs. John Jacob Astor and often advised her on charitable contributions. She organized the Society of the Royal Law, a group that united wealthy benefactors with Church and charitable workers in a common drive to increase employment opportunities for women in churches and church-sponsored institutions.[29]

Dr. Twing's sudden death in 1882 left Mary Abbot a widow at age thirty-nine. Seeking "a time to look about and breathe a little before I tie myself down to any exact or exacting work," she devised for herself the position of honorary secretary of the Woman's Auxiliary, "for the purpose of maturing a system for the training and distributions of women's services in the Domestic Missions of the Church."[30] The Board of Managers appointed her to the position in June 1883. Though she received no salary, she could draw on the Board of Missions' budget for travel expenses. While Julia continued to build up the auxiliary and to strengthen its systems for collecting and distributing funds, Mary Abbot concentrated on developing and publicizing vocational opportunities for women in the Church and tending to the needs of those already so employed. (Her work in this field is discussed further in the following chapter.)

Meanwhile, the Reverend William S. Langford, who had been

chosen general secretary of the Board of Managers in the 1885 reorganization of the Board of Missions, became concerned about the Woman's Auxiliary's growing power. He felt the auxiliary's willingness to fund the special projects of favored missionary bishops threatened the board's ability to set priorities and determine strategy. He probably was also responding to the fact that while Dr. Twing had been the domestic secretary, the Woman's Auxiliary had generally been able to do as it pleased in the national office. Hence, he proposed that the auxiliary be reorganized under a constitution "accurately defining the relations between itself and this Board [the Board of Managers], mapping out with tolerable precision the field of labor proper to such an organization, and providing for the annual and triennial election of officers." The Board of Managers adopted that resolution and placed it on the agenda for the Board of Missions' 1886 general meeting. Emery and Mrs. Twing, however, were suspicious of Dr. Langford's motives and were reluctant to have the auxiliary's work defined by the Board of Missions.[31] So they formulated a strategy that stressed the auxiliary's present contribution to missionary work and suggested means to enhance it.

At the 1886 meeting, both women presented their annual reports. Emery read a long list of special gifts local auxiliaries had contributed but was careful to note that "while the various diocesan Branches express freely their individual preferences in their gifts, they are constantly reminded that they are expected to contribute regularly to the pledged work of the Board."[32] She went on to praise the educational and spiritual value of the special links between individual auxiliaries and specific missionaries, ending with a pledge to encourage members to give systematically to the board's work. Mary Abbot followed with a detailed plan to reorganize the auxiliary to increase its responsibilities by registering all women communicants who did any type of Church work—voluntary or paid—in a systematic program of education and training.[33] Confronted with this extensive and well-developed plan, the Board of Missions took the Anglican *via media* by dismissing Langford's resolution and endorsing the Woman's Auxiliary's present work, "not only to assist the Board in making its regular appropriations, but also to aid all missionary work of the Church."[34] And the redoubtable Mrs. Twing proceeded to carry out most of the recommendations in her report, funding them with money she raised privately or through events sponsored by diocesan auxiliaries.[35]

THE UNITED OFFERING

One step remained, however, to complete the women's effectiveness in plotting missionary strategy: The Woman's Auxiliary needed to control the distribution of the money it raised.[36] The establishment of the United Offering (now the United Thank Offering) at the General Convention of 1889 was the crucial step. There is a legend about the offering's origin. At the Woman's Auxiliary meeting during the General Convention of 1886, about five hundred women were present for the worship service. And yet, when Mrs. Ida Soule, then serving as a delegate from Pittsburgh, helped to count the offering, she found the women had only given a total of eighty-seven dollars. Dismayed at the meager amount, she suggested to Julia Emery that perhaps if the women knew where their money was going, they might be inspired to contribute more generously. Emery agreed and urged her to write a letter suggesting that, just before the next Triennial Meeting, the offering be earmarked for a specific project. Emery would publish the letter in *The Spirit of Missions* and announce the designated recipient of that year's offering.[37]

This version of the origin of the United Offering has been printed innumerable times.[38] A simple laywoman made a very practical observation, repeated it in *The Spirit of Missions* three years later, and women throughout the Church responded generously.[39] A closer look at the circumstances, however, suggests a more complex scenario. In the first place, Ida Soule was more than a simple laywoman. She, too, had been raised in suburban Boston and had known the Emerys for many years. Julia Emery arranged her hotel accommodations at the meeting, in the room next door to Emery and Twing.[40] Moreover, it was uncharacteristic of Emery to delay publicizing such a good idea for three years, unless she had a good reason for doing so. My suspicion is that the threat that the Board of Missions might reorganize the auxiliary at the General Convention had both convinced Emery that her organization must have funds it could control and that she must move cautiously to develop its financial independence.

Furthermore, in her research on women's ministries Mary Abbot Twing had become convinced the Church must officially recognize and define a religious vocation for women in order to validate the many ways in which they already were serving.[41] She had concluded that the office of deaconess had the best chance of being recognized by the General Convention and began to devise a strategy to ensure the passage of the canon on deaconesses at the 1889 convention.[42] Through letters, speeches, and an intense publicity campaign about deaconesses in the 1889 volume of *Church Work*, Twing worked to build support for the proposed canon. Her efforts were successful; the canon on deaconesses was approved by both the House of Bishops and the House of Deputies in 1889.[43] Once that goal had been achieved, both Twing and Emery could shift their energies to raising the United Offering.

At the 1889 convention, then, Julia Emery announced that the offering collected by the women would be used to build a church in Anvik, Alaska, and to send a missionary worker, Miss Lisa Lovell, to Japan. The auxiliary members contributed the needed funds.[44] And throughout the next decade the auxiliary worked to increase the United Offering and to recruit and train women workers. Deaconess training schools were opened in New York in 1890 and in Philadelphia in 1891. (The evolution of the role of deaconess is discussed in the following chapter.) Several women went directly from the training schools to the mission field. By 1900 the Board of Missions sponsored seventy-nine women in domestic missions and seventy-five in foreign missions.[45] The United Offering grew each triennium: 1892—$20,911; 1895—$56,198; 1898—$82,818; and 1901—$107,589. The first two offerings went to endow the missionary episcopate, and the third was used entirely for the training and support of women workers in the mission field.[46]

The United Offering was supplementary; it did not replace the financial support the Woman's Auxiliary gave to the Board of Missions' general budget. The strength of the women's contribution to the Board of Missions is evident in the following figures: For the fiscal year September 1899 to September 1900, the Board of Missions' gross receipts amounted to just over one million dollars.[47] Of this amount, the Woman's Auxiliary contributed directly just over $100,000, or about 10 percent.[48] Legacies from individual women contributed that year amounted to $93,000, or about another 10 percent. That same year, the auxiliary also spent, through specials, an additional $106,374 that was not channeled through the board's budget at all.[49] And the women packed and sent 4,679 missionary boxes, worth $191,434.[50] Thus the direct contribution of the Woman's Auxiliary, aside from the United Offering, amounted to just over $400,000.

Furthermore, one steady source of funds for the board was income from trust funds donated in the past. The 1900 budget lists trusts amounting to $1,242,073, of which 34 percent had been contributed by women, 38 percent by men, and 28 percent by unidentified donors.[51] Though it is impossible to trace which of the female donors were inspired to such charity by the Woman's Auxiliary, the percentage of women's gifts is high for a century in which men were generally in control of financial matters.

WIDENING THE SCOPE OF WOMEN'S WORK

As women increased their financial contributions in the 1890s, they also broadened the scope of their activities. At the 1892 Triennial Meeting, Julia Emery proposed an administrative reorganization of the auxiliary. The 1889 passage of the deaconess canon had established a career for women in the Church, and the founding of the United Offering had provided the auxiliary with a financial base. Emery had come to realize that local auxiliaries needed to broaden their concept of mission work. Though she would have rejected the label, she was moving toward a feminist point of view—urging the recruitment of women and the empowering of Woman's Auxiliary members to plan and direct their own programs. Departing from her general practice of urging support for all the Church's missionary work, she called specifically for gifts "devoted to distinctive woman's work; to the training and support of women as missionaries, to the support of girls at school, to the building of schools for girls, hospitals for women, homes for orphans."[52] Noting that although there were many female missionaries in the field, only one woman had entered that work because of her experience in the auxiliary, Emery urged members to examine seriously their own calls to serve in the mission field and to challenge others to do the same. "It is far from an unlikely thing," she stated, "that some woman, of gifts needed beyond all, is lost to the mission field today, because her modesty prevents her asking for a position that seems to her too great an honor, and no one who has the right calls upon her to take that place and do its work."[53]

To accomplish these tasks, Emery recommended (and the convention approved) the formation of four committees: Systematic Giving, Missionary Publications, Missionary Workers, and Junior Department.[54] The last committee was in charge of the Junior Department, which had been established (at the previous Triennial Meeting) to promote among children and youth the habits of prayer, study, and giving to missions. Diocesan officers in charge of the junior work were appointed, and gradually, in individual parishes, local junior auxiliaries were formed, generally among the young mothers of the parish. They enrolled young people in the children's missionary army, encouraged them to fill mite chests, and taught them about missionaries serving at home and abroad.

Each committee was to be made up of nine Woman's Auxiliary members, with widespread geographical representation. They would meet at least annually, to determine strategy and devise programs. Among the committee members were several women who had been active in auxiliary work for many years—two bishops' wives, Mrs. Tuttle and Mrs. Spalding, both of whom had served as presidents of their diocesan auxiliaries in Utah, Colorado, and Missouri—were on the Publications Committee. On the Missionary Workers Committee were Mary Coles, who had founded the Church Training School for Deaconesses in Philadelphia, Sybil Carter, who had been one of the earliest missionary workers in Minnesota, and New Yorker Cornelia Jay, who had been chairman of the New York Committee on Work for Foreign Missionaries even before the Woman's Auxiliary was founded.[55] The availability of such women to serve on the committees is indicative of the growing number of women volunteers who had developed administrative and organizational skills through their auxiliary work.

The task of recruiting and selecting women missionaries fell to the committee on missionary workers. The committee collected names of potential women workers, screened their credentials, interviewed the most likely candidates, and recommended to the Board of Missions those who should be employed. By the end of its first three years, the committee had received over one hundred applications from women who wanted to serve in the mission field. Six of the applicants were rejected for unsuitability and a few withdrew for personal reasons, but the majority were judged eminently qualified. Twelve women for general mission work and twelve nurses were recommended to the Board of Missions. The board's financial position, however, was such that it could scarcely fund missionaries already in the field; six women were sent out, but there were no salaries for the others. The committee counseled patience, "believing this waiting time may be a school of discipline to test their earnestness and strengthen their zeal," and urged the applicants to enroll in one of the training schools to better prepare themselves for the work ahead. It also pleaded for more financial support from the local auxiliaries.[56]

The committee's experience convinced it that if more women were to be sent into the mission field, women would have to fund their work. At the 1895 Triennial Meeting, it persuaded the auxiliary to devote the entire United Offering for the next three years to the salaries of women missionary workers. And at the 1898 triennial, Julia Emery proudly announced that the offering amounted to $82,743, a 47 percent increase over the previous one—testimony to the widespread approval of funding additional women workers. The next year twenty women were appointed as United Offering missionary workers.[57]

MISSION EDUCATION PROGRAMS

Though many local auxiliaries actively recruited female missionary workers, far more were responsible for mission education. As early as 1874, the New York auxiliary had issued a series of catechisms, written by Cornelia Jay, on China, Japan, and Africa. Creative women such as Harriet Tuttle, Miss Upfold, and Sarah Smiley wrote advanced mission study guides.[58] To publish these materials, two Connecticut auxiliary members, Edith and Mary Beach, in 1891 founded what came to be known as the Church Missions Publishing Company.[59] Over the years, it has published millions of missionary pamphlets and Christian-education booklets, pouring the profits into further mission work.

In 1886 a domestic missionary lending library was established at the national office and the next year was expanded to include works on foreign missions. Lists of the available books were sent to local branches.[60] Diocesan auxiliaries also set up lending libraries that collected reference materials and made them available to local parishes.[61] They developed training courses, bringing together women from many parishes for intensive study of a particular mission field, then sending them back into their parishes to impart the information to local study classes.[62] Such training sessions gradually expanded until, after the turn of the century, they became residential summer sessions for training Church leaders and teachers in the latest materials and methods of Christian education.[63]

Supplementing the auxiliary's Christian-education work were the activities of three other organizations for churchwomen—the Daughters of the King, the Church Periodical Club, and the Girls' Friendly Society. Though these groups were administratively independent of the auxiliary, their links to it were strong. Many Woman's Auxiliary members belonged also to one or more of the other groups. Because all the groups held national meetings concurrent with the General Convention, there was frequent social interaction and cooperation among their national leaders.

THE DAUGHTERS OF THE KING

A Bible class's desire for a deeper form of Christian commitment led to the formation of the Daughters of the King. In 1885 the young women who studied with Margaret J. Franklin at the Church of the Holy Sepulchre in New York City felt called to spread Christ's kingdom among their acquaintances. They adopted a simple rule, promising to pray daily for the blessing of God's Holy Spirit and to reach out to bring others to Christ's kingdom. They called for a return to apostolic simplicity, using as their motto:

> For His Sake . . . I am but one, but I am one
> I cannot do everything; but I can do something
>   What I can do, I ought to do.
> What I ought to do, by the grace of God, I will do.
>   Lord, what wilt thou have me do?[64]

Six women along with Mrs. Franklin began the order and quickly attracted other women to join them in Bible study and prayer. Seeking ways to welcome newcomers into the parish, they stationed themselves in the pews at Sunday services, greeted strangers, and helped them find their way through the pages of *The Book of Common Prayer.* They did not see their organization as in any way supplanting the Woman's Auxiliary or the existing Church guilds but rather as a means to deepen their own spiritual lives and to provide sisterly support of Christ's mission. Soon ladies from other churches heard about the program and sought to copy it. The movement spread slowly at first— six chapters were organized by 1889—but then proliferated rapidly. By 1896 over three hundred chapters had been organized, with a total membership of 11,697 women. The first convention, which met in Baltimore, Maryland, in 1893, attracted delegates from Connecticut, New York, New Jersey, Pennsylvania, Maryland, the District of Columbia, Virginia, North Carolina, Ohio, Tennessee, Georgia, Florida, and Iowa. A national constitution was adopted, and delegates contin-

ued to meet annually until 1901, when they decided to meet triennially at the General Convention.[65]

In the early years, much of the impetus for the organization came
from the Alpha Chapter at the Church of the Holy Sepulchre (which
became the Church of the Resurrection in 1907). Margaret Franklin
served as the national president until 1894; Elizabeth Ryerson and
Anne E. Kragel served, respectively, as secretary and treasurer. From
1891 until 1907 Ryerson also edited the newsletter *The Royal Cross*,
which linked the fledgling chapters through common Bible study as
well as organizational news.

Though the initial emphasis was on evangelism and spiritual development in individual parishes, it was later broadened in response
to a letter, published in the newsletter, from Miss Lily Funsten Ward,
a Daughter of the King from Virginia. She was then serving as a
missionary to China and urged members to unite in prayer for the
Church's work in China. On Miss Ward's untimely death in 1898, the
governing council established a memorial fund in her honor for the
support of women missionaries in China. The following missionaries
were supported by the fund: Miss Charley Warnock, who served in
Wuchang from 1899 to 1902; Miss Annette Burke Richmond, from
1903 to 1916; Deaconess Emily Ridgely, from 1916 to 1927; Miss Eva
Carr, 1922 to 1927; Deaconess Caroline C. Pitcher, 1927 to 1931;
Miss Coral Clark, 1931 to 1934; Miss Gertrude Selzer, 1934 to 1940;
and Miss Elda Joyce Smith, 1937 to 1954 (served the later years in
Hawaii). The examples of these women and their frequent letters in
The Royal Cross inspired other Daughters of the King, many of whom
developed their own ministries as deaconesses, nuns, or lay employees.[66]

A second fund, the Master's Fund, was established at the National
Convention in 1922, to provide scholarships for women to be trained
as church workers, first at the deaconess schools and later at other
educational institutions. To date, over two hundred grants have been
made from it.[67] Thus the Daughters of the King, like the members of
the Woman's Auxiliary, exercised a long-standing commitment to the
education and deployment of women church workers. The seven
founders were impelled by the certainty that Christ's call to service
was extended to women as well as men, that discipleship was not an
exclusively masculine concern. The order's subsequent development
suggests that many other churchwomen wrestled with the question of

their calls to ministry and found ways to exercise that ministry in a wide variety of settings.

CHURCH PERIODICAL CLUB

One form of ministry extensively supported by the Church's women was that of the distribution of written matter. Bibles, prayer books, and Sunday-school texts were routinely included among the supplies the Woman's Auxiliary members sent to missionaries. In 1888 a group of women at the Church of the Holy Communion in New York City organized specifically to send Church periodicals to mission stations in the American West. The driving force behind this newly founded Church Periodical Club (CPC) was Mrs. Mortimer Fargo, the wife of the heir to the Wells-Fargo Company. She was elected president and served in that position until her death in 1892. In that year an endowment, provided through substantial bequest in Mrs. Fargo's honor from her husband, led to the club's incorporation as an independent organization with strong ties to the Woman's Auxiliary. Church Periodical Club members gathered, wrapped, and shipped (via Wells-Fargo) collections of current periodicals to mission stations, beginning with those on the Dakotah Indian reservations and gradually extending the work to other domestic mission stations, schools among the blacks in the South, and western, Church-sponsored, private secondary schools. Similar clubs were formed in other parishes; the minute book recorded that, by 1891, thirty-seven dioceses were working with the Church Periodical Club.[68]

In 1897 Mary Abbot Twing spoke at the club's annual meeting in New York City, praising its accomplishments and urging the members to think "bold thoughts" about their future. She called for further cooperation between the CPC and the Woman's Auxiliary, stressing particularly the need for printed materials in the foreign mission field. Over the next year, club members across the country discussed possible affiliation with the Woman's Auxiliary, and at the next annual meeting the board unanimously approved a plan for cooperation with the auxiliary. It provided that CPC correspondents would be appointed in each diocese and meet with diocesan Woman's Auxiliary officers. Nationally, the CPC's annual report would be attached to that of the auxiliary in the Board of Missions Annual Report. The 1900 report indicated that women from forty-five dioceses had sent over three hundred thousand books and periodicals to missionary outposts.[69]

The Church Periodical Club continued to operate as a quasi-independent agency deriving its financial support primarily from churchwomen and cooperating with the Board of Missions in its distribution of written materials. National board members were elected at triennial meetings held at the time of General Convention and served for three-year terms. This board gradually expanded the CPC's focus to include providing textbooks for seminarians, indigenous clergy, and lay catechists and sending technical and scientific works to Church-sponsored schools and universities at home and abroad. Attesting to the importance of this form of ministry was that during the Church's reorganization in 1919 the Church Periodical Club was designated as one of the cooperating agencies and provided with an annual budget for its administrative work.[70]

THE GIRLS' FRIENDLY SOCIETY

Emily M. Edson was responsible for the organization of the first chapter of the Girls' Friendly Society in the United States. Living in Lowell, Massachusetts, Edson was concerned about the large number of young women employed in the Lowell textile mills. Many of them were living alone for the first time, away from the influence of home and family. Their wages were low and they had few opportunities for entertainment or recreation. Job security was almost nonexistent; an illness or an accident could mean the total loss of income. Churchwomen should reach out to such workers, thought Edson, and provide a combination of motherly care and spiritual guidance to those living in a generally inhospitable environment. As she pondered this problem, an 1875 article in the periodical *The Monthly Packet* caught her eye. It described the work of a newly formed English organization for working women, the Girls' Friendly Society. Edson decided to begin a similar group in Lowell.

In November 1877 she called together a group of women from St. Anne's Church in Lowell to meet with some of the young millworkers. They formed the first American chapter of the Girls' Friendly Society (GFS). Meeting weekly, the group combined intellectual and recreational programs with spiritual direction. The older associates mothered the young workers, providing advice and guidance, instruction in domestic skills, and emergency assistance. Their chief interest was to safeguard the moral and spiritual health of the young workers, many of whom previously had had no contact with the Episcopal Church. Emily Edson, for example, described the organization in these words:

> The society, consisting of ladies as associates, and girls as members, was intended to enlist girls when they were leaving school, or working girls when they were passing into service, so that by watching over them, making friends with them, bringing them to the notice of the clergyman of the parish, and taking an interest in their welfare, the associates might be of essential benefit to the members in the most exposed and trying period of their lives.[71]

As a relationship between the two groups of women developed, however, the local chapters began dealing more directly with the economic, cultural, and social needs of the workers. They set up educational programs, lending libraries, classes in needlework and calisthenics. The variety of programs is evident in this early description of one chapter's work:

> One evening in the week we have a singing-class, and afterwards an hour is spent in discussing subjects such as "Good Manners," "A True Home," "Good Taste," etc. At the other weekly meeting we have a class in embroidery. A book on housekeeping and kindred subjects is read aloud. We are just about starting a saving system, paying three per cent interest.[72]

Two other Massachusetts chapters were formed. In 1879 the three groups met in Boston and joined in a diocesan association, with Emily Edson as president. Within the next few years, the society had spread to Maryland and New York; by 1885 the American chapters had formed a central council and officially adopted the "Three Central Rules" of the English association. Those rules provided that the associates (but not the members) were required to be members of the Church of England and that the organizational pattern would follow that of the Church; that associates and members had to contribute annually to the GFS central fund; and that "no one who has not borne a virtuous character" could be admitted as member or associate—if that character were tainted, the member must forfeit her card.[73] In the next twenty years, chapters were organized in many dioceses, and cooperative enterprises, such as vacation cottages for workers or inexpensive urban rooming houses, were established. Though the Girls' Friendly Society developed its own national organizational structure, it maintained close ties with the Woman's Auxiliary, particularly through the many women active in both organizations. In addition, the American Girls' Friendly Society continued its connection with the parent organization in England as well as with a Canadian branch founded in 1883, urging English immigrants to continue their affiliation with the GFS on the American side of the Atlantic.[74]

The Girls' Friendly Society, then, was another way in which Episcopal churchwomen developed a ministry to the disadvantaged population. Clearly there were strong elements of "noblesse oblige" in the attitudes of the associates who initiated the local chapters, but that the associates cared enough about the young workers to give of their time and resources to develop successful programs was significant. Theirs was a personal ministry; the organization grew and developed by trial and error. Churchwomen created it in response to a need. As working conditions for young women changed, the Girls' Friendly Society's emphasis also changed. Eventually the group focused far more on the daughters of the parish than on women industrial workers and came to be primarily a means of conveying moral and spiritual ideals from one generation to the next. But its early history as a means to reach out to a body of women who had few resources of their own is another example of churchwomen's response to their communities' needs.

THE NEW CENTURY

Thus, by 1900 the Board of Missions heavily depended on the Woman's Auxiliary for financial support, for the collection and distribution of supplies to the mission field, and for the creation and dissemination of missionary education materials. Three other organizations—the Daughters of the King, the Church Periodical Society, and the Girls' Friendly Association—enriched the lives of churchwomen in a variety of ways and served as instruments for the extension of Christ's kingdom both at home and abroad. The Church had officially established a vocation for women—the deaconess—and deaconess training schools were graduating women trained in the religious and practical skills necessary for mission work. Many women were finding employment as teachers, nurses, physicians, and administrators in the growing number of Church-sponsored institutions in the United States and overseas.

As they had grown in experience and organizational skills over the previous two decades, the women active in Woman's Auxiliary work

found they had changed; they had become more assertive, more convinced their talents were useful in extending Christ's kingdom. The
missionary booklets they wrote and published were evidence of this
spirit, as was their increasing involvement in the auxiliary's committee
structure. But above all, the auxiliary leaders' growing determination
to recruit, train, and financially support women workers is evidence
of an evolving feminist point of view. The careful, persistent efforts
of Mary Abbot Twing and Julia Emery had brought about a great
change in women's position in the Episcopal Church. Even the rhetoric with which they described women's roles had lost some of its
submissive quality; a glimmer of hope for a new social order had
begun to appear. Anticipating the turn of the century, Mary Abbot
Twing declared her faith that "the day is sure to come when man's
work and woman's work in the Church will be clearly seen to be only
co-ordinate parts of one great and glorious whole."[75] Neither she nor
her sisters lived to see that day, but their efforts had brought it within
the realm of possibility.

CHAPTER SEVEN

Developing Church Work as a Profession for Women, 1870–1889

Concurrent with the organization of the Woman's Auxiliary was the evolution of another model for female vocations in the Church—the order of deaconesses. In a sense, the movement to establish the order of deaconesses was testimony to the fact that women's work in the Church had come of age. Women had found employment in religious and social-service programs sponsored by the Church. Parishes were eager to hire more of them. But the early workers and the clergy who supervised them sought a clearer definition of their work. Were the women to be primarily teachers or supervisors of volunteer activities, or parish administrators, or spiritual directors? And what skills would they need? A means of education for them needed to be established. Curriculum and training standards needed to be set. And, above all, there was a need for the Church officially to recognize this new vocation for women. By establishing the deaconess as a recognized profession for women in the Church, its leaders imagined they could direct women's natural nurturing tendencies into work that would enhance the Church's ministry.

Historian Robert H. Wiebe has described the widespread movement toward professionalism that occurred in the last two decades of the nineteenth century among physicians, lawyers, teachers, and social workers.[1] This professionalization was characterized by an increasing identification of the individual on the basis of occupation, by the formation of national organizations that limited entry into each occupational field on the basis of specific educational requirements, and by the development of a process of examination to determine the applicant's professional competency. These same forces were at work in the Episcopal Church, producing a demand for an authentic profession through which churchwomen might minister to the sick, the downtrodden, and the dispossessed. Although sisterhoods were one possibility, they were hindered both by a strong current of distrust among many active church members and by the fact that their rigorous requirements of obedience and commitment simply did not appeal to many women. In the search for an alternative professional definition, Episcopal churchwomen began to consider another role model—the deaconess.

The office of deaconess, as the profession developed in the Episcopal Church, was a curious blend of tradition and nineteenth-century sentimentality. The only correlation between the deaconess and her masculine counterpart, the deacon, was that both were understood to exercise a servant ministry. Otherwise the two orders were very different. The office of deacon was understood to be one of the three orders of ministry (along with those of priest and bishop) that had existed since apostolic times. The function of the deacon was

> to assist the Priest in Divine Service, and specially when he minis-
> tereth the Holy Communion, and to help him in distribution thereof;
> and to read Holy Scriptures and Homilies in the Church; and to
> instruct the youth in the Catechism; in the absence of the Priest to
> baptize infants; and to preach, if he be admitted thereto by the
> Bishop. And furthermore, it is his Office, where provision is so made,
> to search for the sick, poor, and impotent people of the Parish, to
> intimate their estates, names, and places where they dwell, unto the
> Curate, that by his exhortation they may be relieved with the alms
> of the Parishioners, or others.[2]

Thus, as stated in *The Book of Common Prayer,* the deacon had well-defined liturgical and educational functions along with that of ministering to the sick and the poor. The deaconess, on the other hand, had no liturgical functions. Her duties were "to assist the Minister in the care of the poor and sick, the religious training of the young and others, and the work of moral reformation." The man was *ordained* deacon by the bishop, who placed his hands on the candidate's head, saying "Take thou Authority to execute the Office of a Deacon in the Church of God committed unto thee,"[3] whereas the woman was *set apart* by the bishop, who shook her hand, saying, "For the service of our Lord we receive thee, to be henceforth known and called by the name and title of a Deaconess in the Church of God."[4] The deacon was given authority; the deaconess was accepted for service.

Futhermore, all men ordained priest had first to serve at least one year in the diaconate. Hence the office of deacon was widely perceived as the preliminary step to priesthood, as a phase through which one passed on the way to becoming a priest. Very few of the men ordained deacon in the nineteenth-century Episcopal Church continued in that office as a lifetime career.[5] Nevertheless, the accepted view of the ordination to the diaconate was that it was a permanent commitment, a lifetime vow that would simply be continued along with the priestly vows if the deacon should consequently be ordained priest. Removal from the office required a complicated procedure and the candidate's renunciation of vows.

The office of the deaconess was shaped, however, by churchmen who were convinced that a woman's highest calling was to marry and that if she did so, she could not serve *both* God and her husband. Hence, though the man's marital state had no bearing on his position as deacon, the deaconess canon clearly stated that the appointment as deaconess "shall be vacated by marriage." This provision was hotly contended between the deaconesses and the Church at large. Most deaconesses felt they were making lifetime vows; the women who taught at the training schools stressed the permanence of their commitment. But they were able to convince only a very few clergy to view the profession their way.

Hence a continued tension prevailed between the clerical view of the deaconess and the woman's view. The clergy saw the deaconess as a religious extension of the ideal of true womanhood—a woman who would be pious, pure, submissive, and domestic, who would simply substitute obedience to the priest or bishop for obedience to a husband. Contrastingly, the women saw the deaconess as a professional church worker—trained in Scripture and theology as well as housekeeping and nursing—who would exercise a vocation of service to the Lord Jesus Christ through the institutional Church. The deaconesses were trained (generally by other deaconesses) to be initiators; the clergy expected them to work as directed. This dichotomy was the basis of most of the difficulties the deaconesses faced in the early twentieth century. These opposing views will become more evident as we trace the development of the office of deaconess in the Episcopal Church.

ENGLISH BACKGROUND

In England, one of the lasting effects of the Oxford Movement had been the recovery of women's ministry in the Church. Although several of the leading Tractarians had founded sisterhoods and were generally supportive of the recovery of the monastic tradition, their emphasis on historical scholarship also led to a renewed interest in the order of deacon. For as they began to read accounts of the beginnings of Christianity with a specific interest in the development of ministries, they discovered the significant role deacons had played in the early Church. Deacons were first mentioned—in The Acts of the Apostles—as a group chosen from among the faithful and charged with a servant ministry, distributing the elements at the Eucharist, visiting the sick and the imprisoned, taking food and clothing to widows and orphans.[6] Always the deacon was under authority—first that of the apostles and later that of the local bishop. Men *and* women served as deacons; scholars pointed to the description, in the New Testament, of Phoebe as a deacon and speculated that the reference in 1 Timothy to the "wives" of deacons should be translated "deaconesses."[7] The writings of such early Church fathers as Ignatius, Tertullian, and Cyprian included references to deaconesses, and the Apostolic Constitutions included rules concerning the latter's work.[8] Canons regulating deaconesses were passed at the Ecumenical Councils of Nicea and Chalcedon. Researchers even discovered an ancient liturgy for the consecration of deaconesses. Such references continued until the middle of the fifth century, when women began to move instead into monastic communities.[9]

Citing historical precedent, some English clergy began to call for the revival of the order of deaconesses in the English Church. The chief spokesman for this point of view was the Reverend John Saul Howson, dean of Chester Cathedral, whose exhaustive study of New Testament evidence, published in 1862, concluded that "the argument for the recognition of deaconesses as part of the Christian ministry is as strong as the argument for the episcopacy." On the strength of Howson's evidence, Bishop Archibald Campbell Tait, of London, admitted Catherine Elizabeth Ferard to the order in 1862.[10] With Tait's support, Ferard founded the North London Deaconess Institute for training other candidates; a similar institute was founded at Middlesborough in Yorkshire.[11] As interest in the new order spread, it produced a demand for an ecclesiastical definition of the deaconess. By

1871 a majority of the English bishops, including the archbishops of Canterbury and York, had signed a statement defining a deaconess as "a woman set apart by a bishop, under that title, for service in the Church."[12] More specific direction of the deaconess, however, was left to the bishop in whose diocese she served. In the next ten years deaconess training institutes were opened in the dioceses of Canterbury, Chester, Ely, London, Salisbury, and Winchester, to train women both for parish work at home and for missionary service abroad.[13] Not until 1891, however, did the Convocation of Canterbury give full recognition to the order, an act affirmed in the 1897 Lambeth Council's approval of the revival of the order of deaconesses.[14]

Concurrent with the revival of the order of deaconesses in the Church of England was Pastor Fliedner's training of nursing deaconesses at Kaiserwerth in Westphalia. English and American clergy interested in developing religious vocations for women used the Kaiserswerth model to support their contention that a religious order organized according to Protestant principles could have practical benefits for the entire Church. The Kaiserswerth model was extremely important to the American Church. As has already been indicated, Anne Ayres and William Augustus Muhlenberg used the Kaiserswerth model for the Sisterhood of the Holy Communion.[15] In 1858, when Maryland's Bishop Whittingham set apart the first seven deaconesses in the Episcopal Church, he used a form of service taken from the manual of the Kaiserswerth deaconesses.[16] On Long Island, Bishop Abram Newkirk Littlejohn used the example of the Kaiserswerth community to strengthen his argument that "the time has come when every parish should have its female Diaconate."[17] Henry Codman Potter, while researching various women's ministries, visited both Kaiserswerth and a hospital run by the Lutheran deaconesses in Alexandria, Egypt.[18] Before opening the Church Training and Deaconess House of the Diocese of Pennsylvania, Mary Coles and Caroline Sanford visited deaconess houses in England and Germany to study their training methods.[19] The success of the Kaiserswerth program proved that such orders could develop in a Protestant Church without leading to the undefined "excesses" Low Churchmen feared whenever the possibility of sisterhoods was mentioned.

EARLY DEACONESSES IN THE UNITED STATES

In the Episcopal church several small groups of women calling themselves deaconesses formed—in Baltimore, Maryland (1855), Alabama (1864), Long Island (1872), Georgia (1874), Nebraska (1875), Boston (1877), Philadelphia (1877), and central New York (1877).[20] Few of these groups were affiliated with any others, and each formed its own code of rules and practices. The Order of Deaconesses of the Diocese of Maryland, for example, began at St. Andrew's Parish in Baltimore, when two women decided to devote themselves to ministering to the poor. Initially they worked from the parish rectory, but as other women joined them, they purchased a house. Soon there were four resident and four associate deaconesses who primarily provided nursing care to impoverished families. They also opened a charity school for "vagrant" children and conducted a church school on Sundays for children of the "more favored classes."[21]

The Baltimore order appears to have been the only one centered in one parish. More often, the early deaconesses served as the residential staff of a charitable institution. In Alabama, for example, they opened an orphanage in Mobile but soon added the overseeing of an infirmary, a widow's home, and a reformatory asylum for their work.[22] In Georgia they ran the Appleton Church Home "for the helpless orphaned daughters of poor soldiers who had fallen in the war."[23] In central New York deaconesses worked at the Shelter for Homeless Girls and Women and at the Hospital of the Good Shepherd.[24] The women trained at the Bishop Potter Memorial House in Pennsylvania had originally called themselves "sisters" but adopted the title "deaconesses" in 1877 as more indicative of the "protestant" nature of their work.[25]

A third form of organization evolved on Long Island. There the bishop, Abram Newkirk Littlejohn, established a diocesan order of deaconesses in 1872 by setting apart seven women to "seek the privilege of living only to serve the widow and the orphan, the sick and the destitute, the wretched and the distressed."[26] His plan was that the deaconesses would not live in community but rather be assigned to individual parishes, where they would assist the priests in works of charity and mercy. Although records of the women's deployment are scanty, it is clear that from the beginning some of them served in charitable institutions rather than in parishes. By 1877 twelve of these women formed the Sisterhood of St. John the Evangelist so they could live in community while continuing their outside occupations. From then until 1891 the total number of deaconesses in the diocese fluctuated between twelve and eighteen, most of the women living in the sisterhood. Bishop Littlejohn's strong support, however, and the order's identification as a diocesan organization provided an organizational model for those who advocated restoration of the diaconate among women.[27]

Although they differed in organization, these various orders were unanimous in their vision of the deaconess's role. She was to "serve the widow and the orphan, the sick and the destitute, the wretched and the distressed."[28] Humility was stressed above all virtues. Maryland candidates pledged to "die to all the pleasures, honors, riches and joys of the world" and "not to seek honor nor praise from man."[29] Long Island deaconesses vowed "docility and orderly obedience" and renounced "all unwomanly usurpation of authority in the Church."[30] Service to the other members of the order was also included in the vow of humility. A devout prayer life would sustain the candidate in her life of service; the knowledge that she followed the path of Christ and his apostles would give her strength. The final prayer for the admission of women to the Maryland Order of Deaconesses provided a vivid vision of the life to which the candidate pledged herself:

> [May Almighty God grant] these Thy handmaidens, such willingness of heart, such humble quietness of spirit and confidence in Thee, such sincerity and godly simplicity in the denial of self and glad endurance of privation, hardship, thanklessness and reproach in the service of Thy poor and the little ones of Thy flock, and such faithful perserverance in meekness, lowliness, and long-suffering, and abounding charity among each other. . . .[31]

Most of these early groups fashioned a distinctive uniform—generally a dark dress, conservatively styled, and a simple veil—short enough to be distinguished from the nun's more elaborate habit. Generally a cross was worn on a necklace.

None of these early deaconess groups was ever large, and several of them disbanded after a few years. Many of the women who joined them, however, continued to serve as deaconesses even after their communities had been dissolved. This was particularly true of the women who had trained at the Bishop Potter Memorial House to work in domestic and foreign missions. Because their initial assignments generally were to lonely, isolated mission stations, those who managed to survive the first few years developed self-reliant lifestyles that enabled them to continue their ministries with very little outside support. Annette Relf's long-time ministry in Minnesota has already been mentioned here. Deaconess Sybil Carter taught lace making to the Chippewa Indians of Minnesota from 1886 until 1890, then returned to New York, where she established a lace-making center that marketed the goods produced at several Indian missions.[32] Deaconess Sophi Petterson worked for years at the Appleton Church Home for Girls in Georgia, only to discover in 1948, when she applied for a pension, that the order of deaconesses to which she had belonged was considered a sisterhood by the Retiring Fund for Deaconesses, making her ineligible for their assistance.[33] These women had been trained for faithful, unquestioning service, and though the ecclesiastical authority over them changed, their inclination was to meet the demands of the work set before them.

NATIONAL RECOGNITION OF THE DIACONATE FOR WOMEN

As the number of informal deaconess organizations grew, Church leaders began to seek ways to regularize their status. As early as 1871 the General Convention charged the Committee on the State of the Church to establish a plan of training and deploying such women. After studying the matter, the commitee finally concluded that because of the "prejudice which identifies every such movement with the false and pernicious system of the Church of Rome," no national plan that did not meet with some opposition could be developed. Hence it urged dioceses to act individually on the matter. A Joint Committee on Reviving the Primitive Order of Deaconesses was appointed and charged with bringing the plan to the next General Convention.[34]

The joint committee included several of the staunchest advocates of women's ministries in the national Church. The bishops appointed were Horatio Potter of New York, Abram Newkirk Littlejohn of Long Island, and Richard Hooker Wilmer of Alabama. Bishop Potter had overseen the organization of the Community of Saint Mary, becoming the first Anglican bishop since the Reformation to bless the formation of a monastic community.[35] Bishop Littlejohn was at the time organizing the Order of Deaconesses of the Diocese of Long Island; in 1872 he admitted seven women to the order. Bishop Wilmer had established the Deaconess Institution in the diocese of Alabama in 1864.[36] Among the priests were the Reverend William Reed Huntington, who later, as rector of Grace Church, New York City, would inaugurate the New York School for Deaconesses, and John F. Spalding, who had introduced—at both the 1868 and the 1871 conventions—the resolution on training schools for women.[37] The laymen included William Welsh, whose work as an advocate for women's ministries both in the parish and in the mission field has already been described.[38]

The committee submitted to the 1874 General Convention a canon providing for the organization of sisterhoods or associations of deaconesses. It proposed that women "of devout character and approved fitness" could be set apart by any bishop for "the care of our Lord's poor and sick, the education of the young, the religious instruction of the neglected and the work of moral reformation." The candidate was required to be at least twenty-five years of age and to present to the bishop, who was the final judge of the adequacy of her preparation, several testimonials to her fitness. Several provisions defined the bishop's authority over the deaconess or sister and required that the latter work only in those dioceses whose bishops welcomed such orders.[39]

Women had high hopes for action by the 1874 convention. The Woman's Auxiliary had been formed in 1872, and many of its new members were present as observers.[40] Because the convention was held in New York City, William Welsh urged the deputies to observe sisterhoods at work in such institutions as the Shepherd Fold, the Shelter for Friendless Girls, St. Mary's Hospital for Children, and the House of Mercy for Fallen Women.[41] The Ladies' Domestic Missionary Relief Association announced that in the past year it had sent boxes of supplies worth over $20,000 to the mission field.[42] But the women's hopes were short-lived. The Committee on Canons urged the defeat of the canon "Of Deaconesses or Sisters" because "it is not sufficiently explicit as to what is to be understood by the word deaconess." The canon had been left deliberately vague, without distinguishing between deaconesses or sisters, in order to establish rules under which diverse orders of women might organize. This vagueness proved a strategic mistake, however, for it aroused among Low Churchmen the suspicion that the canon was simply a ruse for establishing Catholic sisterhoods in the Episcopal Church. So the canon was referred back to committee.[43]

The scenario differed slightly, but the outcome was the same at every General Convention during the next decade: A canon on deaconesses or sisterhoods was presented, discussed, amended, and sometimes passed by one house or the other, but the two houses could never agree on one bill and the proposal was always referred back to committee.[44] Finally, the convention of 1886 did not consider the matter at all.

While the General Convention debated the canons under which religious orders should be organized, the number of the orders continued to grow. The manner in which the sisterhood ideal spread is illustrated by the history of the Order of Deaconesses of the Diocese of Maryland. The Maryland deaconesses began by calling themselves the Sisterhood of the Good Shepherd. Their order disbanded as the Civil War ravaged the state, one sister going to work as a deaconess in Massachusetts, another going to Alabama and beginning the order of deaconesses there. One sister went to Louisville, Kentucky, and in 1869 she opened the Orphanage of the Good Shepherd. Others joined her, and together they founded the Sisterhood of St. Martha, a diocesan sisterhood that then assumed charge of the orphanage. The original sister returned to her community, which had moved to St. Louis, Missouri, to establish its central house there.[45] The mobility and instability of such communities for women was in part due to the lack of a national policy on, or ecclesiastical regulation of, such groups. They were forced to depend on the good will of the bishop of the diocese; a change of bishops, therefore, could bring a change of policy toward them. And because the groups generally had meager financial resources, their subsistence was generally tied to the success of the institution they served.[46]

THE CHURCH CONGRESS

Impressed by the proliferation of such groups, Church leaders were anxious to regularize the former's status. One of the chief forums of public opinion in the Episcopal Church was the Church Congress, which met annually as a forum in which diverging views could be presented. In 1885 the congress addressed the subject of sisterhoods and deaconesses. The clerics who spoke were unanimous in the belief that sisterhoods were "here to stay" and that much of the Church's work "can and will be done in no other way than through their aid."[47] They were less united on the relationship between the Church and the sisterhood. Bishop Doane of Albany held that the bishop of each diocese should have "entire and immediate direction" of any group operating in his diocese, whereas the Reverend Calbraith B. Perry, the Baltimore rector who had worked closely with the Society of All Saints since the inception of its work in his city, pleaded for ecclesiastical authorities to let the sisterhoods alone to "grow, and have full scope, and find their work"; only when the sisterhoods asked for legislation should the General Convention act.[48] Perry was decidedly in the minority, however, for most of the other speakers stressed the need for Episcopal supervision and canon-law provisions.

Most speakers generally used the terms "deaconess" and "sister" interchangeably, to denote committed, ministering women who intended lifelong service in the Christian cause. The question of vows was of great concern. Though each speaker believed some sort of vow was essential, the concept of a lifelong or irrevocable vow was universally rejected. Some mechanism, be it a bishop's release or simply a yearly vow that might or might not be renewed, was necessary to allow for changes in individual commitment or outward circumstances that might cause a sister to leave the order. And yet the clerics agreed that a woman's intention on entering the order ought to be lifelong commitment.[49]

Overwhelmingly, the debate's emphasis was not on the opportunities presented to the Church by the increasing number of women offering themselves for service but on the problem of how to control the women. Who should have authority over their religious communities? Who should control their property? What vows should be required of them? All these were questions of order and control; those about what tasks the women might perform, how they were to be trained, what wages or provisions for their upkeep must be paid, or how others might be attracted to the life were generally ignored. And although by this time many women were searching for a way to express a serious religious commitment without joining a sisterhood, most of the clerics scarcely distinguished between deaconesses and sisterhoods and no one offered a detailed plan for an order of deaconesses. The women were to be the Christlike extension of the ministry to the poor and the suffering, giving totally of themselves and making no demands on those who directed them. One clergyman described this ideal very clearly:

> I am called constantly where I *must go* to minister the consolations of the Gospel and the sacraments, but where I could go with better effect in every way if some holy woman could precede and prepare the way, and remain after to care for some poor daughter of humanity lying alone, and friendless, and helpless.[50]

Why the Episcopal Church should delay regularizing such a sacrificial ministry is hard to understand. The key factor was that though many clergy supported the measure, to none of them was it a matter of ultimate concern. All were busy men and had many other causes for which they worked. For Mary Abbot Twing, however, the development of women's ministries was crucial. As the first general secretary of the Woman's Auxiliary, she had sensed the tremendous potential of the Church's women. She had visited with auxiliaries and women workers all across the U.S. She was particularly sensitive to the needs of working women, knowing from her experience how difficult it was for single women to support themselves on the salaries they were generally paid. And she was extremely sympathetic to their need for official Church approval of their work. She, more than any other person, was ultimately responsible for the General Convention's passage of the deaconess canon.

THE SOCIETY OF THE ROYAL LAW

Indicative of Twing's concern for women church workers was her experience in organizing the Society of the Royal Law. After she had left the position of national secretary of the Woman's Auxiliary in 1876, she began to explore means of promoting Church work as a career for women. While working for the Woman's Auxiliary, Twing had experienced the loneliness of the Church's women workers and had recognized their need for emotional and psychological support. She had also encountered capable women whose talents might be used in Church work but who were prevented from doing so either by limited financial resources or by a reluctance to move into nontraditional fields of feminine activity. To provide the necessary financial and emotional support for these women, Twing organized the Society of the Royal Law.

The society was an association of "women workers" in the Episcopal Church. The term "women workers" was broadly defined to include the following categories: sisters in religious orders; deaconesses; district visitors; officers of guilds or other Church organizations; matrons or managers of Church-sponsored institutions and nurses and other employees of such institutions; teachers in the Sunday schools, sewing schools, and Church-sponsored day schools; and wealthy philanthropists who funded such projects. Even sick and helpless churchwomen were included, for their "churchwork" could take the form of intercessory prayers.[51]

The Society of the Royal Law began in 1880 with a small leaflet passed hand to hand in New York City, Philadelphia, and Boston.

Women who joined pledged to follow the "Royal Law"—"Thou shalt do unto others what thou would have them do unto you"—and to aim toward the "special cultivation of the grace of charity" through daily prayer and charitable works. The society had two functions: (1) to strengthen present church workers and (2) to recruit and support more women for that ministry. Services of instruction, quiet days, and adult study courses met the first function; a correspondence and employment network and free will contributions to support training programs met the second.

The first of the services of instruction was held at the Church of the Holy Communion in New York City on April 21, 1880, with Bishop Frederic Dan Huntington of Central New York as the preacher. "Churchwomen occupied or interested in any branch of Christian work" were invited to attend. Over the next two years, twenty-eight such services were held in parishes in New York, Philadelphia, Detroit, Baltimore, Jersey City, and Washington, D.C.[52] One of their functions was to encourage "fellowship between Christian women living under different advantages and in different circumstances."[53] Wealthy philanthropists such as Charlotte Astor and Catharine Wolfe attended, along with many of the humblest of the Church's workers.[54] Many of the women who ran charitable institutions used the occasion as an opportunity to recruit volunteers for their programs.

In New York City, Boston, Pennsylvania, and Long Island the success of the initial services led to the establishment of monthly meetings on church work for women. The format of the meetings varied, but it generally featured an inspirational address by a clergyman or missionary worker and study groups on specific topics—opportunities for women to share information on the successes and failures of programs they had initiated. In Massachusetts, clergymen from each parish were invited along with the members of the Woman's Auxiliary, providing many clergy with their first chance to participate as equals in women-led discussion groups. The conversation was spirited, Mrs. Twing reported, "the clergy taking the most prominent part, naturally, but the Churchwomen having, from time to time, something to say, sufficient to make the conference worthy of its name."[55]

Though inspiration for mission was one of the speakers' goals, the papers presented were informative and well-reasoned accounts of both the possibilities and the pitfalls of women's work. Mrs. S.I.J. Schereschewsky, who had served for many years with her husband in the mission to China, called for high standards in missionary education, for the joint training of husbands and wives to be sent overseas. She urged the Church to develop a mandatory training program for women workers, including both college education and some supplemental medical training.[56] English Deaconess Charlotte Ransford spoke at one meeting, describing the functions of the diocesan deaconess houses, which combined an ordered communal life with study of the Scriptures and theology and practical training in methods of child care, nursing, Christian education, and institutional and penitentiary work. She offered to train a few American women who might then return to establish similar programs in the United States.[57] Not all the speakers were as optimistic about women's work as Ransford. The Reverend Pelham Williams warned that "the craze for parish machinery may quite disturb the most needful repose of the divine life, . . . what the Holy Ghost declares to be *the* grace of Christian womanhood—viz.: 'The ornament of a meek and quiet spirit.'" He declared that God's priests were ordained to instruct children in the faith "and they can no more delegate this duty to the unordained and unauthorized, than they can rightly vacate the office of feeding the sheep and relegate this duty to a band of good-natured volunteers." In the discussion that followed, several Sunday-school teachers took exception to his words.[58]

The overall effect of such conferences was to inform churchwomen about the wide range of service opportunities already available in the Church and to motivate participants to further action. Drawing members from many churches together fostered unity and established diocesewide support systems for those women ready to embark on ministry. And as Mary Abbot Twing began to mount her campaign to see that the deaconess canon was passed, the conferences proved an excellent forum from which to disseminate information about the order of deaconesses.

The other goal of the Society of the Royal Law had been to encourage women to enter Church work. Twing offered to try to match offers of employment with women desirous of such work and was astounded that over seven hundred women wrote to her. Of those, she found positions for over one hundred in Church-related institutions. The list of those she placed is a veritable catalog of the types of work the women were doing: hospital matrons in Tacoma (Washington), White Earth (Minnesota), and Portland (Oregon); directors of such institutions as the Home of the Innocents (Louisville, Kentucky), the Zion Church Home for Working Girls (Wappinger's Falls,

New York), and the Bee Hive House of the Good Shepherd (Tomkins Cove, New York); nurses and teachers in hospitals and schools throughout the country. About forty of the women were employed in some phase of urban mission work in New York City and Brooklyn. Some were enrolled in vocational training, and several entered sisterhoods or became deaconesses. Interviewing so many women "in such pressing need of employment" strengthened Twing's determination to establish Church work as a viable source of employment for women.[59]

CHURCH WORK

Twing's first step was to establish a communications network broader than the city conferences. In November 1885 she began a monthly journal, *Church Work*, which was sent to church workers in many parts of the United States. The journal included "how-to" articles on organizing day nurseries, clinics, hospitals, parish visiting programs, rural church schools, etc., along with inspirational addresses and news of local sisterhoods and deaconess programs. The offering from the New York City churchwomen's meeting provided the initial funding for the magazine, supplemented by later contributions from wealthy women, chiefly Mrs. John Jacob Astor.[60]

To publish the magazine, the indefatigable Mrs. Twing badgered clergy and women's leaders for reports of their activities. She traveled across the U.S., making six trips to mission fields in the far West and Southwest, collecting information on women's work—visiting mothers' meetings among the Sioux Indians or St. Mary's School meetings in a tent in San Antonio. Featuring articles on sisterhoods and deaconesses, the magazine reflected an editorial policy that favored both as avenues of service for women.

By 1888, however, Twing had become convinced both that a General Convention endorsement of women's work was essential and that there was no chance the measure would pass if it included sisterhoods. Hence she organized a campaign to assure passage of the deaconess canon. Twing instructed her readers about the deaconess movement by publishing in *Church Work* articles about existing deaconess communities and supportive papers by influential clergy. In 1889, during the months leading up to the General Convention, she wrote a series of articles tracing the history of legislation on women's work in the Episcopal Church. It culminated in the recommendation:

If a Canon of Deaconesses similar to that presented during the General Convention of 1880, could be cordially approved and adopted by both Houses, and, more important still, if an "Office for the Reception of Deaconesses," similar to that already in use in the dioceses of Alabama, Long Island and New York, could be added to the "Book of Offices" to be proposed in the General Convention of 1889, no doubt many women would offer themselves for service, under a rule thus clearly set forth, who now hesitate, uncertain as to what the Church really wishes of them, or in what way she desires them to work for her.[61]

While pressing the publicity campaign, Twing wrote privately to influential clergy and bishops, putting together a network of support for the canon on deaconesses. "I shall be very glad to move the necessary Resolution which I would suggest that you draw, yourself, as no one else can know so well precisely what you want to say," wrote Bishop Henry Codman Potter to Mrs. Twing.[62]

In her work for a deaconess canon, Mrs. Twing had two other powerful allies, the Reverend William S. Rainsford and the Reverend William R. Huntington. Both men were rectors of New York City parishes—St. George's and Grace Church, respectively—that had strong traditions of female involvement in charitable and missionary activities, and both were known as innovators. Rainsford already had women working at St. George's to supervise parish visiting and Christian-education programs. Impatient with the national Church's inaction on the deaconess canon, he decided to establish an order of deaconesses on his own.[63] So he trained Julia E. Forneret and, in 1887, presented her to Bishop Henry Codman Potter to be received as a deaconess. She was then employed at St. George's and recruited two other women, Clara H. Simpson and Hildegarde von Brockdorff, who became deaconesses in 1892.[64]

Bishop Potter, still sensitive to the negative attitude toward women's orders, admitted Forneret not by laying his hands on her head—the method of admitting deacons—but by taking the candidate by the hand and saying, "For the service of our Lord we receive thee, to be henceforth known and called by the name and title of a Deaconess in the Church of God." Also he emphasized that she was not making lifetime vows: "Should superior claims to your services arise in your family, or should Providence clearly indicate that your place of duty is elsewhere, . . . you will obey the summons to depart."[65] For her part, Deaconess Forneret vowed to obey those over her, especially the bishop, to perform her duties with a cheerful spirit, and to seek the constant direction of the Lord. (Invariably, in each service to admit a deaconess, the promise to obey her superiors was the first promise she made; in ordinations of deacons and priests, the promise to obey is last.)[66] Rainsford's concept of the deaconess as an active, educated, and organized professional was expressed in the language of some of the prayers: "Give her strength and courage patiently to surmount every obstacle. . . . Give her wisdom and prudence, as well as zeal and love."[67] But the service's overall thrust was to emphasize humility, obedience, docility, and self-denial; the deaconess was to conform to the contemporary image of womanhood, merely substituting service to Christ for service to her family.

Meanwhile, William R. Huntington was also planning to institute deaconesses at Grace Church. In 1877 two sisters contributed $10,000 to the church in honor of their brother. Their donation was to create the Henry P. Campbell Deaconess Fund, the income from which was to be used to support the ministry of deaconesses to the poor and the suffering.[68] The church already had an active social-service ministry centered in Grace Hall, a huge parish house with classrooms, guild-rooms, a library, an industrial school, and a day nursery, all provided and funded through the generosity of Catharine Lorillard Wolfe. Huntington, planning to begin a training school for deaconesses at Grace Hall, wrote to his friend Catherine Meredith, inviting her to lead the project:

> If you really believe in the idea, as I most firmly do, I cannot think of any way in which you could more effectually serve the interests of the Church and of your own sex here in America. My great fear is lest the movement fall into the hands of middle-class women and fail to attract the natural and proper leaders, the women of cultivation and breeding. Your presence at the head of the work, even though you were not able to give much time or effort to personal visitation of the poor, would be a tower of strength to us.[69]

When Meredith proved unwilling to assume the responsibility, Huntington delayed any further action on the deaconess program until after the 1889 General Convention.

THE GENERAL CONVENTION OF 1889

At the convention, Huntington introduced the canon on deaconesses in the House of Deputies, and Henry Codman Potter introduced it in the House of Bishops. The canon was almost identical to that which had been introduced in 1880 and 1883, except it referred to deaconesses only (the clause "and sisterhoods" had been removed). In an article in *The Churchman,* which was distributed to convention deputies, Mrs. Twing explained the rationale for separating the consideration of deaconesses and sisterhoods. She argued that legislation by the national Church would standardize a deaconess program and thus encourage committed women to seek the training necessary for the profession.[70]

The strategy was successful. The canon (with three amendments) was passed by both houses. The three amendments were significant reflections of the prevailing attitude toward professions for women in the Church. The first amendment stipulated that the prospective deaconess must be an unmarried woman, thus guarding against any conflict of interest between a woman's primary duty to her home and family and her calling to serve the Lord. The second amendment increased the required number of testimonials to the fitness of the candidate, from one priest and three lay communicants, two of whom were women, to two priests and twelve laypeople, six of whom were women. Thus the candidate would be thoroughly scrutinized by her peers before being accepted into the order. The third amendment strengthened the bishop's control over the deaconess by granting him the power to suspend or remove her from office following a hearing of the charges against her. Several other resolutions regulating brotherhoods, mission priests, and sisterhoods were presented to the convention, but they were referred back to committee.[71]

Delighted over the passage of the canon, Mr. Pierson, deputy from Albany, predicted: "This measure will promote good, promote religion, win souls to the Saviour, send bread to the hungry, educate the children in the rules and the work of the Church. It seems to me one of the most intelligent and most active elements in the progress of our whole religion."[72] Not even Mrs. Twing was likely to make so extravagant a claim. But the move was significant because it was the first national recognition of women's ministries in the Episcopal Church. Although the canon made no mention of the relationship of deaconess to the three traditional orders of ministry—bishop, priest, and deacon—and made no provision for including her in the Church's organizational structure, it did at least suggest that the ministry was not an exclusively masculine dominion.

CHAPTER EIGHT

The
Order of Deaconesses,
1889–1900

The passage of the deaconess canon gave Episcopal Church sanction to the order and established some general guidelines governing admission. The General Convention had made no provision, however, for the deaconesses' education. Female students were not admitted to Episcopal theological seminaries; the one training school for women workers, the Bishop Potter Memorial House, had ceased operation almost a decade earlier. Hence, the first priority of the deaconess movement's supporters was to establish educational programs.

THE NEW YORK TRAINING SCHOOL FOR DEACONESSES

In New York City, Grace Church had already established the deaconess fund endowment and had made classrooms available in nearby Grace House. There Dr. Huntington began to train candidates in the fall of 1890. He asked Mrs. Twing to take charge of the students' missionary education, which pleased her immensely, for, as she wrote to her brother, "excepting that it is not to be a *resident* school, it is all I could have hoped for in the many years that I have dreamed of some Training School here in New York for the large class of earnest thoughtful women who want to work under authority and yet do not care to be Sisters."[1] To establish the school as an independent agency, Huntington called together a board of trustees, which incorporated the New York Training School for Deaconesses on May 9, 1891. Six of the twelve board members were women.[2] Shortly after the incorporation, an anonymous woman provided a house at 228 East Twelfth Street for a student residence; given "as an act of Faith to a work of Faith," it was called St. Faith's House.[3]

Classes continued to be held at Grace House. The curriculum included Old and New Testament, Theology, and Church History, taught by local priests, and practical courses in household management, ecclesiastical embroidery, and missionary instruction, taught by female church workers. (After only a year, the students requested that the ecclesiastical embroidery class be replaced with instruction in cutting and making wearing apparel, feeling it would be more useful for those who worked with sewing schools.) By 1894 the board had decided to require six months of nurses' training for graduation—the training to take place at St. Luke's Hospital.[4]

Beginning with only four students, the school grew slowly. The requirements for admission were flexible; it was expected that the candidate have a high-school education or its equivalent, be recommended by two persons (one of whom was a clergyman), and produce a physician's statement of good health. The students came from a variety of educational backgrounds. A survey of the school's first nineteen years revealed that of the 284 women who applied for admission, 40 percent had been educated in private (or finishing) schools, 17 percent had some college or normal-school training, 3 percent had only home training by private tutors, and the remaining 40 percent either attended public high schools or did not record their educational backgrounds.[5]

In 1892, the first three graduates of the school—Kate Newell, Mary E. Greene, and Sarah K. Barker—were set apart as deaconesses. All three were hired by Grace Church. Throughout the next decade, an average of four students graduated each year, though several other part-time students were enrolled. In 1902 the graduating class consisted of nine students—a number that remained fairly constant until 1917, when class size began to decrease. Each year there were also several students who did not complete the entire course— women who decided that a religious vocation was not for them, students who needed specialized training in nursing or Bible study, or women who were trained for other positions in the mission field. Although only about half the graduates went on to become deaconesses, most of the others continued to work for the Church.[6]

During the first decade, Huntington remained the spiritual center of the school, guiding and shaping the overall program. Though family prayers were read daily, he was careful to see that the school was not identified with any particular brand of churchmanship. Though known as a Low Churchman, he had a wide knowledge of liturgy and appreciated some aspects of high-church ritual. He hired instructors who represented various styles of churchmanship and insisted that the students worship in whatever manner was most helpful to them. One Friday evening a month, Huntington met with the students, discoursing on theology and sharing his knowledge of the writings of the Church Fathers. The deep mysticism that, according to one student, "always seemed an essential quality of his spirit" was apparent as he sought words to explain the divine mystery of the Eucharist or suggested methods of private prayer.[7]

SUSAN KNAPP, DEAN

Although Dr. Huntington was the guiding spirit of the school, the board had appointed the Reverend Haslett McKim as dean, responsible for the academic program, and Mrs. William H. Hoffman as house mother. When Mrs. Hoffman died in 1897, one of the former students, Susan Knapp, was asked to fill her position. It was a surprising move, but Knapp had already established an unusual reputation at the school. Of an upper-class New York City family, she had remained at home to keep house for her brother, an attorney, after their parents died. When he decided to move to Alaska, she was free to become a deaconess. In 1891, when she first applied for admission (at age twenty-nine), she was thwarted by her physician, who would not sign the health certificate because she suffered from an irregular heartbeat. Determined to pursue her studies, she found another physician who would sign the certificate, was admitted, and completed the course work with distinction. After a year of volunteer work at the Society for the Home Study of Holy Scripture, Knapp returned to the School for Deaconesses to teach the courses in New Testament and Church history. After two years in that position, she assumed the additional duties of house mother.[8]

On May 1, 1899, Susan Knapp was set apart as a deaconess by Bishop Henry Codman Potter. Shortly thereafter, with Deaconess Henrietta Goodwin, she sailed for England to investigate the life of the deaconesses there. The trip was to have great significance for the development of deaconess work in the United States because it put Knapp in touch with the primary theoreticians of the movement in

England, giving her a vision of a worldwide calling and buttressing her opinions with the authoritative stamp of Canterbury. She met Cecilia Robinson, the most outstanding of the English deaconesses, of whom she said, "I found in her an ideal that I never lost sight of."[9] Robinson introduced Knapp to her bishop, Randall Thomas Davidson (who was to become archbishop of Canterbury four years later.) She visited with him and his wife at Farnham Castle, discovering that Davidson's "view of the Deaconess Movement was much more extensive than that of anyone I met in America."[10] This initial meeting began a lifelong friendship between the two—their correspondence forging a trans-Atlantic unity of purpose and administration for the fledgling movement. Knapp and Goodwin stayed at the Rochester Deaconess Institution, which had served as a training school for the past fifteen years, and shared ideas for curriculum and administration with Deaconess Isabella Gilmore, the school's director. While there they met Edmund Stuart Talbot, bishop of Rochester, and his young assistant Cosmo Gordon Lang (who became archbishop of Canterbury in 1928).

Most impressive to Knapp and Goodwin was the control the English deaconesses exercised over their work. The training schools were directed by deaconesses, the clerical wardens serving as advisors. Each diocese had a head deaconess with whom the bishop conferred on matters of recruitment and deployment. To standardize programs, a joint meeting of the bishops and head deaconesses in the ten dioceses in which work was conducted had put forth a series of proposals for further ecclesiastical action.[11] Major decisions about the direction of the work, such as the Rochester Deaconess Institution's decision to extend its work to South Africa, were made by the gathered company of deaconesses rather than by a council of priests or bishops. Such autonomy was an inspiration to Deaconess Knapp, whose only previous experience had been with the New York school firmly controlled by Dr. Huntington. She returned home determined to forge similar instruments of self-control for American deaconesses.[12]

Back in New York, Knapp found Huntington willing to allow her to assume greater responsibility for the training school, and she began to incorporate some of the ideas she had conceived in England. She raised the academic standards, insisting that the students not only learn the subject matter but develop "a clear method of imparting it to others."[13] With Deaconesses Briggs and Goodwin she visited women's colleges, encouraging graduates to consider careers in Church work. By 1903 students from Barnard, Smith, Vassar, Wellesley, and Wesleyan were enrolled at the training school.[14] To give students practical training, she developed summer training internships in local institutions and in the mission field.[15] She organized a chapter of the Church Student's Missionary Association, which she hoped would not only inspire her student's interest in mission work but give them some practical experience in controlling their own organization.[16] In May 1903 the Board of Trustees appointed Susan Knapp to succeed the retiring Dr. McKim as dean of the training school. For the next fifteen years Dean Knapp worked to develop the profession of deaconess, setting high requirements for admission, demanding rigorous academic and practical training, and inspiring in her students and colleagues the highest standards of personal commitment and devotion.

The school was her first priority. Enrollment had increased; during her first decade as dean, about twenty-five students had been enrolled each year. Two houses had been given to the school, to be used for residents, and classes continued to be held at Grace Hall. Plans were underway, however, to move the entire school to the grounds of the Cathedral of St. John the Divine, under construction on Amsterdam Avenue at 111th Street.[17] So Knapp had to manage the existing institution in temporary quarters while planning the permanent facilities. Not until 1910 did classes open in the new building.

Knapp had a fierce pride in her vocation as deaconess, and she sought to instill the same sense of high calling in her students. Rigorous prayer life was at the center of the course, for she felt each candidate must enter "that inner circle where one receives spiritual experience and the knowledge of God's Will for her."[18] The day began with corporate worship, followed by a fifteen-minute period of devotional reading, during which time Dean Knapp would bring the wide range of her spiritual resources to bear on concerns the students voiced.[19] Although she demanded academic excellence, she also stressed the importance of learning to live together, feeling that future deaconesses would need loyalty to each other as well as a spirit of willing obedience to those in authority. Though her standards were high, she tempered them with kindness and concern for the individual. As one student wrote,

> As I think of my years of training under Deaconess Knapp, her many kindnesses stand out clearly. Striking a match and lighting the gas in my bed room to welcome a newly arrived student; supper served to

me in her room as a treat after an illness; a new chair to make me comfortable; her patient listening to complaints and criticisms and the giving of her experienced judgment to set me straight; a scholarship for my second year, not at all deserved. Her keen sense of humor but jokes "must be dignified." The kindness of friends but always keeping the distinction between Head Deaconess and student. Her influence upon my life and work is too great to be put into words.[20]

While Knapp was reshaping the school's curriculum to better prepare women for the office of deaconess, she gradually came to be regarded as the chief spokeswoman for the deaconess movement in the Episcopal Church. Planners of the Pan-Anglican Congress, to be held in London in 1908, invited her to make a major presentation on deaconesses for the section on The Ministry of Women. Her paper was well received by the bishops, priests, and lay leaders who attended the congress, one reporter commenting that she treated the subject "with much clearness and earnestness, combined with a wholesome amount of common-sense, and furtive dry humour of the true American stamp."[21] She reviewed the status of deaconesses in the United States and commented on their training, summarizing her philosophy of education by saying:

> The schools strive to help the woman, by a disciplined life, to the enlightenment of self-knowledge and the joy of self-sacrifice; she learns that a fitness for her calling is her first care, as it is what she is more than what she does which will count in the end. . . . It matters little to the gracious and spirited woman if the authority conferred by her Order is not fully appreciated in that community where God has appointed her a worker. Authority is of value only because of the power it confers, and the woman who radiates harmony and wins love, who walks with God prayerfully and works among men efficiently, has all the power she could crave.[22]

An editorial reviewing the congress's accomplishments singled out seven outstanding presentations, among them "the excellent speeches of women, especially Deaconess Knapp and Miss Constance Smith."[23]

Knapp's reputation as an educational innovator led to an invitation to speak at the 1913 meeting of the Church Congress on "The Relation of Social Service to Christianity." In that presentation she reiterated her belief that inculcating a strong religious faith must be the educator's first priority. Christian social service must be grounded in "absolute devotion to God" and illuminated by a knowledge of God "and of ourselves in relation to Him." Furthermore, the Church must "see to it that her sons and daughters are trained and equipped for that service." Although she acknowledged that better training in the essentials of the faith was necessary, she also suggested that the Church could learn from the work of modern social scientists: "The day has gone by forever when it could be considered part of piety to fear scientific methods in Social Service. We *need* the scientific methods of the great philanthropic organizations, and we *need their thoroughness* also."[24] She buttressed these words with actions by adding to the deaconess training program two courses: one from the School of Philanthropy at Columbia University, on modern methods of dealing with the problems of the poor, and one taught by physicians from St. Bartholomew's Clinic, on modern medical practices.[25]

Knapp's keen analytical ability, however, sometimes led her to make politically unwise statements. At the Church Congress, for example, she warned against "the fantastic spectacle of the rich making intermittent and ill-regulated efforts to take part with the poor in times of crisis." "Believe me," she stated, "to those for whom the drama is not a spectacle, but a rigorous experience, these would-be helpers seem like children running out of luxurious nurseries to play the game of poverty, who may be trusted to run back again at the first touch of hunger."[26]

Such statements reflected an attitude of intellectual and religious superiority that did not endear Knapp to the school's board of trustees. Members of the board often found her high-handed and difficult to control. Though she understood herself as dean to be responsible for the students' education, she felt the board of trustees should confine its attention to the school's finances and the upkeep of the building. While Huntington was alive, he served as the final authority to whom both Dean Knapp and the board deferred. After his death in 1909, however, the Reverend Milo H. Gates was elected warden. Gates, as vicar of the Chapel of the Intercession on Washington Heights, found himself overwhelmed with the responsibility of a growing parish and had little time to devote to the school. So Knapp assumed most of Huntington's responsibilities. She did not, however, serve on the board of trustees and was not always fully informed of the decisions it made.[27]

By 1915 the school had serious financial problems. Construction costs for the new building on the cathedral grounds had run higher than expected. Student enrollment was down. No one on the board of trustees was as successful as Dr. Huntington had been at finding "benevolent ladies" to contribute major gifts to the school. How much of the distressing financial situation was Dean Knapp's fault is difficult to say, but the strained relationship between her and the board is evident in the correspondence and reports. Dean Knapp assumed the reins of government, charged one trustee, "but always declined with decision to accept any responsibility for raising funds."[28] Exacerbating the situation was a growing ideological split with the board (which is described more fully in the later section on "Professional Development"). Basically, Knapp felt deaconesses made a lifetime commitment and they should be subject to the same high professional standards—and granted the same respect—accorded to a priest. Board members tended to be more casual both in their assessment of the requirements for deaconesses and in their view of the deaconess's place in society.

In 1916 the board granted Dean Knapp a leave of absence during which she was to travel to the Orient to visit those graduates serving in the mission fields of China, Japan, and the Philippines. While she was gone, a special committee of the board discussed administrative reorganization. It believed that the solution to the problem would be to appoint a new warden (one who would have time to devote to the school) and to say clearly that he would be responsible for the administration of the school and for representing the school to the "Church outside the School." Because Dean Knapp would then be freed from her duties, the committee suggested she could also act as house mother at the school.[29]

When Knapp returned from her leave of absence and was confronted with this recommendation, she resigned as dean. True to her own high standards of conduct, however, she never disclosed the reason for her resignation or complained about her mistreatment by the board. She moved to Japan, took a house just outside of St. Paul's College in Tokyo, and taught Bible classes to Japanese students. Continuing to correspond regularly with her former students, she sent long letters (describing her activities) to be printed in the semiannual *Alumnae Bulletin*. The closest she came to revealing the state of her mind about leaving was in her first letter, published in the January 1917 *Bulletin* and apparently written in New York about the time she announced her resignation. Without mentioning her plans, she simply described her sabbatical journey to Asia and the deaconesses she visited there. Writing of that region's needs, she ended with the plea:

I pray of you, the Alumnae, see to it that the school does not fail the

East. See to it also that the school does not fail the cause for which
it was founded. These are the days when the Deaconess Movement
is pausing to take a second breath—a crisis in its history. Lift up the
Movement by your influence and do all in your power to send women
for training who, by becoming Deaconesses possessed of the highest
ideals, will contribute toward the permanence of the Order.[30]

There is no record of any correspondence between Knapp and Dr.
William E. Gardner, who was selected as warden in 1917.[31] When
two of her former students, Deaconess Romula Dahlgren and Deaconess Jane Gillespy, "took charge of St. Faith's House," however, she
kept up a steady correspondence with them, Her interest in the deaconess movement continued: her letters are filled with tactical suggestions, information about training, and suggestions for missionary work.
Whenever possible, she arranged her travels to the United States in
order to attend the triennial meeting of deaconesses. The financial
state of several retired deaconesses was of special concern to her. The
Church did not provide pensions for deaconesses, and because most
of these women had worked for such low salaries, they had limited
resources. Knapp shared what she could of her own funds, but finally
they, too, were stretched to the limit.[32] She continued to live in Japan,
teaching Japanese students and maintaining a wide correspondence
until she died in 1941.

Susan Knapp's fate was similar to that of many of the early deaconesses. The same strong will and fierce independence that led her
to pioneer a new profession made her a difficult person with whom
to work. She felt she was called to hold high standards, and she was
unwilling to compromise them. She had enough independent income
to allow her freedom of action; her material wants were few, and she
intelligently chose a lifestyle that could be sustained by her own funds.
But in a Church with no tradition of women employees, and in a
profession that emphasized submission, humility, and obedience,
there were few avenues of support for independent women, few mechanisms of protection for their jobs. Too often, the deaconess was the
expendable person on the church staff. When financial reversals hit
the church, she was dismissed. Her professional pride demanded
humble obedience to the dismissal. The many retired deaconesses
living lives of genteel poverty, forced after decades of work for the
Episcopal Church to depend on the kindness of friends for their very
livelihood, was indicative of the general irresponsibility with which
the Church dealt with its women workers.

Meeting of the King's Daughters, St. George's Church, New York City. In 1906 the garments made at the meetings were sent to an Indian school in South Dakota, two Appalachian missions, the Junior Sea Breeze Hospital, and the Jacob Riis Settlement in New York City. *Source: Year Book of St. George's Church, 1906.*

Sister Hughetta, C.S.M., with several girls who attended St. Mary's-on-the-Mountain, a school founded in 1903 by the Community of St. Mary to educate mountain girls at Sewanee, Tennessee. Sister Hughetta served for many years as the superior of the convent at Sewanee. *Source: Community of St. Mary.*

Black members of the faculty of St. Augustine's School, Raleigh, North Carolina, in 1902. The school was begun in 1867 to educate freed blacks after the Civil War and staffed in the early years primarily by women teachers sent by the Freedman's Commission. College and industrial classes were added later. The school continues today as St. Augustine's College. *Source: Archives of the Episcopal Church, Austin, Texas.*

Indian children with Deaconess Bertha Sabine beside Christ Church, Anvik, Alaska, in 1911. The church was built with a $1000 grant from the first United Offering in 1889 and was often supplied with women workers funded by subsequent UTO collections. *Source: Archives of the Episcopal Church, Austin, Texas.*

Dr. Mary V. Glenton (1862–1923) with Head Nurse Miss Higgins and the women they trained as nurses at Elizabeth Bunn Memorial Hospital in Wuchang, 1910. Dr. Glenton was sent by the United Offering to direct the Bunn Hospital in 1898 and remained there until 1920, when she moved back to the United States to work at St. Agnes Hospital at St. Augustine's School in Raleigh, North Carolina. Earlier she had worked as a missionary physician in Montana and Alaska. [*The Spirit of Missions* 69 (1904):518; *The Spirit of Missions* 85 (1920):633.] *Source: Archives of the Episcopal Church, Austin, Texas.*

Julia Chester Emery (1852–1922) served as secretary of the Woman's Auxiliary
to the Board of Missions of the Protestant Episcopal Church from 1876 to
1916—forty years. Pictured here as a young woman just after she assumed the
national secretary's position. *Source: Dorothy Emery Lyford.*

Mary Abbot Emery Twing (1843–1901), first secretary of the Woman's Auxiliary to the Board of Missions of the Protestant Episcopal Church. Pictured here after the death of her husband, the Rev. A.T. Twing, when she served as honorary secretary of the Woman's Auxiliary. *Source: Dorothy Emery Lyford.*

Attendants at work in the nursery of St. Barnabas' House, New York City in 1922. St. Barnabas' House was a temporary shelter for women and children sponsored by the New York City Mission Society and staffed by Episcopal women workers. *Source: Archives of the Episcopal Church, Austin, Texas.*

Portrait of the first branch of the Girls' Friendly Society (GFS) in America, at St. Ann's Episcopal Church, Lowell, Massachusetts, in 1877. Many of the young women pictured here were employed in the Lowell mills and enjoyed the social, intellectual, and spiritual opportunities offered by the GFS. *Source: Archives of the Episcopal Church, Austin, Texas.*

Miss Clara J. Neely with her first Bible class in Tokyo, Japan, 1900. Neely arrived in Japan in 1899 and retired in 1933. *Source: Archives of the Episcopal Church, Austin, Texas.*

Deaconess Susan Knapp (left, 1862–1941) and Deaconess Edith Hart (right, d. 1927) at St. Phoebe's Training School, which trained Chinese women to serve as deaconesses and Bible women. Although Deaconess Knapp had moved to Tokyo by this time, she continued to visit those graduates of the New York Training School for Deaconesses who were at work in the Orient. *Source: Archives of the Episcopal Church, Austin, Texas.*

Deaconess Gertrude Stewart with her two adopted daughters from the mission station in Hankow, where she served from 1906 until 1927. On her return to the United States, she became dean of the Pennsylvania School for Deaconesses, which she had attended twenty years earlier. Finding she missed the life in China, she went back and served as the director of Bible women's work in the diocese of Hankow until 1941, when the Americans were forced to leave. Back in Philadelphia, she lived at the Leamy Home, which had been founded by Episcopal women a century earlier, and continued to do volunteer work at the Episcopal Hospital until she died in 1965. *Source: Archives of the Episcopal Church, Austin, Texas.*

Miss Cornwall-Legh in 1918 with many of the patients from the leper colony she founded at Kusatsu (District of Tokyo), Japan. The clergy present are the Reverend A.S. Hewlitt (left of Miss Cornwall-Legh), who served as the resident chaplain, Bishop John McKim, and the Reverend P. Daito, the Japanese chaplain. Cornwall-Legh's work at this colony is legendary: Bishop McKim described her as a "self-sacrificing and devoted lady who is giving herself and her possessions to the service of these unfortunate and neglected people." ["Triennial Report of the Board of Missions, 1916," p. 176.] *Source: Archives of the Episcopal Church, Austin, Texas.*

Queen Liliuokalani (1838–1917) of Hawaii, at St. Andrews Priory School in 1915, with Sisters Beatrice and Albertina and Bishop Henry Bond Restarik. The two sisters founded the school in 1867 as a boarding school for native Hawaiian girls and taught there for the next thirty-five years. During the revolution in Honolulu in 1893, they ministered to Queen Liliuokalani while she was under house arrest; she subsequently became an Episcopalian and an active promoter of the school. ["Liliuokalani" and "Rogers, Elizabeth Ann and Ellen Albertina Polyblank" in *Notable American Women.*] *Source: Archives of the Episcopal Church, Austin, Texas.*

Jane Addams, founder of Hull House, with the staff at St. Luke's Hospital in Tokyo, when she visited in 1923. *Source: Archives of the Episcopal Church, Austin, Texas.*

Deaconess Claudine Whitaker with some of her young charges at the House of the Holy Name, a settlement house she and Deaconess Affleck had established in Mexico City. Whitaker began her career as a settlement worker in Philadelphia at St. Martha's House, then trained at the Pennsylvania School for Deaconesses. In 1912 she was sent to Mexico and remained there for the next six years in spite of the unstable political situation and strong anti-American protests. She then returned to the United States and continued inner-city work in New York City. *Source: Archives of the Episcopal Church, Austin, Texas.*

College women who gathered at the Summer Conference on Missions at Hobart College sponsored by the Woman's Auxiliary in 1921. Represented here are the following colleges: Smith, Wellesley, Cornell, William Smith, Syracuse, Vassar, Rochester, Brockport Normal, Mount Holyoke, University of Michigan, Barnard, Wells, Syracuse, Brown, and Johns Hopkins. Such conferences both inspired young women to enter the mission field and taught others who would serve as church-school teachers at home. *Source: Archives of the Episcopal Church, Austin, Texas.*

Mary Elizabeth Wood (1861–1931) flanked by her students and the faculty of the library school at Boone College, Wuchang (District of Hankow). Wood's pioneer work helped establish the public-library system in China; she not only founded Boone Library and its Library Training School but persuaded the U.S. government to use indemnity funds from the Boxer Rebellion to establish a national library (in Peking) with six regional libraries. [John H. Winkelman, "Mary Elizabeth Wood (1861–1931): American Missionary-Librarian to Modern China."] *Source: Archives of the Episcopal Church, Austin, Texas.*

CHURCH TRAINING AND DEACONESS SCHOOL
OF THE DIOCESE OF PENNSYLVANIA

A second school to train deaconesses was established in the diocese of Pennsylvania in 1891, just one year after the New York school opened. The prime mover behind it was Miss Mary Coles, a wealthy Philadelphian who was to oversee the school and provide much of its financial support for the next thirty years. She had been active in the Woman's Auxiliary and, through her close friendship with Mary Abbot Twing, had caught the vision of a cadre of well-educated professional women church workers. Once the deaconess canon was passed by the General Convention, she was determined to establish a training school in Philadelphia. With a group of friends, she raised seven thousand dollars to be used as the down payment on a house that would provide both residential and classroom space for the new school. While the house was being renovated, Coles and Caroline H. Sanford, who was to serve as house mother, traveled to Europe, visiting deaconess houses in England and the Deaconess Training Institute at Kaiserswerth, to evaluate and compare various training methods.[33]

In January 1891 the Church Training and Deaconess House of the Diocese of Pennsylvania opened, with Bishop O.W. Whitaker as its titular head. Financially independent of the diocese, the institution was funded by an endowment managed by a Board of Council consisting of five businessmen. Otherwise, "the financial and outward business of the House, and all matters pertaining to admission" were attended to by the Board of Managers, made up of ten women and Mary Coles, who served as president.[34] Four of these women—Coles, Biddle, Parrish, and Buchanan—also served as faculty members, along with seven local clergymen and one physician. The house mother, Caroline Sanford, was also enrolled as a student; she completed the two-year course of study and was set apart as a deaconess in 1893. She stayed as head deaconess until 1913—twenty-two years.[35] The curriculum included the traditional courses of theology, Old and New Testament, Church history and doctrine, along with a heavy emphasis on practical training. Each woman took a twelve-week nurses'-training course at Episcopal Hospital. She was also required to do field work at a local parish, working with sewing and industrial schools, mothers' meetings, and Church-school classes or assisting with parish and tenement visiting. Each week one member of the board of managers took students to visit various civic institutions—

prisons, hospitals, day nurseries, homes for the elderly. Because most of the board members were actively involved in Philadelphia charitable institutions, they were able to give students an inside view of the institutions' workings. A series of Saturday morning talks on missions was given by women and men who served in the mission field. By graduation, the student was familiar with most of the types of Church work in which women were being employed and she had had practical experience in several of them.[36] In the next two decades, the Philadelphia school developed a reputation for practical training, whereas the New York school placed more emphasis on academic training.

The school began with seven resident students and twenty women who elected to take one or more courses.[37] Enrollment increased gradually; the largest number ever in residence was thirty, during the academic year 1912–1913. Generally, from seven to ten students were graduated each year.[38] The number of special students however, who took only one phase of the training, remained high. Women came from throughout the country to attend the school; the first fourteen students represented eleven dioceses.[39] Graduates found placements easily; the school was beseiged with requests for trained women. "The demand for such Deaconesses is greater than the supply," lamented Bishop Whitaker. "Letters come from all parts of the country asking for graduates of our House, to work in Parishes, and to take charge of Institutions."[40] Two members of the first graduating class stayed in Philadelphia, one went to work among the Indians of Minnesota, one to a hospital in Montana, and one to direct the House of the Holy Comforter in New York City.[41] By 1900 a survey of the graduates showed that fourteen had remained in Pennsylvania, whereas the others were scattered throughout the country— as far away as Spokane and Los Angeles. Fifteen of the forty-three women listed parishes as their work places; four of them served in foreign missions; three taught at deaconess training schools, and two were assigned to other institutions. The others simply listed the city in which they worked.[42]

OTHER DEACONESS TRAINING SCHOOLS

Schools for prospective deaconesses were also established in Virginia and Minnesota, but neither institution operated for very long.[43] In San Francisco, St. Phoebe's Church Training House owed its origin to the ubiquitous Emery family. John Emery (brother to Mary Abbot and Julia) served as archdeacon of California. In that position he was instrumental in establishing St. Phoebe's in 1891. He served as warden and his wife as house mother. The Reverend Edgar Lion was dean of the faculty, and Mrs. A.M. Lawver was in charge of the practical department. The first deaconess to be set apart in California, Helen Reed, was probably trained at St. Phoebe's, for she received her commission in October 1893, just two years after the school had opened. She entered city mission work but served only briefly, for she died in April 1894. In the diocesan journal no further mention is made of deaconesses or of St. Phoebe's House until 1900, when Elizabeth Mary Dorsey, who was trained in the East, was set apart as a deaconess in Sonora, California.[44]

Some years later, in 1908, the Deaconess Training School of the Pacific was established in Berkely, California, as an agency of the diocese. Governed by a board of managers consisting of eight women, with Bishop William Ford Nichols as president and the Reverend E.L. Parsons as warden, the school attracted women from throughout the West. A substantial bequest from one of the original board members, Mary Robertson, led to the purchase of a large home near the University of California. Known as St. Margaret's House in honor of Robertson's sister, the building contained both classrooms and living quarters for the young women. Some years later the Church Divinity School of the Pacific (a theological seminary for men) was moved to Berkely, making it possible for its faculty to teach classes at both institutions. But in the early days, most of the faculty were clergy from nearby churches.[45]

PROFESSIONAL DEVELOPMENT

As the number of women trained to serve as deaconesses increased, the need more clearly to define the profession became obvious. The most perplexing questions centered around the nature of the deaconess's commitment. Were hers lifetime vows? If so, what happened when she married? Would she have to resign her vows, or could she simply cease her ecclesiastical employment but continue to serve the needy in her role as housewife? Or might a married woman even continue to be employed as a deaconess? Were widows eligible to become deaconesses when the canon specified "unmarried women"?

Clearly, the people who were training the early deaconesses were particularly concerned with these issues. William R. Huntington staunchly supported the position that marriage was indeed possible for the deaconess, although he assumed she would not continue to be employed after she married. He compared the lot of a married deaconess to that of a priest who had taken a position as a college professor; both might hold their vows in abeyance as they assumed other responsibilities, but both might also find themselves doing the kind of work for which they had been ordained.[46] Susan Knapp vigorously disagreed with this position, feeling that the deaconess's was a lifetime vocation that must be renounced if the sworn woman should marry. She had been delighted to find strong support for this position among the deaconesses and bishops she met in England and had used their experience to buttress her position.[47]

When Knapp returned from England, she detected a change in Huntington's position on the subject. In his opening address to students that fall, he advised those thinking about becoming deaconesses to put aside the possibility of marriage. Knapp was pleased. "This new unity at the center of things, with the greater confidence placed in me," she wrote to Bishop Davidson, "have made me very thankful and happy, a very different person from the disheartened deaconess who presented herself at Lambeth Castle last August and asked for cheer and counsel."[48]

Knapp may well have exaggerated the extent to which Huntington had changed his mind, for most of the school board was under the impression that he supported deaconesses' right to marry while retaining their office.[49] Nevertheless, because of her daily contact with the students, Knapp was able to impart her vision of a lifetime vocation with such authority that it became the standard expectation of the women she trained. And because she trained a large proportion of the first generation of deaconesses, there was general unanimity on this question throughout the order. On the related issue of whether a deaconess could retract the vows she had made, the deaconesses also followed Knapp's lead. As she wrote to Bishop Davidson,

> Many of our deaconesses hold that the resignation cannot be more than an outward act; but, as these are the deaconesses to whom the wish to resign would never come, no practical difficulty arises, but only perplexity as to the real status of the woman who has vacated her office. I believe the candidates themselves will show increased care each year in examining their hearts and consciences in the matter

and that resignation will become too infrequent to be a cause of disquietude to us.[50]

One means of lessening the possibility that the deaconess might want to marry was to raise the minimum age limit. Because several of the priests and bishops who supported the deaconess movement saw this action as an easy solution to a potentially troublesome problem, the General Convention of 1901 amended the deaconess canon by raising the minimum age from twenty-five to thirty.[51] The move was apparently done with little debate, catching off guard those who favored a lower age. The latter returned to the next convention determined to reverse the requirement.

Two New York rectors, the Reverend L.W. Batten of St. Mark's Church and the Reverend William S. Rainsford of St. George's Church, led the movement to lower the age requirement. Pleading for equal treatment for male and female candidates for the diaconate, both men urged that the age limit be lowered to twenty-one. If the deaconess was to serve as a nurse or a teacher, Rainsford argued, she should be able to begin her service as soon as she was graduated from nursing school or teachers' college. Furthermore, she should be free to marry. "If she serves the Church in the unmarried state during the first bright years of her youth, she cannot fail to get an experience that will make her a blessing to the Church of God, whether she be married or single," said Rainsford.[52] Arthur C.A. Hall, bishop of Vermont, took the opposite point of view, holding that the office of deaconess precluded marriage and required "a dedication to a single life." He stated:

> To send out a young woman . . . to meet her freely in her ministrations the young doctor and the young clergyman (all their sympathies aroused in their work), with no sort of general understanding that she is not to be thought of as marriageable (though *she* may have been led to entertain the idea of a life-long dedication) is both to expose the institution to instability and ridicule, and to expose the individual to unnecessary and . . . unwarrantable difficulties.[53]

To Bishop Hall, a different standard applied to the young doctor or clergyman.

Recognizing there was widespread disagreement about the age at which a woman should become a deaconess, the convention of the diocese of New York petitioned the 1904 General Convention to revise the canon on deaconesses by leaving the age question to the discretion of the candidate's bishop. The bishops, however, rejected such authority. Asserting that "it is inexpedient to add to the burdens of Bishops' discretion in questions so delicate," the committee on canons recommended instead a return to the minimum age of twenty-five. Subsequent action of the General Convention set the minimum age at twenty-three and continued the provision that the deaconess might resign at any time. No further changes were made to the deaconess canon in the next two decades.[54]

EMPLOYMENT OF DEACONESSES

In the mid-1890s, as the first women were graduated from the deaconess training schools, the concept of the institutional parish was just being fully realized. City churches had constructed huge parish houses to be used for the proliferating club meetings, health clinics, immigrant schools, industrial classes, and recreation programs—all staffed primarily by women volunteers. Deaconesses were hired to direct the programs, to act essentially as parish assistants in charge of social-service activities, in positions analogous to those of the head workers at settlement houses. Because they were working in churches with extensive facilities, a space for living on the premises was generally provided. In very large parishes, three or four deaconesses might share living quarters, but generally the parish deaconesses lived alone. Thus the communal style of life did not develop among the deaconesses as it had among the sisterhoods.[55] Instead, the deaconess found her primary identity with the parish she served: Her worship life was centered in the regular parish services; her home was generally on or quite near the church premises; and her primary contacts were with other church members rather than other deaconesses. And because she often remained at one parish through the terms of a succession of clergymen, she became the symbol of stability, the bearer of tradition, and, for good or ill, the arbiter of "the way it was in the beginning, is now and ever shall be." Though she was trained to work obediently and without complaint under the direction of the local priest and bishop, the parish deaconess, fortified by many years of faithful service, possessed formidable authority.

Though there were probably more parish deaconesses employed in New York and Philadelphia than in any other cities, they were by no means limited to the eastern seaboard. Deaconesses worked in the Church of the Incarnation, Dallas; St. Andrew's Mission, Richmond,

Virginia; Trinity Church, Columbia, South Carolina; St. Stephen's Church, Colorado Springs; Emmanuel Church, Boston; Christ Church Cathedral, St. Louis; St. Mark's Church, Minneapolis; and in many other cities.[56] In addition, some Church-sponsored settlement houses hired deaconesses as head workers. Among them were St. Martha's House, Philadelphia; La Grange Settlement, Atlanta; and Neighborhood House, Los Angeles.[57]

Only a limited number of parishes, however, had programs extensive enough to require a full-time deaconess. It soon became evident that other employment must also be found for them. Deaconesses began to be hired as matrons of Church-sponsored institutions, such as hospitals and orphans' homes, and as school headmistresses. As such, they tended to live at the institution, often serving as house mothers as well as administrators. Here also the model of the deaconess as the lone professional woman, intimately identified with the institution she served, prevailed. As administrators, the deaconesses probably had even more power than they had in the local parishes, for most of these institutions were supervised by volunteer boards. With this freedom, however, came a concomitant loneliness and isolation.

For many Church-sponsored institutions in an age of increasing professionalism, hiring the deaconess was the first step in the transition to a professional staff. With some training in administrative procedures and budgets, the deaconess brought some expertise to an office that previously had been held by a woman with little or no academic experience. Her uniform, with its veil and carefully starched collar and cuffs, marked her as a member of an order set apart for service to others.[58] The cross she wore reminded clients of her religious commitment. By her appearance and manner she conveyed the impression that she was a professionally trained religious administrator.

In reality, however, the administrative training the deaconess candidate received was minimal—a typewriting and accounting class, one general course in parish or institutional administration, and on-the-job experience during the required hospital internship and summer work assignments. Religious studies constituted most of her education. By the second decade of the twentieth century, deaconesses began to be replaced as institutional administrators by men and women more specifically trained in office administration and finance. The increasing secularism of the institutions demanded that the re-

ligious character of the administrators be deemphasized. The deaconesses had played their part as transition between the amateur and
professional staffs.

By 1900 deaconesses increasingly sought employment not in city
parishes or institutional administration but in the mission field, where
they could make more extensive use of their talents and training.
There the need for educated workers was so great that deaconesses
were often placed where they were the only representatives of the
Episcopal Church and thus were responsible for meeting the religious, social, and educational needs of their charges. A clergyman or
a bishop might visit sporadically to bring the sacraments and preach,
but the day-to-day ministry was done by the deaconesses. Their training, their uniform, and their identification by the Church as professional religious workers all lent to their work an authority that
theretofore had not been possible for lone women workers. And yet
their very deployment was still heavily dependent on a support network organized and financed by the Church's women. The way in
which the Woman's Auxiliary developed that support network and
championed the employment of deaconesses in both domestic and
foreign missions is outlined in the following chapter.

CHAPTER NINE

Women as Missionaries, 1900–1920

Christians entered the twentieth century convinced that Christ's kingdom was at hand. All the mechanisms for the Church's worldwide expansion had been set in place. Christian missionaries proclaimed the gospel in every land, while in the United States zealous reformers carried messages of spiritual uplift and moral reformation to those segments of society yet untouched by Christ's redeeming love. Strong national Churches supported the missionary enterprise, and Christians from many of them cooperated in a host of ecumenical organizations that transcended denominational boundaries. To mark the new century, thousands of Church members gathered in New York City in 1900 for the Ecumenical Missionary Conference. The general mood of the period was reflected in that body's concluding statement:

> The Conference . . . was held at a time when the political and commercial expansion of Europe and America had directed the thought of Christendom to distant parts of the earth. America had been brought into immediate contact with Asia by the occupation of the Philippines, Great Britain was engaged in war in South Africa, and the clouds of the coming uprising [the Boxer rebellion] were even then gathering in China. Regrettable as were these disturbances in themselves, they widened the circle of thought, and resulted in an increased appreciation of the condition of the non-Christian portions of the world, and deepened the conviction that human progress is inseparably bound up with Christian missions.[1]

Most Episcopal leaders shared the conviction that human progress was "inseparably bound up with Christian missions." Clergy and laity participated actively in the Ecumenical Missionary Conference and assumed leadership in a decade of ecumenical activity that culminated in the Pan-Anglican Congress of 1908 and the World Missionary Conference in Edinburgh in 1910. Episcopal churchwomen served as members of the Joint Committee of Women on the United Study of Missions and supported students in the missionary activity of the Student Volunteer Movement. The Church's General Convention of 1901 was held in San Francisco, both to enable missionaries from the Far East, Alaska, and the western United States to attend and to demonstrate to delegates from the Atlantic coast, as they crossed the continent, the vast missionary frontier of the American West. In the Church, the Missionary Education Movement developed study guides and held training seminars. The Laymen's Forward Movement enlisted churchmen in missionary support; it raised an offering, presented at the General Convention of 1907, of $775,000 for missions. Thirteen new missionary jurisdictions—Puerto Rico, Southern Brazil, Cuba, Honolulu, Mexico, Salina [Kansas], Hankow, Panama, eastern Oregon, Western Colorado, Nevada, Wyoming, and Utah—were established, and the American Church Institute for Negroes was formed.[2]

At the forefront of this missionary activity was the Woman's Auxiliary, which had spent the previous ten years developing mission study programs, raising funds, and recruiting and training women to serve as missionaries. Promotional tools were ready; the women had founded a press to publish them and had established an effective system for distribution both at home and abroad. The United Offering had been built into a fund large enough to support intensive outreach activity.

For the next twenty years, Episcopal churchwomen's work continued with many outward signs of success. The number of women who volunteered to serve in domestic and foreign missions grew steadily, as did the amount of money the auxiliary raised for missionary work. The New York and Philadelphia Deaconess Schools trained more students; new schools for deaconesses were founded in California, Minnesota, and Chicago. Three new sisterhoods were organized, and the existing Episcopal sisterhoods continued to gain members. Religious orders moved into the overseas mission field, establishing communities in China, Hawaii, and the Philippines. Laywomen flocked to summer mission schools and returned home to teach mission study courses to groups of all ages. The Triennial Meeting of the Woman's Auxiliary grew in both participation and program; study courses multiplied, and legislative sessions gave an increasing number of women training in parliamentary procedure and organizational administration.

And yet, in a sense the very success of the women's program was also its greatest flaw, for the Church no longer had to worry about its women; they were taking care of themselves. The local clergyman did not need to recruit women parishioners; they filled the Church in droves. His problem was finding enough for them to do. As Bishop Frederic Dan Huntington testified, in the Diocese of Central New York

> . . . both the original Church life and the survival of it from year to year are owing to women. The first services were often called for and held, the places of worship were provided, the comforts and decencies, and not merely the decorations, were furnished, the money was raised, the church buildings were put up . . . and the clergy have been paid, by the ingenuity, zeal, and toil of women.[3]

Likewise, on the national level the General Convention debates on harnessing the Church's womanpower had ended, for mobilized women were everywhere in evidence. (Means of mobilizing laymen was the current subject of debate.) Increasingly, the Church consisted of separate spheres for men and women, spheres that had little contact with each other.

THE WOMAN'S AUXILIARY TO THE BOARD OF MISSIONS

No one would dispute the success of the Woman's Auxiliary to the Board of Missions. As an organization to unite and mobilize the Church's women, as a means of raising money and supplies and recruiting volunteers for the missionary effort, and as the purveyor of education about mission to the entire Church, the auxiliary had, in twenty-five years, far exceeded the dreams of its founders. By the turn of the century, its chapters had been founded in every diocese and missionary district and in almost every local parish. At least one-third of the missionary budget was provided directly by the women; indirectly they contributed to the other two-thirds.[4] But now that the organization was functioning effectively, its officers found themselves increasingly confronted with the political reality of the situation—they were "auxiliary to" the Board of Missions but had no representation on it and did not participate in its decisions. The history of the next twenty years was shaped by the women's attempts to deal with this crucial problem.

The movement toward greater autonomy had to be made without the leadership of Mary Abbot Twing, for she had died suddenly during the 1901 General Convention. As the most persistent advocate for women's ministries in the Church, Twing had lived to see most of her dreams accomplished: the Woman's Auxiliary, which she began, was thriving; the General Convention had established the order of deaconesses as an official part of the Church's ministry; and a system of recruiting and training women workers had been established. In a sense, it was fitting she died at the convention, where so many of the auxiliary officers, missionary workers, bishops, and clergy whom she had visited in all parts of the world had gathered. These friends filled San Francisco's Grace Cathedral for her funeral, to pay tribute to the small woman whose work had been so important to the Church's missionary effort. In an act that would have pleased her, the auxiliary voted to raise funds to build a dormitory at St. Mary's School in Shanghai in honor of Mary Abbot Twing.[5]

THE UNITED OFFERING

The demand for self-determination first surfaced in the distribution of the United Offering. Presented at each Triennial Meeting since 1889, the United Offering was collected above and beyond the general funds women contributed to the Board of Missions. Though Woman's Auxiliary officers tenaciously clung to the principle that the United Offering would be allocated not by the Board of Missions but by the women themselves, they had generally directed the distribution toward needy areas identified by the board. Thus the offering of 1901 (which came to just over $100,000) had been designated at the 1898 Triennial Meeting to be divided into equal grants for each foreign and domestic missionary bishop, with the proviso that one extra grant be reserved for the Commission for Work Among Colored People in the United States. Though the distribution to missionary bishops was at the suggestion of the Board of Missions, the grant to the commission appears to have been suggested by auxiliary officers, in response to a request from the Auxiliary of the Conference of Workers Among Colored People.[6] From the beginning of their work in the freedom

schools after the Civil War, the Woman's Auxiliary had proved to be
the Episcopal Church's most consistent supporter of work among Negroes. The 1901 grant financed a reorganization of that work. Although it was only a token amount, the symbolic value of equating
the work among Negroes with that done by the missionary bishops
emotionally uplifted the black workers.

Though reserving a part of the United Offering for the work among
blacks was a small assertion of power, the stage was set for a stronger
demand at the next Triennial Meeting. During the 1898 debates, a
letter from Mrs. Tuttle was read. It suggested that before the convention the delegates be informed about possible recipients for the
offering and about the pros and cons of each designation so that they
might more intelligently decide where the money should go.[7] As the
wife of a bishop who served first in Utah and then in Missouri (and
was to serve from 1903 until 1923 as the presiding bishop), Mrs. Tuttle
had been active in Woman's Auxiliary work since its beginning, had
served as president of both the Utah and the Missouri chapters, had
written mission study guides, and had attended most of the auxiliary's
triennial meetings. Her history is typical of the founding generation
of auxiliary members, many of whom organized the first auxiliaries in
their locations, became diocesan officers very early, and then continued to serve in those offices for decades.[8] Through their long association with each other and with the Emery sisters, these women
developed an *esprit de corps* that transcended local boundaries. The
auxiliary work broke down the isolation of the mission field, uniting
the women in a common purpose and bringing them together to
achieve it. The Woman's Auxiliary was the clergy wife's link to the
amorphous institution her husband served; it affirmed that she, too,
was an integral part of the Church's mission. Such women, pleaded
Mrs. Tuttle, should be well informed so they could help decide where
the funds were to be spent.

Meeting in 1901 to decide on the object for the 1904 offering, the
auxiliary had been presented with a Board of Missions request to
divide the funds equally between general missions and women's work.
After due consideration, however, the United Offering Committee
rejected the request, stating:

> With the utmost loyalty to the Board of Missions, the women of the
> Auxiliary wish to exercise this right of an independent judgment. . . .
> They feel that the woman's work, established during the past three

years through the offering of 1898, ought to be supported. . . . They desire, in addition, to do aggressive woman's work for missions. They also wish to help the sick and disabled women workers returning home from the missionary fields in which they have sacrificed their health.[9]

The committee members had learned that the most effective way they could convince the Board of Missions to hire women workers was to provide the funds for their salaries, so they recommended—and the Triennial Meeting voted—to use the entire offering for salaries and medical and retirement benefits for women workers. To mollify the Board of Missions, however, they also urged local auxiliaries to increase their contributions to the general budget, pressing them to raise the national total from $65,000 to $100,000 annually. This action set the pattern for the next two decades; in return for complete freedom in appropriating the United Offering, the Woman's Auxiliary essentially guaranteed to produce $100,000 in general operating funds yearly for the Board of Missions. And each succeeding Triennial Meeting chose to spend most of the United Offering on support for women workers.

As the auxiliary's chief national staff officer, Julia Emery bore the burden of enforcing this agreement. Working in the missions office, she knew the relentless pressure of trying to maintain a missionary program with insufficient funds and sympathized with the Board of Missions' constant need for additional support. And yet, with a feminism based on her association with the women workers, she was convinced that women had unique gifts and talents that made them very effective missionaries. So she clung to the formula, constantly exhorting the women to donate to the general missionary budget and at the same time rejoicing each year as the United Offering increased, refusing to let funds from it be siphoned off to meet existing deficits.[10] It was a supreme balancing act that she performed expertly, thus providing a growing number of jobs for women in the mission field.

WOMEN IN THE MISSION FIELD

The next twenty years saw a gradual increase in the number of women who served in the mission field and a dramatic increase in the percentage of female workers in the field. Seventeen percent of the mission workers sent by the Church were women; by 1916 that percentage had risen to thirty-nine.[11] And because female mission workers were generally paid one-third less than male workers, more could be sent for the same amount of money.[12]

By 1905 the United Offering supported seventy-six women workers and six students in training. (These women were designated as "United Offering workers"; throughout this period there continued to be other women workers in the field who received their salaries from other sources.) They served overseas in Alaska (4 women), China (11), Japan (10), the Philippines (1), Puerto Rico (3), and Liberia (3). In the United States, the largest number (26) worked in the South—in small Appalachian towns or among the blacks in southern cities. Thirteen of the women worked in the Far West, from Oklahoma and Texas to California, generally in schools or on Indian reservations. Five women served in Minnesota and Illinois.[13] As the United Offering grew each triennium (see following table), so did the number of women workers it supported. By 1907 there were 111 United Offering workers.[14] The following year Julia Emery traveled around the world, visiting sixty-six of them—teachers, nurses, deaconesses, physicians, and others—and noted that she missed ninety-six other women whose stations were not on her route.[15]

WOMEN AS DOMESTIC MISSIONARIES

The most noticeable effect of the increased deployment of women was that the Church was able to open mission stations in isolated areas, communities previously considered too poor to support a clergyman. Deaconesses particularly were deployed in this manner; Church leaders felt the women were trained adequately to manage the stations without a resident clergyman. So the women were sent into the sparsely populated valleys of Appalachia, into the mining camps and Indian reservations of the Far West and Alaska, and into the rural villages of China, Japan, and the Philippines. They served on the front lines of mission, generally meeting and ministering to people who had had no previous contact with the Episcopal Church, serving in much the same way as their nineteenth-century sisters had served on the frontier of the Church's ministry to the cities.

Within the United States, the women worked primarily among three groups of people: American Indians, southern Negroes, and Appalachian mountain people. Indian workers were scattered throughout the country. Priscilla Bridge was principal of St. Mary's Indian School, and Deaconess Gertrude Baker was the principal of

UNITED OFFERING, 1889–1919

Year	Amount	Disposition
1889	$ 2,188	$1000 Built church in Anvik, Alaska $1000 Sent Lisa Lovell to Japan as a missionary teacher for one year
1892	20,912	Enrollment fund to endow the episcopate
1895	56,198	Endowment, salary of the Bishop of Oklahoma and Indian Territory
1898	82,743	Endowment, salary of Bishop of Alaska Small gift for a new building at Cape Mount Liberia
1901	107,028	Equal amounts to each missionary bishop with one share to Commission for Work Among the Colored People
1904	150,000	Support, training and retirement of women workers
1907	224,251	$214,251 for women workers $10,000 for training school for women in Sendai, Japan
1910	243,361	$228,361 for women workers $10,000 St. Hilda's School for Girls, Wuchang, China $5,000 girls' dormitory, St. Augustine's School, Raleigh, North Carolina
1913	306,497	$286,497 for women workers $5,000 dormitory, St. Augustine's School, Raleigh, North Carolina $15,000 to rebuild Hooker School for Girls in Mexico
1916	353,620	Support for women workers and students preparing for the work
1919	468,060	$448,060 for women workers $5,000 for school for Navajo, New Mexico $5,000 for hall at Valle Crucis School for Mountain Girls, Asheville, NC $5,000 for All Saints' School, Cuba $5,000 for Chapel at St. Hilda's School, Wuchang, China

Source: Frances M. Young, *Thankfulness Unites* (Cincinnati: Forward Movement Publications, 1979).

St. Elizabeth's Indian School in South Dakota. Elizabeth Buheley ministered to the Utes who came to Fort Duchesne, Utah, to trade. On Wyoming's Wind River Reservation, two women served as field matrons and two others had charge of the Indian School. Miss Marion Roberts, daughter of a missionary physician, was born there and spent her entire life working among the Shoshoni and the Arapaho.[16] In Minnesota, Pauline Colby lived in White Earth among the Chippewas from 1892 to 1922, while Susie Salisbury worked there with the Sioux. "It would be impossible to speak too highly of the heroic devotion and self-sacrifice which Miss Salisbury has shown through these years of her isolation among the Indian People," testified Bishop Samuel Cook Edsall in 1916.[17] In California, Mr. and Mrs. Shea ministered to the Karok Indians in the mountains east of Sacramento. Riding her horse along the mountain trails, Mrs. Shea visited the Indian homes, teaching nursing and hygiene while her husband instructed the converts.[18] Miss Eliza Thacara began work among the Navaho in Fort Defiance, Arizona, in 1895 and served there until her retirement in 1919. There she opened a twelve-bed hospital, which she ran for many years by herself.[19]

In the South, Episcopal women (both black and white) worked among the Negroes, generally as teachers or administrators. Several small industrial schools that trained black girls in sewing, nursing, and domestic service were staffed only by the United Offering worker and perhaps one or two teachers from the community. Many of these schools were short-lived, disappearing when an invaluable worker left, but two of them—St. Augustine's in Raleigh, North Carolina, and St. Paul's in Lawrenceville, Virginia—became normal schools and then colleges. By 1916 schools staffed by missionary workers were operating in Atlanta, Marietta, and LaGrange, Georgia; Greenville, Charlotte, and Raleigh, North Carolina; Lawrenceville, Virginia; San Antonio and Tyler, Texas; Cocoanut Grove, Florida; Keeling, Tennessee; and Charles Town, West Virginia. In the field of health care, one woman worker administered the Good Samaritan Hospital in Charlotte—the first hospital in North Carolina open to Negroes. Elizabeth C. Barber did social-service work at the Sheltering Arms Hospital in West Virginia, one of the few southern hospitals serving both blacks and whites at the turn of the century.[20]

One ministry almost exclusively carried out by women was that in Appalachia. Throughout the Blue Ridge and Smoky Mountains, from West Virginia to Tennessee and South Carolina, women workers—

either alone or in pairs—were sent to live in the isolated valleys to gather around themselves a Christian community. Working generally from small houses they rented or purchased, they called on the mountain people, nursed the sick, taught the children to read and write, prepared confirmation classes, and held Sunday worship services. Intermittently a clergyman would visit to administer the Eucharist; the bishop generally came once a year to confirm those candidates the workers had prepared for the rite.

To the people on the mountain, however, the woman worker was the representative of Christ in their midst. Laura Callaway, for example, arrived in Altamont, Kentucky, in 1902. At the end of her first quarter, she reported that she had visited forty families, begun classes in cooking, sewing, and basketry, organized a mothers' meeting, visited the sick, prepared one woman for burial and read the burial service, opened a Sunday school, prepared thirteen students for baptism, and visited mission schools in Livingston and Corbin.[21] Subsequent reports record that she established a second mother's meeting for Negro women, began confirmation classes and established a small circulating library. During a smallpox epidemic she cared for the sick, supplied needy people with food and clothing, and helped see that all the children were vaccinated. "I have established a reputation as a surgical nurse," she wrote in 1904, "and have been kept busy dressing wounds, and was even called to court as a witness in a shooting affair."[22] She also planted a large garden and taught her charges how to can its produce.

Similar work was carried on in many parts of the South. Deaconess Adams and Deaconess Maria V. Williams served in the diocese of southern Virginia. Caryetta Davis and Agatha Saunders reported in 1916 that their day school was attended by 105 scholars and their Sunday school by 147 pupils in Callaway, Virginia. Mamie Montgomery reported that St. Elizabeth's Day School had 40 pupils and their Sunday school had 95. In West Virginia, Miss Fisher ran a hospital, its chapel, a Sunday school, and various organizations in the Kanawha coal fields. "This hospital is perhaps the greatest missionary agency in the diocese, reaching nearly all nationalities and creeds," wrote the bishop.[23] Women also worked in mining communities in other parts of the country. Three women served among the coal miners of Thayer, Virden, and Glen Carbon, Illinois, and Deaconess Knight served in the gold mining town of Canyon City, Oregon.[24]

In addition to others' work among Negroes, American Indians, and

Appalachian people, a few women exercised unusual ministries in urban settings. Women staffed Atlanta's La Grange Settlement, which ministered primarily to the poor white families that had moved to the city from rural areas. In Los Angeles, Deaconess Sophie R. Miller worked with Indians who had moved into the city, and Mary L. Paterson founded a center for Japanese immigrants, offering English-language instruction and a kindergarten along with regular church services and Bible classes. In San Francisco, outreach programs to both the Japanese and the Chinese communities were staffed by women workers. In 1913 Deaconess Jane Hall founded a home for young actresses on Forty-Sixth Street in New York City. Later known as The Rehearsal Club, it provided living quarters at reasonable rates for actresses for the next half-century.[25]

Also chiefly in the hands of Episcopal women were the Church-sponsored educational institutions. *Whittaker's Church Almanac* for 1899 listed eighty such schools for girls, all of which were staffed primarily by women.[26] One of the most interesting schools was St. Andrew's Priory, established in Hawaii at the request of Queen Emma in 1864 to educate native girls. Founded by the Sisters of the English Society of the Most Holy Trinity, it came under the control of the Episcopal Church in 1902 and eventually was run by the Community of the Transfiguration, providing college-preparation courses for young women of the various Hawaiian racial strains.[27]

Such schools might be sponsored by the diocese or by the local parish or run by one of the religious orders, but most of them were able to exist primarily because of the long-term dedication of the women who served as faculty, administrators, and house mothers. Viewing this work as their unique ministry, many of these women devoted their lives to the schools, though their remuneration was negligible. For a generation of girls for whom higher education was a distinct possibility, these teachers provided the best college-preparatory courses available in many cities. Ruth Benedict, the anthropologist, attended such a school (St. Margaret's, Buffalo), as did Grace Abott (Brownell Hall, Omaha), who would become director of the U.S. Children's Bureau, and Miriam Van Waters (St. Helen's Hall, Portland), who led the movement to reform women's penal institutions.[28] A half-century earlier, diarist George Templeton Strong had credited women's petition to attend classes at Columbia University to the influence of the Community of St. Mary: "The school of the Sisters of St. Mary finds great favor with the 'strong-minded' womankind, because the 'Sisters' carry out the theory of 'woman's rights' in doing their noble work thoroughly and well without masculine aid."[29] His words point to the important role such schools continued to play in introducing a feminist point of view to their students. Many of the teachers and administrators imparted to their pupils a sense of confidence in their own abilities and a tradition of academic excellence that served them well as they moved into new fields.

Though the years between 1900 and 1920 were characterized by the development of the new domestic ministries described above, the work of institutional parishes and Church-sponsored institutions continued to be conducted primarily by the Church's women, either as volunteers or as paid staff members. There were some changes of emphasis—e.g., the "rescue work" of the nineteenth century evolved into programs of care, counseling, and adoptive services for "unwed mothers." Recreation and educational programs for young working women were developed through the Girls' Friendly Society (GFS), an Anglican association of girls' clubs. GFS chapters built a network of vacation homes with rooms to rent to women at nominal cost. And Woman's Auxiliary members continued their efforts to recruit women to serve as missionaries either at home or in the foreign mission fields.

WOMEN AS FOREIGN MISSIONARIES

By 1900 the Episcopal Church had established missionary districts in Liberia, China, Japan, and Haiti and had additional work in Mexico, Cuba, and Brazil. Church services were held regularly at over two hundred mission stations in those countries. The next year, districts were established in the Philippine Islands, Cuba, Puerto Rico, and Hawaii. Work began in the Panama Canal Zone in 1906 and in the Dominican Republic in 1913.[30] The mission station in each region generally consisted of a site for church services, several homes for mission workers, and, often, a school—either for local children or for Bible women and catechists, or both. Many of the larger stations also included health-care facilities that ranged from one-room clinics to modern, well-equipped teaching hospitals such as St. Luke's Hospital in Shanghai.[31]

By the turn of the century, a growing sense of professionalism was evident among the women missionary workers. The increased deployment of deaconesses in the mission field was evidence of that trend; as educated professionals they generally worked as administrators of the various institutions—orphanages, schools, clinics, child-care centers—that evolved around the mission stations. There was also a move to recruit women with special skills, e.g., teachers and nurses and doctors. Some outstanding women physicians—such as Dr. Mary Gates and Dr. Ellen Fullerton in Shanghai and Dr. Mary V. Glenton in Wuchang—served overseas for long periods of time. Their skills were used not only to deliver health care to women patients but to organize nurses'-training programs for native workers.

The Woman's Auxiliary Committee on Missionary Workers systematized its work. Recruitment and interview processes were formalized; successful candidates were recommended to the Board of Missions for appointment. No longer were good intentions and pious, motherly inclinations adequate preparation for missionary service. Though the Board of Missions required no specific training of the workers, the auxiliary committee recommended that candidates prepare for overseas service at one of the deaconess training schools. As their report stated:

> These women, often young, with zeal and courage, need to be instructed in *practical* knowledge to enable them to make the most of *small things.* The training in our Church training schools . . . inculcates self-denial, self-restraint, obedience, all essential qualifications for the difficult and blessed work they desire. . . . Shall we not *do* our duty, train our women, send them out and pay their salaries?[32]

The committee also arranged scholarships for those women who could not afford the cost of the training.

Once a woman was accepted for a mission field, she was generally sent first to the largest mission station in the country, where she might spend one to three years gaining proficiency in the indigenous language while she taught or worked with natives who already spoke some English. When she attained fluency in the language, she was sent wherever the need was greatest, generally (but not always) living with a more experienced woman worker at the station. As in the domestic field, the deaconess was generally given a greater degree of autonomy from the beginning and moved directly into very responsible positions. Each year, workers received vacation time within the country and, every six years, a six-month furlough to return to the United States.

Although teaching and nursing were their primary occupations, some women did more unusual work. Miss Frances Bartter directed an Industrial School and Exchange among the Moros on the Philippine Islands, selling the student-made products to support the educational program. Miss Cornwall-Legh ministered to the lepers at Kusatsu, Japan, "giving herself and her possessions to the service of these unfortunate and neglected people."[33] One investigator wrote of her work that "it is the most impressive evidence of God's grace that I saw in Japan. . . . Eighty-five lepers confirmed out of a total of two-hundred; fourteen more confirmed at the time of my visit . . . the whole leper-church filled with joy and missionary zeal."[34] In Mexico City, among "a very squalid and destitute portion of the city's population," Deaconess Claudine Whitaker ran the Settlement House of the Sacred Name, offering a kindergarten, mothers' meetings, classes for young men and women, and a rudimentary health-care program.[35]

Instead of trying to obliterate the native cultures, many of the women workers tried to preserve them. In Hankow, Miss Holand wrote a musical setting for the liturgy based on the Chinese scale and taught it to the Bible women in training there.[36] Margaret Waterman first learned the Igorot language in the Philippines, then wrote an Igorot grammar that could be used in the native schools. She and Deaconess Margaret Routledge prized the native weaving and arranged for their students to export it.[37] Mary L. James indicated her appreciation for Chinese culture when she wrote to the national missions office:

> I feel that the undue haste with which some of the *men* medical missionaries and Rockefeller workers in China wish to revolutionize social customs, constitutes a serious menace to the Christian work undertaken by the various churches. . . . Until we build up, from childhood, a Christian social background with ideals as well as liberties, we are indeed rash to smash the old Chinese customs which protect the girl. Certainly American Civilization, as I see it on this furlough, does not fill me with the desire to transplant its social licenses and liberties wholesale to China. . . . It seems to me we should try to give China Christianity, but to err on the safe side when it comes to our "civilization." I am not so sure that China has not got some things over us.[38]

Increasingly, the emphasis was on training native workers. Nurses' training schools for the native women were established at mission hospitals in Shanghai, Hankow, Tokyo, Manila, and several other locations. Sarah E. Conway went one step further. Working in Liberia, she saw the need for a hospital. Later, on furlough in the United

States, she persuaded a wealthy Philadelphia woman to provide the necessary funds, then returned to Cape Mount where, while serving as a visiting nurse in the surrounding countryside, she supervised the construction of Liberia's first hospital.[39] A nurses' training school for Liberian women was later established at the hospital.

Although it is difficult to determine, the emphasis on educating other women seems to have come primarily from the women missionaries themselves. In her quarterly report, for example, Deaconess Edith Hart indicated she had spent most of her time on educational projects—moving the training school for Bible women into new quarters, arranging for a trained nurse from the hospital to teach the women hygiene, establishing a boarding and day school that would offer academic courses to older women (married as well as single), and planning for a week-long institute for Bible women already at work in the field. With all these responsibilities, she wrote, "it is not surprising that the parish work for which I am responsible is done in a most superficial manner."[40]

Obviously, the education of native women was a high priority for Deaconess Hart, as it was for Miss Suthon. In Aomori, a fishing village in northern Japan that often was isolated by snowstorms from November through May, Miss Suthon, with a Japanese catechist and a Bible woman, established a mission. They opened a small day school and began Sunday-school meetings. Soon they also began to teach English to the men and women of the village, so that their first pupils would eventually establish other schools throughout the village.[41] Deaconess Elizabeth M. Deane was sent as a nurse to Grace Hospital in Circle City, Alaska, a gold-rush boom town on the Yukon River. The doctor who supervised the hospital there proved incapable and had to be reassigned, leaving the deaconess in charge of both the hospital and the mission church. "Miss Deane will be alone this winter," wrote Bishop Peter Rowe, "and she will do all that one devoted soul can do for Christ's sake. She is respected and loved by all for her good work's sake."[42]

For some, the isolation and loneliness of their positions proved difficult. From Aomori, Irene P. Mann wrote:

> I am living alone, and the language and people are so new and strange, that at times the isolation and loneliness of Aomori is appalling. I suppose homesickness is only natural and to be expected under the circumstances. Pray for God's blessing upon me in the work here, that I may be to these people all that He would have me be.[43]

From Japan Deaconess Carlsen wrote to Dean Knapp at the training school:

> Oh, Deaconess, isn't there someone who is nice and wants to come out here who can come soon? I would so love to have someone with me. I do love Hirosaki and the work here but one does get most awfully lonesome when there is no one to talk to or get help or inspiration from.[44]

Serving as the only white woman in the Indian village of Allakaket, Alaska, Deaconess Bertha B. Mills "broke down nervously" and had to be evacuated by dogsled to Tanana, a 150-mile journey.[45]

Partly to allay such loneliness, the women workers replicated in their mission stations the organizations of their home parishes. As one woman wrote from the interior of China:

> At noon each day the girls use the prayers of the Junior Auxiliary, which have been translated for them. There is a branch of the Woman's Auxiliary also, which works for the United Offering and support the girls' day-school at Hunan. Several of these women have mite-chests in which they put a little money day by day. The children, too, have boxes, and are learning to pray and give for Missions. In the two schools eight, only, of the thirty-six girls have unbound feet, but the people are beginning to rectify this evil, and it is growing less.[46]

Needlework classes were a popular mode of reaching the local women. Chinese women embroidered silk, Philippine women made lace, and women from many lands constructed and mended garments. Not only was needlework a traditional feminine occupation but it offered the opportunity for quiet conversation and a means of breaking through the barriers of shyness and restraint. None of the women workers seemed to question their roles as purveyors of domesticity. Though their lives often contradicted the proper image of a Victorian lady, the women workers conveyed the virtues of piety, submissiveness, and domesticity to their female charges.

For themselves, however, many of the foreign missionary workers found the freedom from social constraints and expectations one of the chief *advantages* of missionary life. The number of women who spent most of their lives as foreign missionaries testifies to the satisfaction they derived from their posts. The independent spirit of these women is evident in their correspondence. As Deaconess Hart testified, "Indeed, I have often said to Bishop Roots, that, in view of the trouble women missionaries make, if I were a Bishop, I would not have one of them in my diocese; unless, of course, I wanted to have some work done."[47]

Not only did the women missionaries have more freedom of action abroad than they would have had at home but they forged for the native women with whom they worked a larger share in the Church's administration. A 1924 survey of women's position in the mission field revealed that in most mission areas, native women *and* missionaries had a greater share in Church government than did their counterparts in the United States. One respondent indicated there was "very much more real democracy in the matter of voting and acting as delegates in Church Councils than in the U.S.A." Another reported, "In this diocese, women are members of vestries in certain parishes, and are eligible to election in the Diocesan Synod. Both Chinese and foreign women are members of our Diocesan Council." The only negative reply in the survey came from Bishop Hulse in Latin America: "The position of women in the church here is exactly as it is in the North. They do the larger part of the work and the men hold the offices."[48]

SUPPORT FOR MISSION CONSTRUCTION FROM THE AUXILIARY

Although the most significant use of the United Offering was to support the women missionaries, each Triennial Meeting also set aside funds for building. These gifts had the strategic value of enabling the women to shape a program by constructing and equipping a building for a specific purpose. For example, in 1907 the United Offering was used to build a training school for Japanese Bible women and kindergarten teachers. The choice of this project indicated the women's growing emphasis on sharing ministry, on training others to carry on their work.

The training school was built in Sendai, a city about two hundred miles north of Tokyo. Deaconess Ranson and her assistant, Miss Correll, were in charge of the students—from twenty to forty women from throughout Japan. Instruction was in Japanese, which both the American women had learned. A kindergarten was operated at the school for the practical training of student teachers; each weekend the latter moved into the surrounding villages, holding classes for women and girls on Saturdays and teaching Sunday schools for children the next morning.[49] By working through the children, the missionary women were able to reach the basic family unit. In his study of Protestant missions' effects on Japan, Charles W. Inglehart claimed the kindergartens "became the most effective seed-plots for Christian nurture, and ran their rootlets into neighborhood families as no other Christian institutions could quite do."[50]

Other buildings built primarily with funds from the Woman's Auxiliary included a girl's dormitory at St. Augustine's School; a college for Negroes in Raleigh, North Carolina; the Hooker School for Girls in Mexico; a school for Navajo Indians in New Mexico; a dormitory at the Valle Crusis School for Mountain Girls in Asheville, North Carolina; a classroom building for All Saints' School in Cuba; a chapel for St. Hilda's School in Wuchang, China; St. Mary's Hall in Shanghai; St. Agnes' School for Girls in Kyoto, Japan; St. Luke's Hospital in Tokyo; and the Church General Hospital in Wuchang, China. The first six gifts were from the United Offering, for buildings that could be made with the allotted sums; the last four, however, were far more expensive projects, which the auxiliary was reluctant to support with United Offering funds for fear of diverting needed money from the support of women workers. Instead, women volunteered to chair committees to raise the necessary funds: Mrs. Walter Alexander of New York raised over $75,000 for St. Agnes's School, whereas Miss Littell raised over $195,000 for the hospital in Wuchang.[51]

Thus the first two decades of the twentieth century saw a gradual increase in the number of women serving in both foreign and domestic mission fields and a broadening of the variety of tasks they undertook. The work was marked by an increasing professionalism, both on the part of the missionary workers themselves and on the part of the Woman's Auxiliary Committee on Missionary Workers. Concurrently, the deaconess training schools enlarged and revised their curricula to provide more comprehensive training for those about to enter missionary service. And undergirding all these changes was the steady work of the Woman's Auxiliary, raising funds, recruiting and training volunteers, and providing missionary education programs for the entire Church.

ORGANIZATIONAL DEVELOPMENT IN THE AUXILIARY

As the auxiliary's work expanded and grew more complex, more intricate systems of communication and administration were needed. Most significant was the Triennial Meeting's evolution from an informal gathering of interested churchwomen into a representative assembly. Members of the Woman's Auxiliary had met together at each General Convention since 1874. The first meetings had lasted just one day and were open to all women at the convention. In 1883 a second day's conference of diocesan officers was added. The auxiliary president of the diocese in which the convention was held presided over these triennial meetings, which gradually began to make policy decisions, passing resolutions that shaped the administrative structure and determined how the United Offering was to be used. Membership in this assembly, however, was informally defined until 1907, when those present voted to limit the membership to women serving as officers of their diocesan auxiliaries (the diocese determining which of its officers would be sent).[52] No numerical limit was set on the diocesan delegations to the Triennial Meeting until 1910, when each diocese was granted no more than five representatives, chosen by either the bishop or the diocesan auxiliary. If possible, one of the five was to represent the Junior Department of the diocesan auxiliary.[53]

As the officers' conference evolved into a representative assembly with legislative powers, the Triennial Meeting expanded to include several other gatherings. Meetings of other Church-related organizations for women, such as the Church Periodical Club, the Daughters of the King, the Girls' Friendly Society, and the St. Barnabas Guild for Nurses, were held in conjunction with it. Throughout this period, the meeting's chief focus continued to be on education rather than legislation. All women at the convention were invited to attend the educational sessions on such topics as: "The Board of Missions and Its Care of the Missionaries," "Our Juniors in the Mission Field," "The Devotional Life of the Auxiliary," and "Appropriations and Apportionments" (the latter led by Board of Missions treasurer George C. Thomas).[54] These discussion groups dispensed information and enabled delegates from many parts of the world to exchange suggestions and discuss organizational and strategic techniques. Daily Bible-study classes and worship services and elaborate visual displays of missionary activity throughout the world completed each Triennial Meeting's program.

TRIENNIAL MEETING, 1916

The Triennial Meeting of 1916 proved to be a major turning point for the Woman's Auxiliary. It was the second meeting to consist of duly elected representatives, many of whom were eager to define the triennial's role as a decision-making body. Military actions in Europe and the Far East lent a spirit of urgency to the deliberations; reports from China of missions closed and schools disrupted tied the faraway areas of mission study to the pressing international news of the day. Although the United States had not yet entered the war, the presence at the meeting of many English visitors kept the European conflict before the delegates. Bishop Montgomery, the secretary of the Society for the Propagation of the Gospel (SPG) and the archdeacon of Worcester, England, led prayers of intercession for the peace of the world. Miss Forbes and Miss Soulsby of the SPG addressed the women's meeting, describing the ways in which English churchwomen were ministering to the needs of soldiers on the front.

The gravity of the international situation and the collective sense of frustration at not being able to control events led the delegates to evaluate their past work, wondering if any of the study groups or money-raising projects had been worthwhile. Coupled with this self-analysis was a call to a stronger prayer life, a sense that in the midst of world upheaval, Christians must find their strength and guidance through prayer. Hence the national secretary, Julia Emery, called on the gathered delegates to join her throughout the next year in a "Pilgrimage of Prayer." Plans to dispense information about the "pilgrimage" were made, and a committee was appointed to revise the United Offering prayer and write a prayer for the Woman's Auxiliary, to be used as a sign of unity by its chapters throughout the world.[55]

Auxiliary organization was also a topic of concern. Although the Triennial Meeting had become a representative assembly, rules governing its procedures had never been adopted. A system of committee reports and proposed resolutions had evolved, but there was an increasing desire to formalize them. The custom of asking the auxiliary president of the diocese in which the convention was held to preside over the Triennial Meeting was also questioned. After much discussion, the Committee on the Woman's Auxiliary was asked to draw up suggested procedures for consideration by the 1917 meeting of the auxiliary's officers. Another committee was appointed, in response to a Board of Missions request, to confer with the board on the training and deployment of women workers.[56] The triennial, however, further requested that the Board of Missions appoint a committee "to confer with a committee of our body on the whole subject of the relation between the Woman's Auxiliary and the Board of Missions."[57] Clearly, the women were beginning to question the administrative arrangement that provided that all decisions regarding the Woman's Auxiliary be made by the Board of Missions (on which they were not even represented).

Meeting concurrently, the General Convention was also in the process of evaluating the structure of the Board of Missions, which essentially functioned as the only national administrative structure of the Church. Although several reorganization plans were presented, the convention delegates ultimately voted to maintain the status quo for the next three years, reelecting Bishop Arthur S. Lloyd as president of the board and postponing administrative reorganization until the 1919 convention.

RESIGNATION OF JULIA EMERY

Immediately after the 1916 Triennial Meeting, Julia Emery resigned her position as national secretary of the Woman's Auxiliary—a position she had held for forty years. Although she had considered leaving for some time, she waited until the election of the Board of Missions' president before deciding. Once Bishop Lloyd was reelected and the drastic reorganization of the Board of Missions postponed until the 1919 convention, Emery felt free to leave. Characteristically, she managed to resign with as little fanfare as possible. She submitted her resignation to Lloyd, asking him to present it to the board on the final day of the convention, then quietly returned to New York without informing anyone else, giving no one the opportunity to dissuade her.[58] For she was convinced that the next three years would bring about a major change in the Church's administrative structure, and she wanted to allow Lloyd to plan with freedom. As she explained to her brother:

> Woman's work is sure to be coming more and more under the consideration of the Church. He [Bishop Lloyd] has to plan big things. This gives him the chance to take the possibilities of the whole in review and see how the Church's work for Missions—men and women together—may best be done at this particular time. . . . It leaves him free and less bound by the traditions and methods though it may increase his work.[59]

Emery's resignation forced the auxiliary to establish an orderly procedure for choosing her successor. Forty years before, Emery's appointment had been arranged by the Board of Missions with no input from the auxiliary, as had the few appointments subsequently made in the office. Although the Board of Missions reluctantly accepted Emery's resignation and appointed her assistant Grace Lindley to serve as acting secretary, at the next meeting the auxiliary's officers assumed they would choose the new general secretary, asking the Board of Missions Committee on the Woman's Auxiliary to recommend a procedure for making the choice. The committee suggested that the secretary be nominated by the auxiliary and appointed by the Board of Missions to a six-year term that would correspond to the term of the Board of Missions' president.[60] The appointment would be made at the next General Convention, Grace Lindley acting as secretary in the interim.

Apparently some of this procedure was simply part of the auxiliary's growing demand for self-determination, for Grace Lindley was the obvious candidate to succeed Emery. She had "come up through the ranks," serving as an officer of her local parish auxiliary and then as secretary in charge of "junior work" in the dioceses of Newark and New York. When Julia Emery left the New York office to attend the Pan-Anglican Congress in London in 1908 and then to continue around the world, visiting mission stations all along the way, Grace Lindley was asked to help in the national office and was later hired full-time as assistant secretary.[61] Thus she had worked with the Woman's Auxiliary program long enough to assure the conservatives that she would not bring a radical departure from the past, and yet she had also shown considerable initiative in developing the Junior Auxiliary program and working for missionary education. Her leadership style probably would not differ markedly from that of Julia Emery; it would be gracious, inclusive, and self-effacing.

Besides, Emery would remain closely affiliated with the national office. Her sister, Margaret Theresa, continued to serve as box-work secretary; working daily in the office, she could keep Emery informed about whatever was happening. Emery became the coordinator of the "Pilgrimage of Prayer," keeping up a steady stream of correspondence with Woman's Auxiliary officers throughout the U.S. She also began to work on another project—writing the history of the Board of Missions. Thus, that Emery maintained close relations with the office and that the continuing auxiliary staff had served a lengthy apprenticeship under her greatly reduced the likelihood of any radical change in the auxiliary's structure.[62]

Actually, Emery's resignation was just one of many indications that women's position in the Church structure was changing. In Christian education, for example, the women had developed an extremely successful mission study program including not only printed materials—study guides, mission reference aids, children's stories, and workbooks—but an extensive schedule of teacher training—short parish and diocesan courses and longer residential mission study courses held each summer at such scenic retreats as Sewanee, Tennessee, and Wellesley, Massachusetts.[63] In 1910 the General Convention had appointed a General Board of Religious Education to try to develop Christian-education resources for the entire Church. Though the next few years were marked by territorial squabbles among the general board, the educational secretary of the Board of Missions, and Emily C. Tillotson, the assistant secretary in charge of the Woman's Auxiliary's educational work, the women were confident that the success of their efforts would lead to women's greater involvement in planning the national educational program.[64]

Another indication of women's changing position in the Church was their increasing involvement in the Christian social-relations programs developing on diocesan and national levels. This involvement was the direct outgrowth of the social-service ministries women had exercised both as volunteers and as paid staff members over the preceding quarter century. But there was a growing militancy in their demand that the Church act to correct social ills; they began to verbalize the social gospel they had manifested in their vocational choices. Through their work (described above) in both domestic and foreign missions, the churchwomen had gained substantial experience in working with economically and educationally deprived populations. They had also gained confidence in their ability to counter that deprivation. Their attempt to interpret that vision for the Church at large is the subject of the next chapter.

CHAPTER TEN

The Social Gospel

The first two decades of the twentieth century saw Episcopal women making the social gospel a reality *through their actions*. As volunteer parish workers, deaconesses, nuns, matrons and principals of a wide variety of hospitals and schools, these women, motivated by a spirit of Christian love, were caring for the sick, the poor, the uneducated, and the dispossessed. In developing Church work as a profession for women, they had chosen subservient models, focusing on the goals they wanted to accomplish rather than on their own needs or requirements.

The concept of the social gospel, however, entails more than the delivery of services to those in need; it also entails a recognition of the corporate nature of sin and the radical demand that society restructure itself to respond to the inequities it has created. In one sense, many of the women workers were reshaping the limited spheres in which they worked—requiring their parishes to respond to immediate needs, demanding more services from the Bureau of Indian Affairs on the reservations, providing vocational training for Appalachian women. By living in disadvantaged communities, they also were gaining experience about the nature of poverty, racial discrimination, and economic exploitation. But to move from these limited activities to a more direct challenge to the system itself was inconceivable to many of them. One of the reasons such a challenge was unthinkable was the relative isolation of most of these workers. City workers lived and worked at the institutions they served, most of which had very small staffs. Rural workers were geographically isolated. Foreign missionaries were far from the mission office that deployed them. The women workers had no place in the Church structures that governed the institutions; though many of the trained workers (especially the deaconesses) felt their vocations were similar to those of the priests, the latter generally did not share their opinion and made no effort to include them in clergy conferences or diocesan conventions.

It was their affiliation with another group of women—the settlement-house workers, similarly isolated because their residence was also their place of work—that began to break down this separation, establishing an informal network of women involved in social service. A significant number of the first settlement-house workers were Episcopalians, including Ellen Gates Starr of Hull House, Helena Stuart Dudley of Denison House (Boston), Mary Kingsbury Simkhovitch of Greenwich House (New York), and Vida Scudder and Mary Van Kleeck of the College Settlement Association. Several of these women had first experienced social work through volunteer activities in their local parishes, and they continued to maintain strong Church ties.[1]

The objective of this study is not to chronicle the development of the settlement-house movement but to suggest the connections between that movement and the Episcopal women workers. Many of the first social settlements were begun by Episcopal Churches (and some continued under Church sponsorship), whereas others were intentionally founded as nondenominational institutions. Of the 38 religious settlements established before 1900, 11 were Episcopalian. By 1910, of the 167 religious settlements listed by Woods and Kennedy, 31 were Methodist, 29 Episcopal, 20 Presbyterian, and 10 Congregational.[2] Women who trained at the Church Training and Deaconess House in Philadelphia studied social-work methods at St. Martha's House, a settlement established in 1901 and directed by Deaconess Jean W. Colesberry. Graduates went on to work at other settlements, such as St. Agnes House in Philadelphia, St. Monica's Home in Des Moines, Iowa, and the Neighborhood Settlement in Los Angeles.[3] Many of the women workers found in social settlements another place to invest their energy and altruism—but with a higher degree of professional reward. Lavinia Dock, whose later efforts as founder and editor of the *American Journal of Nursing* would shape that profession, first applied for a job as a visiting nurse at Grace Church, New York. When she informed Dr. Huntington that she could not live on the proposed salary of $300 per year, he asked her whether she was working for *money* or for the *Lord*. She merely observed how unjust it was that "the employers of poorly-paid agents should pride themselves on philanthropy or charity when it is really the worker who is the philanthropist."[4] She moved instead to Henry Street Settlement and continued nursing from there.

THE SOCIETY OF THE COMPANIONS OF THE HOLY CROSS

Though both the early experience of settlement workers in voluntary Church-sponsored programs and the employment of some church workers at settlement houses forged links between the two areas of employment, the most important connection was an unusual organization, the Society of the Companions of the Holy Cross. The driving force behind it was Emily Malbone Morgan, who, with Harriet Hastings, organized the group in 1884. The only daughter of a wealthy family in Hartford, Connecticut, Morgan grew up with a strong religious conscience. Influenced by the works of John Ruskin and Sir Walter Besant, she visited Toynbee Hall in London and was very impressed with what she saw there. She returned home determined to dedicate herself to helping working women. Adopting a very simple lifestyle, she poured all her resources—income from her family and royalties from the several books she wrote—into the purchase and maintenance of vacation cottages for workers. The remainder of her life was centered around her two consuming interests—the welfare of working women and the Society of the Companions of the Holy Cross.[5]

Morgan organized the society in 1884 as a group of laywomen dedicated to maintain a Christian lifestyle with an emphasis on intercessory prayer. Its members were Episcopal women who agreed to certain central ideals—the Way of the Cross, the Life of Intercession, Social Justice, Christian Unity, Simplicity of Life, and Thanksgiving.[6] The commitment was to both prayer and action as Morgan explained:

> We are an order of women living in the world with a desire for the stronger development of the spiritual life in ourselves and others, and we must develop that life along the lines of the world in which we live. . . . Any pseudo-nunlike life would be at best but a weak imitation of those who possess a sacred vocation to which most of us have not been called. What we must try to understand by our association together is our own vocation as that of women living in the world and having individual influence, social or otherwise, banded together to

meet the serious religious, educational, and social problems of our age, first by prayer and then by battle.[7]

The first Companions were from New England, but the society gradually grew to include many of the leaders of the settlement movement as well as Episcopal church workers (both at home and in the mission field), deaconesses, and even a few Episcopal nuns.[8] By 1894 Ellen Gates Starr (cofounder of Hull House), from as far away as Chicago, had joined. Women were accepted as members, after a year's probation, on another Companion's recommendation to Emily Morgan. Vida Scudder directed the probationers from 1909 until 1942, whereas Morgan remained companion-in-charge until her death in 1933, summarizing each year's activities in an annual letter sent to members around the world. By 1897 there were 143 members, with chapters in Hartford, Boston, Philadelphia, and San Francisco; by 1908 there were 252 members. Several black women were among the early Companions. Missionaries such as Margaret Waterman in the Philippines and Dr. Marybai in India spread word of the order to other lands. An English society was also formed. Others were in China, Puerto Rico, and Alaska.[9]

Central to the society's life was its annual conference, which brought the scattered Companions together for ten days each summer. Begun in 1896 at Beulahland (one of the workers'-retreat houses Morgan sponsored), the conference in 1901 was moved to Adelynrood, a country farmhouse at the Drummer Academy in South Byfield, Massachusetts. In 1913 the society purchased land in South Byfield and erected a building (still in use today) as a conference center and retreat house, transferring the name Adelynrood to it. Since 1914 the Companions have met there annually for a program of lectures, discussions, and recreation within a daily schedule structured around morning, noon, and evening worship services.[10] Though guest speakers such as Jane Addams, Walter Rauschenbusch, Father James O.S. Huntington, and Emily Greene Balch were often invited, the programs were primarily offered by the Companions themselves, who shared their intellectual and social concerns. Vida Scudder presented her research on the social commitments of St. Francis; Genevieve Cowles spoke of her work for prison reform, and Maud Foley, a member of the Garment Workers of Boston, urged other Companions to join the Women's Trade Union League. From Vida Scudder comes this picture of the Adelynrood during the conference:

In the little house oratory, a half-dozen women cherishing devotional methods accredited by the ages would now and again supplement the required chapel offices of prime and compline by the use of terce and nones. . . . At the same time, another group sitting peacefully on the wide porches looking westward might be holding a prayer meeting, studying the Greek Testament, or practicing the Quaker method of silent fellowship. . . . Here, a group might gather around a Companion, recounting her adventure in addressing a strike meeting—possibly that of 1912 at Lawrence; on another occasion people might listen to a passionate appeal from someone who had been visiting a mining area, or to report a strike in Chicago. E.M.M. [Morgan] tells gleefully in 1915 of her bewilderment on hearing that the socialist Companions, of whom there were always a few, were meeting to discuss vestments; and of her relief when it turned out that their topic was investments, and the possibility of a white list to salve the Christian conscience.[11]

For the Companions, these annual conferences and the conferences led by the Committees on Social Justice and Christian Unity were a time of reflection and recreation—a chance to integrate their spiritual life into social action. The yeasty mixture of women who were employed as professors, doctors, social workers, and religious workers, whose common ground was their membership in the Episcopal Church, led to stimulating conversations and a collective impulse to reform both the social order and the Church. A high percentage of the Companions were professional women, and many were forging new opportunities for women in their chosen fields. For the unmarried members, the society became a supportive family; for the missionaries, it became a home to which to return in the United States. The roll of members was a veritable *Who's Who* of professional women—settlement workers Helena S. Dudley of Denison House, Ellen Gates Starr of Hull House, Mary Simkhovitch of Greenwich House, and Mary Van Kleeck of College Settlement; college professors Vida Scudder (Wellesley), Adelaide Case (Teachers College), and Alice van Vechten Brown (Wellesley); social workers Mary W. Glenn, president of the National Conference of Social Workers, Katherine Coman, economist, Emily Sophie Brown, the first woman to serve in the Connecticut State Legislature, Caroline B. Wittpenn of the New Jersey Charities Aid Association, and Miriam Van Waters, prison reformer; religious workers Grace Lindley, national secretary of the Woman's Auxiliary, Reverend Mother Florence Teresa of the Community of Saint John Baptist, Sister Ruth Magdalene of the Community of the Transfiguration, Deaconesses Susan Knapp and Jean Colesberry and Dorothea Carlson; missionaries Grace Crosby (China) and Margaret Waterman (Philippines), and Harriette Keyser and Margaret Lawrance, organizers of the Church Association for the Interests of Labor.[12] Also associated with the society were several priests and bishops, including Floyd Tomkins of Philadelphia, James O.S. Huntington and Edward H. Schlueter of New York City, Charles H. Brent, who became bishop to the Philippines, and Bishop Arthur C. Hall of Vermont.[13]

Although some Companions probably regarded the society primarily as a spiritual resource for busy women, the interaction between the various disciplines they represented forged an understanding of the social gospel unique in the Episcopal Church in the early twentieth century. That understanding not only inspired the Companions to individual and corporate activities in their own fields but led them on several occasions to challenge the Episcopal Church to come to terms with social issues. For example, in 1907 Harriette Keyser shared with the annual conference her dismay that the Committee on Capital and Labor, which had been appointed at the General Convention of 1901, had never even issued a report or brought before the convention any consideration of the labor unrest then prevalent in America. Jane Addams, who was one of the guest speakers at the conference that year, described her experience in dealing with labor problems at Hull House and her conviction that the Church must address those issues. The ensuing discussion led to a petition to the General Convention that the Church "take some action which shall bring [it] into fuller knowledge and closer truth with the industrial and social problems of the day." Specifically, the document requested the reappointment of the Commission on Capital and Labor, with the stipulation that it bring suggestions for specific action to the next convention.[14]

Bishop Arthur Hall agreed to present the petition to the House of Bishops, and some Companions lobbied for the bill through correspondence and meetings with deputies to the General Convention. Cognizant of the importance of their activities, the women wrote, "In venturing so serious a step as bringing itself to the notice of the Church, the Society realizes that it has reached a new stage in its corporate life, but it was felt that our pledge to constant prayer for the reconciliation of classes inevitably led to this step, at a juncture when there seems a real chance of quickening the social conscience of the Church."[15] The petition was successful. The commission was reappointed and in 1910 became the Joint Commission on Social Service, stimulating and coordinating social-service programs throughout the Church. Significantly, this was the first commission of the General Convention to include women as members; Deaconess Knapp, Vida Scudder, and Mary Simkhovitch served along with Robert A. Woods, Seth Low, J.M. Glenn (whose wife was a Companion), and several other clergy and laymen.[16]

In 1909 the Companions devoted their entire annual conference to the subject of "The Church and Social Justice." The conference committee, led by Anna Whitcomb, summarized the social-action programs of six other Protestant denominations, the Roman Catholic Church, the Federal Council of Churches, the YMCA and the YWCA, and suggested areas of cooperative action. Harriette Keyser reported on programs in the Episcopal Church, including the Church League for Industrial Democracy, the Girls' Friendly Society, diocesan social-service commissions, and C.A.I.L. (Church Association for the Interests of Labor). Both documents were reprinted, widely circulated in the Episcopal Church, and used as guides for developing diocesan social-service commissions.[17]

In 1916 some of the Companions sent another petition to the General Convention, urging

> that the service of the community and the welfare of the workers rather than private profits should be the aim of every industry, and the test of its value; and that the Church should seek to keep this aim and this test constantly before the mind of the public; and that Christians as individuals are under the solemn obligation on the one hand, conscientiously to scrutinize the sources of their income, and on the other hand, to give at least moral support and prayer to every effort to secure fair conditions and regular employment for wage earners, and the extension of true democracy to industrial matters.[18]

With only a few stylistic changes, the resolution was adopted by the entire convention. Later it formed the basis for an expanded resolution adopted by the Bishops of the Anglican Communion meeting in Lambeth in 1920.[19]

Some Companions also worked for minimum-wage and hour laws to protect working women and for anti-child-labor legislation. During the 1911 coal strike, Companion Margaret Shearman moved into the coal camps near Pittsburgh to help the miners' families. When she called for assistance, Lucy Watson of Utica and Margaret Lawrance of New York joined her, whereas others sent relief funds.

On another issue, several Companions—Helena Dudley, Vida Scudder, Florence Converse, Geraldine Gordon, Lucy Sturgis, and Grace Hutchins—sent a strong protest to the House of Bishops committee that had recommended censuring Bishop Paul Jones. (Jones was the bishop of Utah whose staunch antiwar statements and support of the pacifist movement during the saber-rattling period just prior to the United States's entry into World War I angered many of his diocesan leaders. In 1917 Utah requested that he be removed as bishop. The House of Bishops discussed the case at two successive meetings, finally resolving the situation by both affirming Bishop Jones's freedom to express his opinion *and* accepting his resignation.) But many of the Companions continued to believe that the bishop's pacifism was thoroughly consistent with his Christian beliefs and that he ought to be lauded rather than censored.[20]

In 1918 they wrote to President Wilson, requesting a new trial for labor leader Thomas J. Mooney. The next year they petitioned both the president and the attorney general, asking for the immediate release of conscientious objectors serving prison terms. Through these and many other activities, members of the society expressed their commitment to social justice.[21]

Far more could be said about the Companions as initiators of social-service programs, as champions of interdenominational cooperation, and as advocates for social justice. One has only to begin to read the biographies of these women to be impressed by their commitment to, and their realization of, social-gospel ideals.[22] Their accomplishments in terms of meaningful social change would easily stand alongside the work of such social-gospel reformers as Walter Rauschenbusch and Richard T. Ely. Their long-term dedication to the Episcopal Church is ample evidence of the important part their religious convictions played in shaping their dedication to an improved society.[23] And yet, because of the privacy of their religious life, their work has been neglected by Church historians; and the religious dimension of their concern for social justice has been ignored in historical studies of the progressive period. Through both their individual commitments and their corporate activities as Companions, these women voiced a strong social conscience within the Episcopal Church, a conscience that often pushed the Church into social action projects. As educated professionals pursuing careers in social work and as active, involved churchwomen, they played a significant role in shaping the Episcopal Church's response to the demands of the social gospel.

CHAPTER ELEVEN

Defining Membership Rights for Women in the Episcopal Church

The years between the General Conventions of 1916 and 1919 were critical for the Church's women because many of the flaws inherent in the then present system of organization began to become evident. Few people realized, for example, how dependent the deaconess movement had been on Susan Knapp's leadership. Her Far East tour, followed by her abrupt resignation and move to Japan, left a void not only at the New York school but in the nationwide movement, for there was no one else who had such a broad grasp of the problems and possibilities of the work. Although Dr. Gardener, Knapp's successor at the school, tried to suggest changes in the role of deaconess, he was viewed as an outsider by the women Knapp had trained, and his words carried little weight with them.[1]

Knapp had hoped a strong leader would emerge from among the deaconesses, but there were few mechanisms for producing one. Although Knapp and Caroline H. Sanford, head of the Philadelphia school, had been good friends and had worked together frequently, the graduates of the two schools rarely had contact with each other. (Sanford had retired in 1913, and Clara M. Carter, who succeeded her, focused her energies more directly on the school than on the deaconess movement.)[2] Deaconesses who had trained elsewhere were even more isolated. Initially, the deaconess training schools had served as professional centers for their graduates, encouraging them to return each year for alumnae retreats and serving as employment bureaus for those women in need of jobs. In cities like Chicago, however, where graduates from various training schools were working, groups of deaconesses had just begun to form local associations for study and companionship.

In 1916 Deaconess Anna Gray Newell, who served on the staff of Christ Church Cathedral in St. Louis, organized a day-long meeting for those deaconesses attending the St. Louis General Convention. The meeting led to a call for a national organization of deaconesses that could serve as a forum for discussions about the order and promote the profession more effectively to possible candidates. A committee consisting of the heads of the three schools and four other deaconesses was appointed to formulate plans for an association and to establish a comprehensive directory of deaconesses and their work. All the deaconesses were invited to gather at the next General Convention, to consider the committee's report.[3]

At subsequent regional meetings over the next three years, the growing frustration at not being able to attract more women to the order became evident. At the New York meeting, for example, Deaconess Ellen Humphreys asked:

> How shall recruits be won to our cause? How shall women who have given unstinted service in Patriotic work be influenced to take up this form of service? It is the burning question of the day. This can only be answered by the Church making as strong an appeal to the minds and hearts of women as the Red Cross has done. Surely the varied fields of work open to the Deaconesses with the attendant joy of service should offer such an appeal.[4]

Her listeners found these questions perplexing, because as a general rule they were quite content with their lives as deaconesses and could not understand the different expectations of a more secular generation of women. More options existed for women seeking careers in 1917, however, than had been available to them just a decade before. Even women who sought careers in social service could find "respectable" positions outside Church-sponsored agencies. The deaconess's conservative dress and, probably more important, the centrality of religion to her life, seemed outmoded to a generation more secularly and scientifically oriented.

The other concern the deaconess movement faced was finding a way to provide for those women who retired. Salaries for deaconesses were abysmally low; very few of the parent churches or institutions made any provision for pensions. Though many of the earliest deaconesses had been women of independent means who often paid their own living expenses, others were not so fortunate. Both the New York and the Philadelphia schools had small retirement funds, but the amount of assistance they could provide was miniscule. A New York deaconess, for example, contributed ten dollars per year to the fund and was eligible to draw on it after twenty years, if she could demonstrate need.[5] Clearly a more substantial means of providing pensions was needed. After discussing various options, the deaconess central committee decided to appeal to the 1919 General Convention to include deaconesses in the Church Pension Fund already available to clergy.

UNEASINESS IN THE WOMAN'S AUXILIARY

The Woman's Auxiliary also found itself in an uncertain period. Julia Emery's retirement was symbolic of a general change in the auxiliary's leadership. The first generation of Woman's Auxiliary leaders, who had proven to be such loyal, long-term supporters of the work, was dying off. Miss Sallie Stuart, who had organized the auxiliary in the diocese of Virginia and had served as its president since 1890 and also had chaired the national committee on missionary workers, died in 1916.[6] Mrs. A.E. Ketchum, who had organized the Scranton Auxiliary, and Miss Fanny Schuyler, who had been an active worker in the New York branch for over fifty years, died the following year.[7] Many of the younger generation were clubwomen like Mrs. Powell Clayton, who had had extensive experience with the Red Cross in Tennessee, and Mrs. Cowles, who had served as president of the Federation of Women's Clubs—women for whom Church work was just one of many community activities in which they participated.[8] Even in the churches themselves, other organizations had proliferated—chapters of the Girls' Friendly Society, the Daughters of the King, and the Guild of St. Barnabas, all of which competed with the auxiliary for women's time and attention. In addition, there was rising concern about the number of women who, though nominally church members, were "entirely unbusy about it."[9]

To determine what plans were best calculated to bring about the interested action of those "unbusy" women, to elicit cooperation between the various churchwomen's organizations, and to assess the general state of the auxiliary, a questionnaire was sent to each auxiliary. The Committee on Cooperation spent long hours collecting and

tabulating the results. The initial distrust and suspicion with which
the questionnaire was greeted signified the erosion of the spirit of
unity that had characterized earlier churchwomen's activities. As
Lucy C. Sturgis, the committee's chairman, explained:

> There has been, and there still is, a wide misunderstanding of the
> reasons why this committee was appointed, and a consequent mis-
> conception of its purpose. . . . . "Why," women have asked, "should
> the Auxiliary have anything to do with the increased membership or
> the missionary activity of the Daughters of the King or the Guild of
> Saint Barnabas?" "In an every-member canvass would you actually go
> so far as to advise a young woman to join the Girls' Friendly Society
> instead of the Woman's Auxiliary?" The answer to both these ques-
> tions surely is that if we are to be truly loyal to the Board of Missions
> to which we are auxiliary, we will be supremely desirous of gaining
> the most widespread possible support for its work.[10]

What Sturgis did not mention but which was abundantly clear from
the tabulated returns, however, was that many churchwomen questioned whether their goal was "to be truly loyal to the Board of Missions." "Give women representation in the Church; don't keep them
as an appendix," wrote one president. "The Woman's Auxiliary should
have a national constituion and by-laws to govern all its actions; above
all it should have a representative on the Board of Missions," wrote
another.[11]

The question of women's representation on the Board of Missions
was due to come before the 1919 General Convention. The president
of the board, Bishop Arthur Selden Lloyd, had become convinced the
board should include women. In 1917 he urged the addition of eight
women (one representing each province) in the Board of Missions
reorganization plan to be submitted to the convention, and he solicited
the auxiliary's opinion about the proposal. With its customary thoroughness, the auxiliary studied the matter, asking each local chapter
to discuss whether women should serve on the board and to send to
the Triennial Meeting women prepared to vote on the issue. The
ensuing discussions demonstrated that Episcopal women were certainly not unanimously in favor of the proposal; many considered it
improper for women to enter political arenas.[12]

THE COMPANIONS OF THE HOLY CROSS

Along with other Episcopal women, the Companions of the Holy
Cross found themselves in a period of uncertainty. Many of the mem-

bers felt the activism of the past few years was interfering with the society's spiritual goals. Others resented the organization's notoriety. This feeling was reinforced when, during the 1918 summer conference, agents from the Federal Bureau of Investigation visited Adelynrood daily, ostensibly to check on the activities of those members who had become outspoken Christian pacifists. [13] Unwilling to be identified with the Companions' increasingly radical stance, Bishop Hall resigned his position as general adviser to the society, prompting the following message from Emily Morgan, in her yearly letter to the membership:

> The Companions must decide at the next conference about the wisdom of too many petitions being signed at our Companion house, or by us as members of the Society, or as to the publicity being given to them in press notices. I am not expressing any opinion. I would ask you, however, to consider whether by indulging unthinkingly in such a policy we are not trying to do two incompatible things: to provide a quiet place for prayer and refreshment and at the same time to seek a publicity, even in righteous causes, that will in the end destroy the spirit of both prayer and quiet. [14]

Part of the difficulty was that the society had grown to a membership of over four hundred and Morgan was no longer able to dominate its activities. To share the leadership, standing committees on religious unity and social justice had been formed, but in their righteous zeal they sometimes offended other members. After a lengthy discussion of the social-justice committee's recommendation that the society endorse a proposed new child-labor law, the 1918 conference decided to refrain from taking a stand, leaving it to individual members to contact their legislators about the measure. [15]

Over the next ten years an uneasy truce reigned in the society. The social activists did not refrain from bringing items to the membership's attention, but petitions and stands were generally signed by individuals—without affixing the name of the companionship. In 1919, for example, many members of the order signed a memorial, sent to the General Convention, urging that the Church constitution be amended to permit women to serve in the councils of the Church— but it was a petition from individuals, not from the order. [16]

Thus, by 1919 a spirit of uncertainty and uneasiness prevailed among many churchwomen. Deaconesses, Companions and Woman's Auxiliary members were, for a variety of reasons, dissatisfied with women's work in the Church. Some thought organizational reform was needed; others hoped to capture the attention of the Church's young women by emphasizing the "Spirit of Service for Christ's Sake."[17] But all looked to the 1919 convention as the place where momentous decisions would be made.

THE 1919 GENERAL CONVENTION

An atmosphere of expectancy prevailed among the delegates to the General Convention as they met in Detroit in October 1919. The Great War was over; the world was safe for democracy (and Christianity). The Peace Conference at Versailles had fashioned a new world-order that most Americans welcomed; the bitter battle over membership in the League of Nations was yet to be fought. Although President Woodrow Wilson had collapsed the week before the convention opened, the extent of his disability was not evident to the deputies as they passed a resolution assuring him of the Episcopal Church's "confident hope for his speedy restoration to complete health."[18]

The spirit of expectancy extended to ecclesiastical matters also. The 1916 General Convention had considered several proposals to revise the administrative structure of the national Church, but the wartime uncertainty prompted the delegates to defer decisions until a more propitious time. All signs at the beginning of the 1919 convention indicated that that moment had arrived. Church structure must be modernized, many delegates felt, to meet the demands of the twentieth century. Among the many issues to be addressed—the office of the presiding bishop, the national Church's role in Christian education, the system of financial support for missions—that of women's position in the Church had a low priority for most deputies.

For the delegates to the Triennial Meeting of the Woman's Auxiliary, however, the question was critical. In 1919 women in the United States were on the threshold of a new world: Universal woman was almost a reality; many states had already extended the franchise to women, and in June, Congress had passed the Nineteenth Amendment to the Constitution, prohibiting the denial of the right to vote because of sex. State assemblies were rapidly ratifying the amendment. Was this not the time for the Church, also, to grant women full membership in the ecclesiastical body? Should women not also be able to vote at Church meetings and to serve as representatives in Church councils?

Two major proposals concerning women were already on the convention's agenda. One was to enfranchise women, granting them the right to vote in Church assemblies and to serve as elected deputies to the Church conventions. The other was the proposal to seat women on the Board of Missions. Because they perceived their function only to be concerned with missionary matters, the Woman's Auxiliary officially debated only the latter proposal.

THE 1919 TRIENNIAL MEETING OF THE WOMAN'S AUXILIARY

As the women assembled in Detroit, they began to realize what a momentous decision lay before them. Aware of the weighty responsibilities on the members of the Board of Missions, they wondered if women were ready for those responsibilities. When the matter finally came up for debate, the strong feelings on both sides of the issue surfaced. As one observer reported:

> Mrs. Monteagle of California said that the introduction of women to do the work of men was unwise—she knew of instances when it had proven so. Miss Corey moved a reconsideration of the question. . . . Miss Delafield deemed this a movement to kill the motion. She said that the Auxiliary had been thinking about this matter for three years, that they had all been consulted about it, and this was the time to pass the measure. . . . Speeches waxed fast and furious. Pros and cons were thick as leaves in Vallombrosa. The official gavel demanded order again and again. Women rose in their seats and what they might have said was drowned by cries of "louder," We can't hear a word," "Please turn this way," etc.[19]

Finally, to restore order the chairwoman asked Mrs. Cowles, the president of the Federation of Women's Clubs, who was in charge of dispatch of business, to take the gavel. Mrs. Cowles stepped to the platform, saying, "Ladies, this is a matter which can be settled and be settled right," and then, with parliamentary insight, called for a moment of silent prayer. Once quieted, the delegates sat through the closing speeches to the final vote, which was overwhelmingly in favor of electing women to the Board of Missions. With the decision established, the auxiliary went on to elect eight of its members to serve on the Board of Missions, conditional on the General Convention's approval.[20] And the women thus elected, very properly dressed in their church-going suits and hats, posed for a photographer, proud to be taking this new step in the Church's history.

Because the Triennial Meeting was scheduled for the first few days of the convention, however, many of the women delegates had returned home before the matter of female representation on the Board of Missions came before the House of Deputies. Bishop Lloyd's proposed reorganization of the Board of Missions was only one of many proposals to change the Church's administrative structure. After lengthy consideration, the General Convention designed a totally new national structure for the Episcopal Church—government by presiding bishop and council. Between General Conventions, the council would be the responsible governing body, and it would consist of members elected by the General Convention and the provinces. And women were again omitted; the canons specifically provided that only men could be elected to the council.[21] The latter body was divided into five departments—Missions and Church Extension (which replaced the Board of Missions), Religious Education, Christian Social Service, Finance, and Publicity. Each department could appoint additional members—men or women—to serve on its governing board, with seat and voice in the department but not in the council. So two women, Ada Loaring Clark from Tennessee and Mrs. R.W.B. Elliott from New York, were appointed to the Department of Missions and Church Extension.[22] They were token members—two women on a board with a total membership of twenty—and although Ada Loaring Clark had at least been one of the women the auxiliary elected to serve on the Board of Missions, Mrs. Elliott was not, and does not appear to have been active in Woman's Auxiliary work at all.[23] Thus, the auxiliary's carefully considered decision to elect representatives to serve on the Board of Missions was essentially ignored in the reorganization of the Church's national administrative structure and women were barred from participation in the National Council. Not until 1934 were women granted membership on the council.[24]

VOTING RIGHTS FOR EPISCOPAL WOMEN

The second women's question before the General Convention was even more significant, for by granting women the right to serve as deputies to the General Convention, the deputies would be conferring on them full membership rights in the Church.[25] The measure had first been proposed by Robert H. Gardiner of Gardiner, Maine, at the 1916 convention, at which the committee on constitutional amendments judged the measure "inexpedient" and tabled it.[26] Realizing that a stronger showing of public support was needed to bring the matter to the floor, Gardiner organized a three-year petition campaign that garnered over a thousand signatures from priests and laymen and women in favor of allowing women to serve as deputies. The previous summer, Gardiner had taken his petition to the annual meeting of the Companions of the Holy Cross, and many of the women there had signed it and written letters in support of it. Gardiner himself was an important supporter whose Episcopal credentials were impeccable. A long-time vestryman of his parish, he had been a deputy to each General Convention since 1903 and had represented the Episcopal Church on the Joint Commission on Faith and Order. His commitment to including women in Church councils may have been strengthened by the example of his sister, who, as Sister Eleanor of the Community of St. Mary, served as superintendent of the Trinity Infirmary in New York City for many years.[27]

The resolution Gardiner presented to the 1919 General Convention amended the constitutional provision that each diocese was to be represented at the convention by four presbyters and "not more than four Laymen, communicants of this church." Gardiner moved to delete the word "Laymen" so the section would read "not more than four communicants of this church." (Women, as well as men, were included in the category of "communicants.") Supporting the resolution, he pointed to the work of the deaconesses, sisterhoods, and women missionaries, noting:

> A very large part of the social work which is being done with increasing efficiency and with growing influence upon social and industrial questions is left to women. Why should they not vote as to the relation of the Church to those questions? Churchwomen have a very large and important part in that social work. The Church is letting them do it without restraint or advice. If they were part of the legislative body of the Church, they would be guided and, if necessary, restrained by the opinion of the whole Church.[28]

Despite the argument's negative connotations, it testified to the significance of women workers in social-action ministries. "Women are allowed to do most of the work of the Church," Gardiner continued, "in prayer, in teaching, in Sunday Schools, in boys' clubs as well as girls', in money for missions, charity and parochial support. Why should they not share with lay men the direction of that work?"[29]

Other supporters of the measure pointed to the national movement toward women's suffrage, most notably that Congress had passed the Nineteenth Amendment, which granted women the right to vote. The Church of England had extended suffrage to women by deciding that the electoral roll of each parish should be made up of all who "are baptised and declare that they are members of the Church of England."[30] And the previous year, the General Conference of the Methodist Episcopal Church, South, had granted women the right to serve as conference delegates.[31] The Episcopal Church needed "an infusion of the idealism of woman, of her swift intuition of righteousness, of her readiness to spend herself to the utmost," stated one petitioner.[32]

Repeating its 1916 action, the committee on constitutional amendments refused to suspport Gardiner's proposal. By suggesting a slight change in the resolution's wording, Gardiner managed to bring the matter to the floor and spoke fervently in favor of broadening the membership to include women. When put to a vote, however, his resolution lost by an overwhelming majority. A similar amendment was introduced in the House of Bishops, where it was defeated without debate.[33] Instead, a joint committee of deputies and bishops was created to study "the whole matter of Woman's Work in the Church"—a committee made up entirely of men.[34] "Incidentally," chided the editor of *The Churchman*, "where had the House of Deputies mislaid its sense of humor the day it created a commission on . . . churchwomen and forgot to put on it a single churchwoman?"[35]

Thus the hopes many women and men had for a new order in the Church were crushed by the 1919 convention's action. Indeed, in the process of rewriting the canons to establish the new national Church structure, the words "male" and "laymen" were inserted wherever the terminology had been ambiguous, making the exclusion of women from Church councils definite and specific.[36]

The consequences of the rewritten constitution and canons were extensive, for they defined two forms of membership in the Episcopal Church. Both men and women as communicants were expected to work and pray and give for the spread of Christ's kingdom, but only men served as political representatives. Men made the decisions women were expected to help carry out. And once the segregated system was written into the constitution, its subsequent amendment required a majority vote of both houses in two succeeding General Conventions.[37] With only men as delegates to the convention, it was difficult for women to get a hearing. Not for another fifty years were they seated in General Convention, years that saw slow progress toward equality in Church membership. Gradually, diocese by diocese, women won the right to vote in parish meetings and to serve on vestries and in diocesan conventions.[38] In 1934 four women were added to the National Council, not as regularly elected members but as representatives elected only by the women at the Triennial Meeting. Not until 1970 were women deputies seated as deputies of General Convention.[39]

THE DEACONESS PETITION

The only women successful in their approach to the 1919 General Convention were the deaconesses. Prior to the convention, members of the central committee of deaconesses—which included representatives of the training schools in New York, Pennsylvania, and California—had considered means of modernizing the profession, of making it more appealing to "the large number of intelligent and progressive women who are seeking or might be led to seek community service."[40] This group appealed to the House of Bishops to establish a joint commission that would consider recruitment, standardization of requirements for the office of deaconess, a means of examining candidates, and the establishment of a pension plan.

At the convention Bishop Philip Mercer Rhinelander of Pennsylvania introduced a resolution urging the trustees of the Church Pension Fund to amend their charter to make the fund available to deaconesses and to establish terms and conditions for pensions. The resolution easily passed both houses, as did the resolution establishing a joint committee on adapting the office of deaconess to present-day tasks of the Church. For the second time in its history, the General Convention appointed women to one of its committees: Deaconesses Clara M. Carter, head of the Philadelphia School, and Anna G. Newell of Missouri, along with laywomen Mrs. Augustus M. Hand, a long-time board member of the New York School for Deaconesses, Mary Van Kleek of the Russell Sage Foundation of New York, and Elizabeth Matthews, auxiliary president of the diocese of southern Ohio, were appointed to serve along with Bishops Rhinelander, James Henry Darlington of Harrisburg, and Thomas Frederick Davies of western Massachusetts; and priests William E. Gardner, Edward L. Parsons, and George Lynde Richardson, who served as wardens of the New York, California, and Pennsylvania training schools.[41]

Perhaps the most striking fact about the 1919 meeting was the almost total lack of communication between those attending the Triennial Meeting and those at the General Convention. The intensity of the Woman's Auxiliary's interest in membership on the Board of Missions never got communicated to the deputies. Indeed, few of the deputies realized how significant was the women's contribution to the missionary work of the Church, for the latter's general pattern of humble and quietly efficient service attracted little notice. The deaconesses were able to engage the convention delegates' attention because of the unique relationship between the order of deaconesses and the bishops. The canon stipulated that the deaconess was "under the direct oversight of the Bishop of the Diocese in which she is canonically resident," a stipulation that at least implied some responsibility on the part of the bishop for the deaconess's welfare. So it was to his advantage as well as hers to regularize some form of pension.[42] That fact, along with careful advance work by the deaconess central committee, accounted for the convention delegates' willingness to set up a committee that included women. Unfortunately for the deaconesses, the pension fund trustees decided against including them in the fund. Not until 1971 were deaconesses declared eligible for coverage.

The 1919 General Convention aptly demonstrated that the Episcopal Church was not yet ready to accept women as equal members of its political structure. Women shared the responsibility for this decision, for they were willing to be obedient and absorbed in service to others. That they had developed administrative and fund-raising skills that could be useful to the entire Church was a conclusion very few of them had yet reached. One man in a position to understand the scope of the women's activities was the Board of Missions' president, Bishop Lloyd, who made a powerful plea for involving women more fully in policy-making councils:

> The Church's experience makes evident the loss resulting from the separation of the women from their natural relation to the work intrusted to the whole Body of Christ, while the illustration afforded by the nation's history during the years just past is abundant proof of the added vigor and effectiveness of administration which may be expected from the counsel of wise women in the practical affairs of the Church.[43]

But his plea fell on deaf ears; the Victorian ideal of separate spheres for men and women still held sway in the Episcopal Church.

CHAPTER TWELVE

The Question of Ministry

The *fact* of ministry is established for each Christian at baptism. The *question* of ministry is an ongoing dialogue—as individuals seek to discern the form their ministry should take—a dialogue heavily influenced by history, culture, and circumstance. For Episcopal churchwomen in the period between 1850 and 1920, there is abundant evidence of their response to the *fact* of ministry. The *question* of ministry—its place, its form, its reception—created a dynamic that often led to frustration and disappointment. Yet in addressing it, women set a pattern both original and profound, one that broadened the concept of ministry for the entire Church.

The work of Episcopal women from 1850 to 1920 transformed the Church. By 1920 the standard expectation for parish life included a host of activities designed to reach out to the community: boys' and girls' clubs, women's guilds, parish visitation programs—calling on shut-ins, assisting at the hospital, volunteer work at an orphanage—and correspondence with people in the mission field. This pattern of parish life was decidedly different from that of 1850. The change had been brought about primarily by the women who voluntarily organized and staffed the majority of these programs. Education was their special province—a few men taught Sunday-school classes, and generally the superintendent of the Sunday school was male, but the majority of the Church-school teachers and those responsible for the ongoing educational program of the parish were women. Education about the Church's missionary outreach—the advance of Christianity in foreign lands and needy regions at home—was almost totally in the hands of women, both as teachers and as developers of curriculum materials. Women knew more about the Church's worldwide mission than did the men; they were more involved in the deployment of missionaries and the support systems, too.

Although women were almost universally excluded from diocesan political structures, their activities on a diocesan level were significant. The strong networks of communication and support forged by churchwomen's organizations—primarily the Woman's Auxiliary, but also other groups such as the Daughters of the King and the Girls' Friendly Society—fostered a diocesan rather than a parochial identity and strengthened the cohesion within each diocese. Again, there was an educational component to these networks, in that the women taught their local parishes about the various diocesan programs—the youth camps, the Appalachian work, the inner-city clinics, the fresh-air excursions. In addition, most dioceses owned and operated several institutions—hospitals, orphanages, homes for the aged, schools—that depended on women as staff members, publicists, case-workers, and financial supporters. The diocesan involvement in social-service ministries would have been severely curtailed without churchwomen's untold hours of voluntary labor to administer, support, and maintain the institutions.

This period also saw the development of various vocations for women in the Church. Several sisterhoods were founded, communities based on distinctive interpretations of vocation and obedience. They offered women the opportunity of lifetime devotion to God's work and of service to others in a form widely perceived (because it appealed to only a limited number of women) as nonthreatening to established patterns of Church life. A second vocation for women— that of the deaconess—was established by the national Church and professional standards and educational requirements for it were developed. Though it was designed to appeal particularly to the college-educated woman who would be attracted by high professional standards, it also included strict obedience requirements that protected the traditional social hierarchy. A third vocation—that of the missionary worker—was less clearly defined and thus offered women the opportunity to establish their own ministries. This vagueness, however, left the missionary workers with little status in the ecclesiastical organization, forcing them to rely on the Woman's Auxiliary to provide financial support (including disability benefits and pensions), to set standards of recruitment and training, and to serve in Church councils as the primary advocate for missionary workers.

Thus, the importance of the support networks the women forged becomes clear. The strong link between the auxiliary and the missionary workers supported and defined those workers' roles. The tie between the auxiliary and the women missionary workers also linked the local parish to the mission field, giving Episcopalians in Chicago, for example, a glimpse of Church life in Mexico through Ds. Whitaker's eyes or a sense of the Church's presence in Kyoto through correspondence with Marietta Ambler. Less apparent but equally significant were the close relationships among many of the sisterhoods. The All Saints Sisters stayed in New York City at the house of the Community of St. Mary on their way to begin work in Maryland. When yellow fever struck Memphis, a nursing sister from the Society of St. Margaret joined the St. Mary's sisters who had hurried to Memphis to help the women there. The intricate web of social and religious workers that made up the Society of the Companions of the Holy Cross is yet another example of the empowerment such support networks conferred. For example, Jane Addams compared programs with the missionary staff of St. Luke's Hospital, Tokyo, and Margaret Shearman sought the assistance of other Companions to minister to the needs of striking Pennsylvania coal miners. A common religious purpose united these diverse religious and settlement-house workers.

In the years between 1850 and 1920, Episcopal women had developed their own form of ministry. Recognizing their powerlessness in the Church's political order, they had identified with other powerless groups in a ministry of care and concern. This identification reflected the contemporary social expectation that women should be wives and mothers, caring for the young and helpless, and emotionally sustaining the family. Emotional and intuitive responses were well within the social boundaries set for women. And yet, as these churchwomen gradually enlarged the scope of their action, caring for those beyond the boundaries of their families, their social classes, even of their local communities, they began to recognize the dual nature of their ministry—a ministry of individual action *and* of support networks, one that must reaffirm other ministers as well as initiate new programs. Education was a critical component of the reaffirmation; one had to know about and understand the work in order to support it. Hence the strong emphasis, in so many of the churchwomen's programs, on both teaching *and* doing.

In her essay on female institution building, historian Estelle Freedman stressed the importance of the development of strong organizations that both gave women an arena in which to act and provided a network of other women to support them.[1] She persuasively argued that female support networks are a necessary component of the movement toward equal rights for women. To abandon the women's organizations before the attainment of those rights is to risk leaving in a very vulnerable position those in the forefront of the struggle. Though Freedman wrote primarily of the women's-club movement in the period between 1880 and 1920, her conclusions are equally applicable to the development of women's work in the Episcopal Church.

Although operating as auxiliary to the Board of Missions implied a subservient status for Episcopal women, that form of organization did have certain advantages over that of a completely independent entity. "Women's work" was perceived as an integral part of the Church's mission. Handling from the same office the deployment of men and women missionaries made sense from budgetary and administrative viewpoints and gave the women missionaries a higher status than they might have had were they representing only the Woman's Auxiliary. The auxiliary's clever manipulation of the United Offering funds to ensure that women were hired for missionary posts accomplished a feminist goal within a supportive posture. The women had a great deal of freedom in developing their own organization, in recruiting, and in establishing training programs for women workers.

Yet the *question* of ministry continued to challenge them, often at a barely conscious level. Most of the women workers thought of themselves as full members of the Church, as people called to proclaim Christ's saving love to all the world. That call was empowering; it enabled them to scorn custom, to develop new ministries, to forge unusual lifestyles for themselves and their sisters. Many of the women who served as nuns, deaconesses, nurses, missionaries, parish volunteers, or social workers did so out of deep commitment to a gospel they perceived as egalitarian. And that egalitarianism was part of the message they proclaimed to the people with whom they worked—the sick, the poor, the uneducated, and those in foreign lands.

Though Freedman's emphasis on the importance of female networks is certainly valid, I am convinced there comes a time, especially for a women's organization within a larger institution, when it must see that women are allowed access to the controlling power. To do so, the women's organization may have to surrender some of its autonomy in exchange for a share of the decision making. Otherwise, it runs the risk of imprisoning women in a restricted sphere within the institution and rendering their work increasingly marginal.

For women in the Episcopal Church, such a time came in 1919. The Women's Auxiliary had become a powerful association engaged in fund raising and logistical support for missions and Christian education and outreach at home. Women professionals were working in the Church in a variety of fields; they had skills and experience that could be useful in a larger context. Nationally, the women's suffrage amendment to the United States Constitution was on the verge of ratification. Because the Episcopal Church was in the midst of an extensive administrative reorganization, to include women in that reorganization, giving them the status of equal members of the household of God (a status implied at their baptism), could have been done with few changes in the wording of the revised canons.

But the change did not occur. The 1919 General Convention defeated both the suffrage resolution and the plan to elect eight women to the Board of Missions. The women's organization was sentenced to remain "auxiliary to" the Church's political councils. This action confronted Episcopal women with their marginal position in the Church. It was plain to see that although they thought of themselves as equal laborers in the vineyard, the deputies of the convention had a hierarchical rather than an egalitarian view of the vineyard.

Women responded to the results of the 1919 convention in a variety of ways. Some were angry, some just disappointed. The majority were probably oblivious to the decision and merely continued in the ministries they were already exercising.

Many circumstances in the next twenty years changed the character of women's work in the Church. Vocational opportunities for women expanded in the 1920s. The revolution in popular culture made Church work seem rather old-fashioned compared to other, more glamorous opportunities. Wars and civil unrest in Asia disrupted many mission stations. The rise of the Community Chest, with its emphasis on funding only nonsectarian organizations, led some settlement houses to cut their ties with the Episcopal Church. The economic depression of the 1930s eliminated most of the women workers' paid positions in local parishes, taking a terrible toll particularly on the employment of deaconesses. For these and many other reasons, women's position in the Episcopal Church shifted. To blame it solely on the results of the 1919 General Convention would certainly be inaccurate, but that no change in women's status took place during the reorganization made subsequent amendment more difficult to accomplish.

With the reorganization of the national Church, the Woman's Auxiliary voted to become "Auxiliary to the Presiding Bishop and Council," a decision that enabled it to widen the scope of its activity by including Christian education and Christian social relations along with its long-standing emphasis on domestic and foreign missions. But the broadening tended to diffuse its energy; the certainty and sense of high purpose that had characterized the earlier days of auxiliary work waned. More time seemed to be spent on the maintenance of the organization itself, less on attaining its goals.

The next fifty years saw few changes in the official status of women in the Episcopal Church. Some women continued to seek vocations as deaconesses or members of sisterhoods; others went into missionary service either at home or abroad. The 1920s' emphasis on educational methods led to a new profession for women in the Church—that of the director of religious education. The deaconess training schools adapted their curricula to prepare women for Christian-education work, and a new school—Windham House—was founded to train women church workers. The Bishop Tuttle Training School was established in Raleigh, North Carolina, to train Negro women in parish and social work. Initiated and almost totally supported by the Woman's Auxiliary, it was yet another example of the churchwomen's deep interest in ministry to the black community. Like so many of their missionary sisters, women from the Bishop Tuttle School often held black congregations—urban and rural—together, functioning as pastors, teachers, and administrators, performing all but the sacramental roles of priesthood for long periods of time.

Women continued to enter missionary work as teachers, nurses, physicians, and administrators, and the proportion of women missionary workers continued to rise. In 1920, 28 percent of the domestic and foreign missionaries sent by the Episcopal Church were women; in 1930, 30 percent were women; and in 1940, 42 percent of foreign missionaries were women. (None of these figures includes missionary wives unless the latter were employed by the Church. Employed or not, the missionary wife played a significant part in the Church's work in most mission stations.) If one looks only at the foreign field, the proportion of women is much higher. By 1920, of the missionaries sent from the United States, women outnumbered men in Alaska,

Hawaii, the Philippines, Puerto Rico, China, and Japan. Of the overseas dioceses in which over ten missionaries worked, only Liberia and Cuba listed missionary staffs with a higher number of men than of women. In the next twenty years, the proportion of women in foreign missions continued to rise.[2]

Political rights for women in the Church evolved very slowly. A few dioceses granted women the right to vote in parish and diocesan meetings and to serve on vestries or as delegates to the diocesan convention, but not until the 1950s was there any widespread movement in that direction. As late as 1961, women served on vestries in only 31 of the 104 dioceses and they were elected as delegates to only 47 diocesan conventions.[3] The 1934 General Convention provided that four women, nominated by the Woman's Auxiliary, serve on the National Council (along with twenty-eight men), but even they were elected by a General Convention that excluded women deputies.

The struggle to open the General Convention's membership to women continued for the next fifty years. Every General Convention from 1946 to 1964 defeated a resolution to interpret the term "laymen" (as defined in the membership requirements) to include women as well as men. Mrs. Randall Dyer was elected as a deputy to the convention in 1946 by the Diocese of Missouri; the House of Deputies offered to seat her without voice or vote—an "honor" she declined. In 1949 three women—Mrs. Edmund V. Cowdry from Missouri, Mrs. Elizabeth Davis Pittman from Nebraska, and Ruth Jenkins from Washington State—were elected as deputies. When offered seats without voice or vote, they responded, "The real issue is not courtesy to women but that of the right of women to represent in its councils the Church they are proud to serve. We therefore decline the courtesy offered to us."[4] At the next convention (1952), the Triennial Meeting of the Woman's Auxiliary proposed that it be declared the third house of the General Convention—a proposal the convention also defeated. Not until 1967 did the General Convention finally vote to allow women to serve as deputies to it. Even then, before it became official the vote had to be reaffirmed by the next convention. That reaffirmation was voted at the beginning of the 1970 convention, and twenty-eight duly elected women deputies took their seats—over fifty years after the acceptance of women as deputies had first been proposed.[5] That same convention finally granted the women who served as deaconesses a status equivalent to that of the male deacons—membership in the first order of ministry.

The crucial question for women in 1970, as it was for the women in 1919, was that of ministry. What is the ministry of the Church? Who are the Church's ministers? To whom are they sent? What authenticates their work? In the period between 1850 and 1919, women developed a wide range of ministries, and yet neither they nor the Church recognized their work as ministry. Symbolically, the women were viewed as handmaidens, as those who prepared the way for the priests, the Church's authentic ministers. In local parishes they served as the altar guild—those who could set the table but not serve the meal. They instructed children in the fundamentals of the Christian faith but were not allowed to present those children to the bishop for confirmation. In these and many other ways, Episcopal women played their servant role in the Church. Not until they finally recognized that a theological doctrine of ministry based on gender was contrary to the egalitarian stance of the gospel was it possible for them to challenge the Church to live up to its ideals. Once women realized they would always be second-class citizens in an institution that limited its priesthood to men, they were able to confront the Church with its own claim of the equality of all people before God.

The campaign for the ordination of women to the priestood began (slowly) in the 1960s, supported by a wide range of Church leaders, both men and women. Ironically, the first General Convention to vote on admitting women as candidates for ordination to the priesthood (1970) was also the first to include women as voting delegates. The measure failed then, and again in 1973, but it was passed in 1976. By opening the priesthood to women, the Episcopal Church had finally recognized the validity of the former's ministries.

Once ordination was possible, priesthood became the primary vocational choice for many women who felt called to ministry. Some who had served as nuns, deaconesses, directors of religious education, or missionary workers sought ordination. Others, without previous Church-related employment, became priests. Since 1976 over seven hundred women have been ordained to the priesthood.[6] Their presence in the order of priests has already begun to alter the shape of that vocation. Though some women priests have become parish rectors, a high percentage of today's women priests are filling social-service positions similar to those their sisters held a century earlier. Women priests are working as hospital chaplains, as teachers and principals in Church-related schools, as administrators of social-service institutions, as priests in marginal parishes of the inner city or the rural heartland, and as directors of such Church-related institutions as alcohol- and drug-treatment centers, youth ministries, and shelters for battered women and abused children.

An oversupply of clergy—and the unwillingness of many parishes to hire women rectors—have contributed to the extensive deployment of women in social-service positions. The testimony of this history suggests, however, that these are not the only causes. Episcopal women of the nineteenth and early twentieth centuries recognized and responded to a different call; they chose to enter social-service ministries, and, with very little support from Church authorities, they developed their own ministering vocations. In the process they shaped a Church that was responsive to social needs and involved in the community. The ordained women who today continue social-service ministries are following a tradition forged by their antecedent sisters.

Notes

ONE: THE WOMAN'S SPHERE

1. Mary Abbot Twing, "Fourth Triennial Report of the Honorary Secretary of the Woman's Auxiliary to the Board of Missions," 1895, p. 18, Woman's Auxiliary Collection, Archives of the Episcopal Church (hereafter cited as AEC), Austin, Texas.

2. For information about the Emery family, I am indebted to Mrs. Twing's nieces, Violet Emery and Dorothy Lyford. *The Reminiscences of Violet Emery and Dorothy Lyford*, 14 April 1980, in the Oral History Collection, AEC; *see also* the large collection of Mary Abbot Emery Twing's correspondence in the Emery Collection, AEC; John A. Emery, "From the Forecastle to the Pulpit: The Story of Fifteen Years of Unusual Preparation for a Ministry and of Forty Years in the One Diocese of California," n.d., Diocese of California Archives, San Francisco.

3. Rosemary Ruether and Eleanor McLaughlin, *Women of Spirit: Female Leadership in the Jewish and Christian Traditions* (New York: Simon and Schuster, 1979), pp. 19–20.

4. Theressa Hoover, *With Unveiled Face: Centennial Reflections on Women and Men in the Community of the Church* (New York: Women's Division, General Board of Global Ministries, The United Methodist Church, 1983), p. 13.

5. Elizabeth Howell Verdesi, *In But Still Out: Women in the Church* (Philadelphia: The Westminster Press, 1976), pp. 73–77, 85–89.

6. Helen Emery Falls, "Baptist Women in Missions Support in the Nineteenth Century," *Baptist History and Heritage* 12 (January 1977):26–36.

7. Harry Leon McBeth, "The Role of Women in Southern Baptist History," *Baptist History and Heritage* 12 (January 1977):3–25.

8. Sister Elizabeth Kolmer, A.S.C., "Catholic Women Religious and Women's History: A Survey of the Literature," in Janet Wilson James, ed., *Women in American Religion* (Philadelphia: University of Pennsylvania Press, 1980), pp. 127–40.

9. Mary J. Oates, "Organized Voluntarism: The Catholic Sisters in Massachusetts, 1870–1940," in Janet Wilson James, ed., *Women in American Religion* (Philadelphia: University of Pennsylvania Press, 1980), pp. 141–70.

10. Kenneally claims that though both priests and women idealized women as

Mary, only the priests were concerned with the image of woman as Eve. James J. Kenneally, "Eve, Mary, and the Historians: American Catholicism and Women," in Janet Wilson James, ed., *Women in American Religion* (Philadelphia: University of Pennsylvania Press, 1980), pp. 191–206.

11. Heather Huyck has summarized the period from 1920 to 1976 in "To Celebrate a Whole Priesthood: The History of Women's Ordination in the Episcopal Church" (Ph.D. diss., University of Minnesota, 1981). *See also*: Emily Hewitt and Suzanne Hiatt, *Women Priests: Yes or No?* (New York: Seabury, 1973); Norene Carter, "Entering the Sanctuary: The Struggle for Priesthood in Contemporary Episcopalian and Roman Catholic Experience," in Ruether and McLaughlin, *Women of Spirit*, pp. 356–72; Shirley Sartori, "Conflict and Institutional Change: The Ordination of Women in the Episcopal Church" (Ph.D. diss., State University of New York at Albany, 1978).

TWO: ENLARGING THE SCOPE OF THE CHURCH'S MINISTRY

1. Henry Anstice, *History of St. George's Church in the City of New York, 1752–1911* (New York: Harper and Brothers, 1911), pp. 350–56; George Hodges and John Reichert, *The Administration of an Institutional Parish* (New York: Harper and Brothers, 1906), pp. 16, 25–34, 42–47, 76–99; Diocese of New York, *Convention Journal*, 1900, p. 169.

2. Anstice, pp. 198–231; *The Spirit of Missions* 15 (1850):293.

3. George Wolfe Shinn, *King's Handbook of Notable Episcopal Churches in the United States* (Boston: Moses King Corporation, 1889), pp. 65–68, 241–43. Among the other churches with social-action programs that Shinn mentions are: St. George's Church, Newburg, N.Y.; St. Stephen's Church, Philadelphia; Grace Church, New York City; Christ Church, Raleigh, N.C.; St. John's Church, Detroit, Mich.; St. Stephen's Church, Providence, R.I.; Trinity Church, Toledo, Ohio; St. Luke's Church, San Francisco; Calvary Church, New York; St. John's Church, Cohoes, N.Y.; St. Mark's Church, San Antonio; Trinity Church, Boston; and St. Mark's Cathedral, Salt Lake City. *See also* pp. 45–47, 50–51, 83, 88–90, 94–96, 97–103, 105, 112–15, 129–30, 132–33, 137–38, 139–41, 146–47, 151–53, 160–63, 170–74, 179–86, 199–202, 254–57.

4. Episcopal Diocese of New York, *Convention Journal*, 1850. Data regarding Sunday schools for this period are difficult to find, for many dioceses did not yet include such information in their annual convention journals. Most churches in the diocese of Pennsylvania report Sunday schools in 1850, whereas in Maryland only 23 of 104 churches reporting listed Sunday schools. Diocese of Pennsylvania, *Convention Journal*, 1850, pp. 79–137; Diocese of Maryland, *Convention Journal*, 1850, pp. 155–57.

5. Carroll Smith-Rosenberg, *Religion and the Rise of the American City* (Ithaca: Cornell University Press, 1971), pp. 125–63; New York Protestant Episcopal City Mission Society, *Annual Reports*, 1832–1844, Diocese New York Archives (hereafter known as DNYA).

6. Charity Organization Society, *New York Charities Directory, 1900* (New York: The Knickerbocker Press, 1899).

7. *Whittaker's Church Almanac* (New York: Thomas Whittaker, 1899), 292–343.

8. Shailer Mathews, "Social Gospel," in Shailer Mathews and G. B. Smith, *A Dictionary of Religion and Ethics* (New York, 1921), pp. 416–17.

9. Charles Howard Hopkins, *The Rise of the Social Gospel in American Protestantism, 1865–1915* (New Haven: Yale University Press, 1940), p. 318.

10. Ibid., p. 14.

11. Ibid., p. 251.

12. Ibid., p. 321.

13. *See* particularly Aaron I. Abell, *Urban Impact on American Protestantism, 1865–1900* (Hamden, CT: Archon Books, 1962); Paul A. Carter, *The Decline and Revival of the Social Gospel* (Hamden, CT: Archon Books, 1971); Robert T. Handy, ed., *The Social Gospel in America* (New York: Oxford University Press, 1966); Henry F. May, *Protestant Churches and Industrial America* (New York: Octagon Books, 1963).

14. George Hodges, *Henry Codman Potter* (New York: The Macmillan Company, 1915), p. 70; Hopkins, *Rise*, p. 35.

15. *An American Cloister: An Account of the Life and Work of the Order of the Holy Cross* (West Park, NY: Holy Cross, 1917), pp. 22–23; James B. Simpson and Edward M. Story, *Stars in His Crown* (Sea Bright, NJ: Ploughshare Press, 1976), pp. 85–101.

16. Charles Thorley Bridgeman, *The Trinity Church Association and Trinity Mission House, 1876–1956* (New York: Trinity Church Association, 1956), pp. 13–14.

17. Diocese of New York, *Convention Journal*, 1965, pp. 162–99.

18. Anne Ayres, *William Augustus Muhlenberg* (New York: Thomas Whittaker, 1889), pp. 298–305; George B. Roberts, "Christ Church Hospital," *Historical Magazine of the Protestant Episcopal Church* 45 (1976):89–102; Diocese of Chicago, *Convention Journal*, 1900; Sister Catherine Louise, *In the House of My Pilgrimage* (Glenside, PA: Littlepage Press, 1973), p. 21; Charles Silliman, *The Episcopal Church in Delaware, 1785–1954* (Wilmington: Diocese of Delaware, 1982); Diocese of California, *Convention Journal*, 1892, p. 92; Allen du Pont Breck, *The Episcopal Church in Colorado, 1860–1963* (Denver: Big Mountain Press, 1963), pp. 80–81; John H. Davis, *St. Mary's Cathedral* (Memphis: Chapter of St. Mary's Cathedral, 1958), p. 83.

19. James Thayer Addison, *The Episcopal Church in the United States, 1789–1931* (New York: Charles Scribner's Sons, 1951); Raymond W. Albright, *A History of the Protestant Episcopal Church* (New York: The Macmillan Company, 1964); John E. Booty, *The Church in History* (New York: The Seabury Press, 1979); W.W. Manross, *History of the American Episcopal Church* (New York, 1950).

20. Addison, *Episcopal Church*, p. 282.

21. Albright, *History*, p. 316.

22. Ibid., p. 323.

23. Addison, *Episcopal Church*, p. 168.

24. Albright, *History*, p. 317.

25. Booty, *Church*, p. 181.

26. Ibid., p. 186.

27. Hopkins, *Rise*, p. 150.

28. Henry F. May, *Protestant Churches and Industrial America* (New York: Octagon Books, 1963), p. 184.

29. Hopkins, *Rise*, p. 152; Ronald C. White, Jr., and C. Howard Hopkins, eds., *The Social Gospel* (Philadelphia: Temple University Press, 1966), p. 72.

30. C.A.I.L. Scrapbook, DNYA; Harriette A. Keyser, *Bishop Potter: The People's Friend* (New York: Thomas Whittaker, 1910), pp. 37, 89–97; Huntington, *Memoir*, pp. 357–58.

31. *See* references to Keyser's investigations of child labor in New Jersey and the

South, of tenement-house manufacturing of clothing, and of the fishing industry on the Maine coast. *Hammer and Pen,* December 1902, July 1903, November 1903.

32. Keyser, pp. 36, 78, 80–87.

33. May, *Protestant,* p. 182. *See also* Hopkins, *Rise,* p. 318; Handy, *Social Gospel,* p. 12.

34. Ibid., p. 5; Hopkins, *Rise,* p. 38; May, *Protestant,* p. 182.

35. I am grateful to my colleague Cynthia McLean, whose current research on China substantiates this point in terms of the Episcopal missionaries there. Cynthia McLean to Mary S. Donovan, 30 January 1985.

THREE: THE EPISCOPAL CHURCH IN 1850

1. James Elliott Lindsley, *This Planted Vine: A Narrative History of the Episcopal Diocese of New York* (New York: Harper and Row, 1984), p. 162; Van Wyck Brooks, *The World of Washington Irving* (New York: World, 1944), p. 31; Perry Miller, *The Raven and the Whale* (New York: Greenwood Press, 1956), p. 23.

2. Addison, *Episcopal,* p. 138; *The Episcopal Church Annual* (New York: Morehouse-Barlow, 1976), p. 18; Lindsley, ibid., 171.

3. E. Brooks Holifield, *The Gentlemen Preachers: American Theology in Southern Culture* (Durham: Duke University Press, 1978), p. 29.

4. H. Caswell, *America and the American Church,* pp. 64, 296, quoted in Addison, *Episcopal,* p. 138.

5. M.R. Babcock to John Young, 24 May 1855, Young Papers, U.N.C., Chapel Hill, quoted in Holifield, *Gentlemen Theologians,* p. 14.

6. Joan R. Gunderson, "The Non-Institutional Church: The Religious Role of Women in Eighteenth Century Virginia," *Historical Magazine of the Protestant Episcopal Church* 51 (1982):347–57.

7. Victoria Hunter Clayton described instructing her slaves: "As to their religious training, every Sunday morning the mothers brought their little one up to see me. Then I could satisfy myself as to the care they gave them, whether they had received a bath and suitable clothing for the holy day. Later the larger children presented themselves to be taught the Catechism. . . . When the evening meal was over my dining room was in readiness for the reception of all the grown [slave] members of the family. They gathered there and took their respective seats. They were taught the Creed of the Holy Apostolic Church, the Lord's Prayer, and the Ten Commandments; that is, all who could be taught, for some of them never could learn to repeat them, but understood the meaning sufficiently to lead a right life. Sometimes I would read a short sermon to them. They sang hymns, and we closed with prayer to our Heavenly Father." Henry Thomas Malone, *The Episcopal Church in Georgia, 1733–1957* (Atlanta: The Protestant Episcopal Church, 1960), p. 88.

8. Carroll Smith-Rosenberg, "The Female World of Love and Ritual: Relations Between Women in Nineteenth Century America," in Esther Katz and Anita Rapone, *Women's Experience in America* (New Brunswick: Transaction Books, 1980), pp. 259–92.

9. "The Ministration of Public Baptism of Infants," in *The Book of Common Prayer* (New York: Thomas Nelson and Sons, 1896), p. 248.

10. Catharine Beecher to Leonard Bacon, 24 April 1862, quoted in Karen Kish Sklar, *Catharine Beecher* (New Haven: Yale University Press, 1973), p. 260.

11. *See* biographies of Catharine Beecher, Harriet Beecher Stowe, Emma Willard, Almira Hart Lincoln Phelps, Sarah Josepha Hale, Emma Dorothy Eliza Nevitte Southworth, and Lydia Sigourney in Edward T. James, ed., *Notable American*

Women (Cambridge, MA: The Belknap Press of Harvard University, 1971). For her investigation of the beginnings of mass culture, Ann Douglas chose thirty ministers and thirty middle-class women "who were among the leading literary propagandists for a sentimentalized culture." Of the thirty women, ten converted to the Episcopal Church: Emma Willard, Sarah Josepha Hale, Lydia Huntley Sigourney, Catharine Beecher, Harriet Beecher Stowe, Delia Bacon, Lucy Larcom, Adeline D.T. Whitney, and Elizabeth Stuart Phelps. (Ann Stephens, a cradle Episcopalian, was also on the list.) Ann Douglas, *The Feminization of American Culture* (New York: Avon Books, 1978), pp. 111–12, 402–9.

12. Barbara Welter, "The Feminization of American Religion: 1800–1860," in *Dimity Convictions* (Athens: Ohio University Press, 1976), pp. 86–89.

13. Of the sixty-five sermons Cott surveyed, at least a third were from Trinitarian Congregationalists, whereas Unitarian Congregationalists, Presbyterians, Episcopalians, Baptists, and others made up the rest. She states, however, that denominational differences did not perceptibly change the ministers' assessments of women's roles. Nancy Cott, *The Bonds of Womanhood* (New Haven: Yale University Press, 1977), pp. 126–59.

14. Of the thirty clergy Douglas included in her sample, only one, Frederic Dan Huntington, was an Episcopalian, and she includes only one reference to him in the text. Douglas, *Feminization*, pp. 116, 228, 412–13.

15. Douglas, *The Feminization*, pp. 111–12.

16. *See also* Mary P. Ryan, *Cradle of the Middle Class: The Family in Oneida County, New York, 1790–1865* (New York: Cambridge University Press, 1981); Anne M. Boylan, "Evangelical Womanhood in the Nineteenth Century: The Role of Women in Sunday Schools," *Feminist Studies* 4 (October 1978):62–80; Keith Melder, "Ladies Bountiful: Organized Women's Benevolence in Early 19th Century America," *New York History* 3 (July 1967):231–53.

17. Joint Commission on the Revision of the Hymnal, *The Hymnal 1940 Companion* (New York: The Church Pension Fund), pp. 150, 258, 272, 288, and 438.

18. Such statements begin to appear in the 1880s. William S. Rainsford, who began work at St. George's Church in 1893, warned, "There is great danger that public worship may be left to women, clergymen, and the uneducated." *A Preacher's Story of His Work* (New York: The Outlook Company, 1904).

19. There are very few records of such groups. Dr. Joanna Gillespie has discovered references to the following associations: Auxiliary to the Education Society, founded 1821, Randolph County, Virginia; The Society for Educating Pious Young Men for the Episcopal Ministry, 1818, New York and New England; Female Tract Society of Worthington, Ohio, 1822; Newark Female Bible and Prayer Book Society, 1817; Episcopal Women's Common Prayer Book Society of Wilkes Barre, Pennsylvania, 1818; Ladies Circle of Industry, Immanuel Church, Bellows Falls, Vermont, 1827. See *The Education Society to Its Members and Auxiliaries* 1825, AEC; *The Christian Journal and Literary Register* 1 (1817):43, 236; 2 (1818):200.

20. Mrs. A.T. Twing, *The Woman's Auxiliary to the Board of Missions* (New York: Church Missions House, n.d.), pp. 1–6, pamphlet in Woman's Auxiliary File, DNYA. For typical associations, *see* Female Missionary Association of Trinity Church, Southwork, "Report to the General Missionary Society of the Protestant Episcopal Church," Philadelphia, 30 April 1829, and Female Missionary Society of St. Andrew's Church, Mount Holly, Pennsylvania, "Constitution," 18 February 1829, Domestic and Foreign Missionary Society Collection (hereafter cited as D&FMSC), AEC.

21. Lindsley, *This Planted*, pp. 170–75.

22. Keith Melder, *Beginnings of Sisterhood: The American Woman's Rights Movement, 1800–1850* (New York: Schocken Books, 1977); Alma Lutz, *Crusade for*

Freedom: Women in the Antislavery Movement (Boston: Beacon Press, 1968); Gerda Lerner, "The Political Activities of Antislavery Women," in *The Majority Finds Its Past: Placing Women in History* (New York, 1979).

23. Addison, *Episcopal*, p. 192.

24. The Reverend Stephen Elliott of Beaufort, South Carolina, owned 190 slaves. Holifield, *Gentlemen*, p. 30. Dr. Samuel Seabury, rector of the Church of Annunciation in New York City, published his book *American Slavery Distinguished from the Slavery of the English Theorists and Justified by the Law of Nature* in 1861, just before the outbreak of the war. Samuel Seabury, *American Slavery* (New York, 1861). Bishop John Henry Hopkins of Vermont defended slavery on scriptural grounds, insisting that even Jesus "did not allude to it at all." "In the relation of master and slave we are assured by our Southern brethren that there is incomparably more mutual love than can ever be found between the employer and the hireling," he claimed. John H. Hopkins, *Scriptural, Ecclesiastical, and Historical Review of Slavery* (New York, 1864), pp. 30–32.

25. Albright, *History*, p. 254.

26. Diocese of Delaware, *Journal*, 1849, p. 12, quoted in Charles A. Silliman, *The Episcopal Church in Delaware* (Diocese of Delaware, 1982), p. 77.

27. *Pastoral Letter*, pp. 10f., in William A. Clebsch, ed., *Journals of the Protestant Episcopal Church in the Confederate States of America* (Austin, TX, 1962), Part III, p. 226; Albright, *History*, p. 253.

28. George E. DeMille, *The Catholic Movement in the American Episcopal Church* (Philadelphia: The Church Historical Society, 1941), pp. 24–52; William Wilson Manross, *A History of the American Episcopal Church* (Milwaukee: Morehouse Publishing Company, 1935), pp. 266–90.

29. Charles P. McIlvaine, *Oxford Divinity, Compared with that of the Roman and Anglican Churches* (London, 1841), p. 538.

30. Of the 1,976 clergy ordained between 1822 and 1855, 29 entered the Roman Catholic Church. For a survey of the churchmanship controversy, *see* George E. DeMille, *The Catholic Movement in the American Episcopal Church* (Philadelphia: Folcroft, 1950); Albright, *History*, pp. 226–52; and Addison, *Episcopal*, pp. 152–63.

31. The composition of the Board of Missions was changed several times, but generally a committee of about thirty men—bishops, priests, and laymen—exercised administrative control between General Conventions. In 1871 the name of the committee was changed to "Board of Managers," with the understanding that "Board of Missions" was to refer to the entire General Convention. Julia Emery, *A Century of Endeavor, 1821–1921* (New York: The Department of Missions, 1921), pp. 64–67, 190–92.

32. Various formulas were used to determine self-sufficiency at various times.

33. Emery, *Century of Endeavor*, pp. 353–70.

34. Emery, *Century of Endeavor*, pp. 352–57, 400–23, 438–38. *The Spirit of Missions* 15 (1850):91, 230, 237, 260, 289.

35. Roland Foster prepared a chart of Episcopal Church communicant strength from 1860 through 1976, divided according to provinces. According to his figures, by 1860 the Church was made up of a total of 150,591 communicants, of whom 4,481 (.029%) lived in the western provinces. Typescript manuscripts in author's possession.

FOUR: EPISCOPAL SISTERHOODS, 1850–1920

1. Anne Ayres, *Evangelical Sisterhoods* (New York: T. Whittaker, 1867), pp. 20–21.

2. Henry Codman Potter, *Sisterhoods and Deaconesses at Home and Abroad* (New York: E.P. Dutton & Company, 1873), p. 92; Thomas J. Williams, "The Beginnings of Anglican Sisterhoods," *Historical Magazine of the Protestant Episcopal Church* 16 (1947):350–72.

3. Geoffrey Rowell, *The Vision Glorious* (New York: Oxford University Press, 1983), p. 110.

4. Peter Anson, *The Call of the Cloister* (London: Society for the Propagation of Christ's Kingdom, 1955), p. 595.

5. Anne Ayres, *The Life and Work of William Augustus Muhlenberg* (New York: Thomas Whittaker, 1889), p. 188; Alvin Skardon, *Church Leader in the Cities: William Augustus Muhlenberg* (Philadelphia: University of Pennsylvania Press, 1971), pp. 126–37.

6. Ibid., p. 189.

7. Ibid.

8. Ibid., p. 190.

9. Ibid., p. 197.

10. *See* advertisements for the school in *The Churchman*, 17 March 1849, 15 December 1849.

11. Anne Ayres, *Practical Thoughts on Sisterhoods* (New York: T. Whitaker, 1864), p. 10.

12. Anne Ayres, *Thoughts on Evangelical Sisterhoods* (New York, 1862). Muhlenberg wrote the introduction to this pamphlet, which was circulated privately and republished in 1864 at the request of Bishop Alonzo Potter of Pennsylvania. Ayres, *Muhlenberg*, p. 252.

13. Ibid. The Sisters of Charity of St. Joseph's in the Roman Catholic Church was an order founded by Elizabeth Bayley Seton, who had been an Episcopalian member of the Trinity Parish for many years before she joined the Roman Catholic Church. Annabelle M. Melville, *Elizabeth Bayley Seton, 1774–1821* (New York, 1951).

14. Ayres, *Evangelical Sisterhoods* (New York, 1867), p. 17.

15. Unfortunately for the historian, the sisterhood's requirement of humility and the public suspicion of religious orders both militated against record keeping. Most of the religious communities have very little biographical information and no personal letters or papers from the first sisters. In fact, it is often difficult even to find a sister's original name. Because of the fear that "particular friendships" would develop between two women, many orders forbade correspondence between sisters (other than that from the sister to the mother superior). The letters to the mother superior are rarely accessible to the researcher.

16. Lavinia L. Dock and Isabel M. Stewart, *A Short History of Nursing* (New York: G.P. Putnam's Sons, 1938), pp. 113–14.

17. The Daughters of Charity of St. Vincent de Paul opened a hospital in Baltimore in 1823, followed by several others in eastern cities. The Congregation of St. Joseph of Carondelet had established work in Illinois, Pennsylvania, Minnesota, Virginia, and New York before 1860. The Sisters of Mercy established Mercy Hospital in Pittsburgh in 1848 and added work in Washington, D.C., in 1852. Gladys Sellew and Sister M. Ethelreda Ebel, O.S.F., *A History of Nursing* (St. Louis: C.V. Mosby Company, 1955), pp. 252–58. Four Lutheran deaconesses from Kaiserswerth had come to America in 1849 to establish work at Pittsburgh, but their enterprise did not flourish. Catherine M. Prelinger and Rosemary S. Keller, "The Function of Female Bonding," in Hilah F. Thomas and Rosemary Skinner Keller, *Women in New Worlds* (Nashville, TN: Abington Press, 1981), vol. 1, p. 318.

18. Dock and Stewart, *Short*, p. 126. Cecil Woodham-Smith, *Florence Nightingale* (New York: McGraw-Hill, 1951), pp. 268–80.

19. *History of the St. Luke's Hospital Training School for Nurses* (New York, 1938), pp. 28–29. Because Ayres wrote much of the early history of the hospital and was determined to belittle her own role in order to exalt that of Dr. Muhlenberg, it is difficult to assess her work. Observations like the following, however, indicate the crucial role she played in formulating and teaching nursing procedures: "The Sisters have been steady at their posts, doing what only voluntary service for Christ's sake can do; and at what post has not their head been found—The First Sister and House Mother from the beginning—to whose motherly and affectionate solicitude, by day and by night, with singular administrative ability, is due the whole interior economy of the household, confessedly, a pattern of its kind. . . ." Ibid., p. 19. *See also* Dock and Stewart, *Short*, pp. 145–46.

20. Ibid., pp. 153–54. Sellew and Ebel, *History*, pp. 274–76. Sister Helen's move to Bellevue was complicated by the fact that her religious vows required obedience to the Mother Superior in England. The women organizing the school spent an anxious period waiting for letters of explanation and approval to cross the Atlantic. While working at Bellevue, Sister Helen also established a similar training school at Blackwell's Island. All Saints Sisters of the Poor, *As Possessing All Things* (Catonsville, MD, 1972), pp. 4–6.

21. Sellew and Ebel, *History*, p. 278.

22. Ayres, *Evangelical*, p. 18; Ayres, *Muhlenberg*, pp. 275, 302–5; *Annual Report of St. Luke's Hospital*, 1860, p. 16, DNYA.

23. *An Account of St. Luke's Hospital, 1860* (New York: Robert Craighead, 1862), pp. 24–25, DNYA; *History of the St. Luke's School for Nurses* (New York, 1938), pp. 21–26, 34; *Second Annual Report of St. Luke's Hospital, 1860*, p. 29, DNYA.

24. *History of St. Luke's Hospital Training School for Nurses* (New York, 1938), p. 26; H. Boone Porter, Jr., *Sister Anne: Pioneer in Women's Work* (New York: The National Council, 1960).

25. *Chronicle of the Church of the Holy Communion* (New York, 1901), pp. 37–44, 50–52, pamphlet found in the library at St. George's Church; *Forty-seventh and Forty-eighth Annual Reports of the Shelter for Respectable Girls*, October 1919, miscellaneous file #12, DNYA; Ayres, *Muhlenberg*, pp. 398–444.

26. Community of St. Mary, *The Sisterhood of St. Mary, Its Life and Work* (Peekskill, NY: Convent of St. Mary, 1941), p. 7; Skardon, *Church Leader*, pp. 133–35; John Punnett Peters, *Annals of St. Michaels, 1807–1907* (New York: G.P. Putnam's Sons, 1907), pp. 302–6.

27. As the wife of the Reverend William Richmond, Mary had accompanied him as he visited the prisoners on Blackwell's Island. Disturbed by the plight of the women and girls she met on these visits, Mary began to seek ways to help them. After her husband's death, she continued the ministry and, in 1853, founded the House of Mercy as a residence for homeless women. She was also instrumental in the founding of St. Barnabas House and the New York Infant Asylum. When the sisters who had left Holy Communion approached Dr. Peters, Richmond was glad to have them take over the House of Mercy, for she was dying of cancer and feared there would be no one to take her place. John Punnett Peters, ed., *Annals of St. Michael's, 1807–1907* (New York: G.P. Putnam's Sons, 1907), p. 420.

28. William Augustus Muhlenberg, ed., *Evangelical Sisterhoods* (New York: Thomas Whittaker, 1867), p. 47.

29. Morgan Dix, *Instructions on the Religious Life Given to the Sisters of Saint Mary* (New York: Community of St. Mary, 1909), p. 23.

30. Ibid., p. 39.

31. Community of St. Mary, *The Sisterhood of St. Mary, Its Life and Work* (Peekskill, NY: Convent of St. Mary, 1941), pp. 7–8; Sister Mary Hilary, *Ten Decades of Praise* (Racine, WI: DeKoven Foundation, 1965), pp. 44–48, 80–83; John Punnett Peters, ed., *Annals of St. Michael's, 1807–1907* (New York: G.P. Putnam's Sons, 1907), pp. 304–5. Isaac Henry Tuttle, rector of St. Luke's Church, was the first chaplain, but he resigned in 1866.

32. Sister Jane to E. Folsome Baker, 4 November 1863, Community of St. Mary Archives (hereafter cited as CSMA), Peekskill, New York. Potter himself wrote to Baker, "I assume no responsibility in regard to it [the question of admission] and . . . I reserve that and all other questions connected with the Sisterhood for further consideration." Horatio Potter to E. Folsom Baker, 4 November 1863, CSMA.

33. Diocese of New York, *Convention Journal, 1865.*

34. Sister Mary Hilary, C.S.M., *Ten Decades of Praise* (Racine, WI: DeKoven Foundation, 1965), pp. 31–32.

35. "The ministers opposed to the sisterhood have held several meetings in their rooms at the Bible House, and they have resolved to present the whole subject before the Diocesan Convention," reported the *New York World.* Ibid., p. 48.

36. Hilary, *Ten Decades*, pp. 47–52.

37. Ellen Hulme to Dr. Peters, 8 April 1967 and 24 April 1867, in "New York Protestant Episcopal City Mission Society Minutes, 1831–1869," pp. 320–25; St. Barnabas House Register, Episcopal City Mission Society Collection, DNYA; Sisterhood of the Good Shepherd, *Annual Reports, 1870–1887*, Columbia University Library (hereafter cited as CUL), New York; Olin Scott Roche, *Forty Years of Parish Life and Work, 1883–1923* (New York: Friebele Press, 1930), pp. 148–49. In 1886 the Sisterhood of the Good Shepherd moved to the Chelsea area and worked out of St. Peter's Parish.

38. The letter was signed by William F. Morgan of St. Thomas' Church, H.E. Montgomery of the Church of the Incarnation, Samuel Cooke of St. Bartholomew's Church, E.A. Washburn of Calvary Church, and Henry Codman Potter of Grace Church. Hilary, *Ten Decades*, p. 66.

39. Ibid., pp. 72–78.

40. Twelve Roman Catholic sisters and brothers also died in the Memphis epidemic, as did two Episcopal priests who worked with the sisters. Ibid., pp. 95–109; John H. Davis, *St. Mary's Cathedral, 1858–1958* (Memphis: St. Mary's Cathedral, 1958), p. 76; *The Sisters of St. Mary's at Memphis, With the Acts and Sufferings of the Priests and Others Who Were with Them During the Yellow Fever Season of 1878*, CSMA.

41. Ibid., pp. 111–16.

42. The Poor Clares of Reparation and Adoration, comp., *Religious Communities in the American Episcopal Church and in the Anglican Church in Canada* (West Park, NY: Holy Cross Press, 1945), pp. 75, 79, 87, 97, 102; George DeMille, *A History of the Diocese of Albany, 1704–1923* (Philadelphia: The Church Historical Society, 1946), pp. 98–102.

43. All Saints' Sisters of the Poor, *As Possessing All Things* (Catonsville, MD: All Saints Convent, c. 1972), pp. 3–12.

44. Sister Catherine Louise, S.S.M., *The House of My Pilgrimage* (Glenside, PA: Littlepage Press, 1973), pp. 21–34.

45. James B. Simpson and Edward M. Story, *Stars in His Crown* (Sea Bright, NJ: Ploughshare Press, 1976), pp. 34–42.

46. In 1882 Sister Ruth Margaret left the Society of St. Margaret to establish the Sisterhood of the Holy Nativity, with the Reverend Charles Chapman Grafton as

spiritual adviser. A branch of that community moved with the latter to Wisconsin when he was elected Bishop of Fond du Lac, and branches were later opened in several other cities. Williams, *Beginnings*, p. 371; Sister Catherine Louise, *House*, pp. 19, 22, 39. The best description of the daily life of an Episcopal religious community was written about the Sisters of the Holy Nativity: J.G.H. Barry, *From a Convent Tower* (New York: Edwin S. Gorham, 1919).

47. Simpson and Story, *Stars*, pp. 50–56, 80; All Saints' Sisters, *As Possessing*, p. 13.

48. Simpson and Story, *Stars*, p. 20.

49. Hillary, *Ten Decades*, pp. 71–75.

50. Simpson and Story, *Stars*, p. 117.

51. Listed in *The Living Church Annual*, 1899–1900, pp. 125–28. The date marks the founding or beginning of work in the United States. A few other small communities with work in only one location also existed at this time.

52. The Sisterhood of the Good Shepherd provided each sister with $150 yearly for personal expenses; each of the other communities had a fund from which needy sisters might receive aid. Potter, *Sisterhoods*, pp. 7, 237.

53. Boards of Managers were generally all male, but by the 1880s females began to appear on some of the boards. *See* listings for the Home for Aged Women, the Gallaudet Home, St. Mark's Day Nursery in Charity Organization Society, *New York Charities Directory, 1900* (New York: The Knickerbocker Press, 1899), pp. 107, 192, 249; Endowment Fund Trustees in Lucius A. Edelblute, *The History of the Church of the Holy Apostles* (New York: printed by author, 1949), p. 251, General Theological Seminary Library (hereafter cited as GTS), New York City.

54. The Committee on Dismission of the Board of Lady Managers of the Church Home for Orphan and Destitute Children in Boston was charged with the "special duty of providing suitable homes . . . , for ascertaining the character and circumstances of those applying for children, and seeking homes for others for whom there had been no application." Each woman kept in touch with one or more children who had left the institution and reported semiannually on the child's condition. The Church Home Society, *The Challenge of a Heritage* (Boston: Thomas Todd Company, 1955), p. 8.

55. *Forty-Seventh and Forty-eighth Annual Reports of the Home for Respectable Girls* (New York, 1919), DNYA file #12; Sister Catherine Louise, *House*, p. 78; Community of St. Mary, *Mount Saint Gabriel Series Number One: Historical Papers* (Peekskill, NY: St. Mary's Convent, 1931), p. 57, CSMA; Sister Mary Hilary, *Ten Decades*, pp. 130–32.

56. "Register of the Community of St. John Baptist," CSJB.

57. Sister Mary Hilary, *Ten Decades*, p. 148. In 1906 the Community of St. Mary divided into an eastern and a western province. A 1980 survey of religious orders reported that the eastern division had professed 186 sisters since 1865; the western division had a total membership of 100. Other communities reporting their total membership since founding were: Community of the Transfiguration, 102; Sisterhood of the Holy Nativity, 115; and Society of St. Margaret, 169. Evangeline Thomas, CSJ, ed., *Women Religious History Sources* (New York: R.R. Bowker Company, 1983), pp. 51, 92, 121, 135, 138.

58. All Saints, *As Possessing*, pp. 8–13.

59. *Chronicle of the Church of the Holy Communion, 1901*, GTS.

60. Morgan Dix, *Lectures on the Two Estates: That of the Wedded in the Lord and That of the Single for the Kingdom of Heaven's Sake* (New York: Pott, Young and Cox, 1872), p. 98.

61. "Little Katie Hassett" became Sister Catharine (the administrator of St.

Mary's Hospital), whom sister Mary Hilary described as "astute business woman and hospital administrator, pioneer in pediatrics and thoughtful observer of medical and surgical advances, beloved colleague of New York greatest doctors." Hilary, *Ten Decades*, p. 130. Williams, "Beginnings," p. 364.

62. Barbara Welter, "The Cult of True Womanhood," *American Quarterly* 18 (Summer 1966):150–74.

63. Barry, *From a Convent Tower*, p. 32.

64. "As a business woman, she would have taken a high place among men of that class; thoroughly vested in whatever she needed to know, wisely administering the financial affairs of the Sisterhood, watchful, prudent, forecasting," wrote the Reverend Morgan Dix, the rector of Trinity Parish, Wall Street, about Reverend Mother Harriet Starr Cannon of the Community of St. Mary. Dix, *Harriet Starr Cannon* (New York: Longmans, Green & Company, 1896), p. 95.

65. For an account of the long-term work of Episcopal sisters in an urban ministry, *see* Bridgeman, *Trinity Church Association*.

FIVE: THE CHURCH'S FIRST HIRED WORKERS, 1865–1879

1. Allan Nevins and Milton Halsey Thomas, *The Diary of George Templeton Strong*, vol. 3 (New York: Octagon Books, 1974), p. 239.

2. Ibid., p. 238.

3. Virginia Lieson Brereton and Christa Ressmeyer Klein, "American Women in Ministry: A History of Protestant Beginning Points," in Rosemary Ruether and Eleanor McLaughlin, eds., *Women of Spirit* (New York: Simon and Schuster, 1979), pp. 304–6.

4. Carolyn DeSwarte Gifford, "For God and Native Land," in Hilah F. Thomas and Rosemary Skinner Keller, eds., *Women in New Worlds* (Nashville: Abingdon, 1981), Vol. I, p. 310; Ruth Bordin, *Women and Temperance* (Philadelphia: Temple University Press, 1981).

5. The Freedmen's Commission was made up of thirty-one members—bishops, priests, and laymen—who also served on the Board of Missions. A general agent was charged with administration and fund-raising because the work was not financed by the Board of Missions. In 1874 the Commission's name was changed to Home Mission for Colored People, and four years later the body was dissolved. Minutes of the Freedmen's Aid Commission of the Domestic and Foreign Missionary Society Executive Committee, 1865–1878 (hereafter cited as Freedmen's Commission Minutes), D&FMS Records; Emery, *Century*, pp. 172–75.

6. *The Spirit of Missions* 32 (1867):87 (hereafter cited as *Spirit*).

7. Ibid., p. 858.

8. Oliver Otis Howard to Isabella James, 12 April 1867 and 19 April 1867; G.K. Noble to John Ely, 1 May 1867; Ada W. Smith to Isabella James, 2, 9, 14 March 1867, Isabella Batchelder James Collection, Arthur and Elizabeth Schlesinger Library (hereafter cited as AESL), Cambridge, Massachusetts.

9. Josiah King to Isabella James, 20 April 1867, ibid.

10. Ada W. Smith to Isabella James, 14 March 1867, ibid. Of the twenty-four teachers supported by the Pennsylvania Branch in 1867, thirteen were black and eleven white. *Spirit* 33 (1867):858.

11. Few records of this phase of mission work are available, possibly because the general agent kept an office apart from the Board of Missions. In the D&FMS records payroll records and quarterly reports from the teachers are not included with those of the other domestic missionaries. The primary sources are letters from the teachers

printed in *The Spirit of Missions* and the Minutes of the Freedmen's Aid Commission. Tracing the number of teachers employed is also difficult, because some teachers were sponsored directly by parishes or Freedmen's Aid Auxiliaries and hence never listed as employees of the Commission, e.g., *see* Almira Hesketh's letter: "For several years my salary was paid by Church friends in Hartford, Connecticut, who also furnished a large amount of books and clothing; and that of my associate by friends in New Haven, Connecticut. I may say that all we had in Wilmington—money, books and clothing—came from these two parishes." *Spirit* 37 (1872):511. Elizabeth Knapp, teacher in Wilmington, North Carolina, was supported by a Dorchester, Massachusetts, parish. Freedmen's Commission Minutes, 12 March 1868. *Spirit* 32 (1867):91; *Spirit* 33 (1868):161.

12. *Spirit* 32 (1867):86–89, 858. Freedmen's Commission Minutes.

13. "Annual Report of the Executive Committee of the Commission of Home Missions for Colored People," *Spirit* 38 (1873):795.

14. *Spirit* 32 (1867):861.

15. Ibid., p. 863.

16. Ibid., p. 862.

17. Ibid., p. 861.

18. Ibid., 37 (1872):189.

19. Ada W. Smith to Isabella James, 2 March 1867, AESL.

20. *Spirit* 37 (1872):133.

21. Ibid., p. 313.

22. Ibid., p. 314.

23. Ibid., p. 189.

24. Freedmen's Commission Minutes, 25 January, 19 April, 24 May and 20 September 1866.

25. Ibid., 13 February 1868. The teachers who assisted the Reverend John Clark in Talcott, Virginia, also served "gratuitously." *Spirit* 32 (1867):89. Anne W. Phillips of Boston taught "at her own expense." Jacqueline Jones, *Soldiers of Light and Love: Northern Teachers and Georgia Blacks, 1865–1873* (Chapel Hill: The University of North Carolina Press, 1980), p. 39.

26. Freedmen's Commission Minutes, 2 April 1868.

27. By matching notices of appointment in the Freedmen's Commission Minutes with letters that subsequently appeared in *Spirit,* I have attempted to calculate length of service. Because this method only provides information on those whose letters were published and does not indicate that the women left the year their letters were published, it underrepresents the longevity of the total goup. Among the longer terms were those of Amanda Aiken, Petersburg, Virginia, 1866–1870; Mrs. C.A. Atwell, Petersburg, 1870–1876; Miss Dawson, Charleston, 1865–1872; Mrs. A.C. Hall, Fayetteville, then Wilmington, North Carolina, 1867–1872; Augusta and Catharine Hammond, Raleigh, North Carolina, then Charleston, South Carolina, 1867–1872; Almira Hesketh, Wilmington, 1866–1872; Miss Hicks, Newbern, North Carolina, 1866–1872; Eliza Kennedy, Wilmington, 1867–1871; Kate Savage, Charleston, 1867–1876; S.G. Swetland, Newbern, North Carolina, 1866–1872.

28. *Proceedings of the Board of Missions of Domestic and Foreign Missionary Society of the Protestant Episcopal Church in the United States of America* (hereafter cited as Board of Missions, *Proceedings*) (New York: Board of Missions, 1889), p. 41.

29. *Spirit* 32 (1867):326–27.

30. *Spirit* 34 (1869):756.

31. *Spirit* 37 (1872):508.

32. Ibid., p. 511.

33. Ibid., p. 509.

34. Freedmen's Commission Minutes, October 1877; Emery, *Century*, pp. 174–75; *Spirit* 32 (1867):89, 37 (1872):507–9, 884; G.K. Noble to John Ely, 1 May 1867, Isabella James Collection, AESL.

35. Ada W. Smith to Isabella James, 9 March 1867, AESL.

36. Clergymen who worked in the mission field often faced the same economic insecurity; but they at least had bishops to whom they might complain and the possibility of seeking work in another diocese where economic conditions were better.

37. George Freeman Bragg, *History of the Afro-American Group of the Episcopal Church* (Baltimore: Church Advocate Press, 1922), pp. 132–34.

38. Theodore DuBose Bratton, *Wanted—Leaders! A Study of Negro Development* (New York: Presiding Bishop and Council, 1922), pp. 196–97.

39. For further information about the growth of black congregations, *see* ibid., pp. 198–206.

40. Ibid., pp. 153–55; Bragg, *History*, pp. 133–34, G. Maclaren Brydon, *The Episcopal Church Among the Negroes of Virginia* (Richmond: Virginia Diocesan Library, 1937), pp. 10–12.

41. Bratton, *Wanted*, pp. 152–55.

42. Bragg, *History*, pp. 180–82; Oscar Lieber Mitchell, *In Memoriam Mary Amanda Bechtler*, c. 1918, AEC.

43. Joyce Howard (Cheverly, Maryland) is currently collecting interviews of the women workers trained at the Bishop Tuttle School. For further information about women's involvement in the development of black colleges, *see* Arthur Ben Chitty, "Women and Black Education: Three Profiles," *Historical Magazine of the Protestant Episcopal Church* 52 (June 1983):153–65; Mary Elizabeth Johnston, *Across a Stage: The Extra Clap* (Oberlin: Oberlin College Press, 1982); J. Kenneth Morris, *Elizabeth Evelyn Wright: Founder of Voorhees College* (Sewanee, TN: The University Press, 1983; Tollie L. Caution, "The Protestant Episcopal Church: Policies and Rationale upon which Support of its Negro Colleges Is Predicated," undated clipping from *The Journal of Negro Education*, Henry Knox Sherrill Resource Center, New York City.

44. Mary Maples Dunn, "Saint and Sisters: Congregational and Quaker Women in the Early Colonial Period," in Janet Wilson James, ed., *Women in American Religion* (Philadelphia: University of Pennsylvania Press, 1980), pp. 27–46; Sydney V. James, *A People Among Peoples* (Cambridge: Harvard University Press, 1963).

45. Minutes of the First Meeting of the Society, quoted in "Centennial Year of Female Prayer Book Society," *The Church News of the Diocese of Pennsylvania*, February 1934, p. 152.

46. M.A. DeWolfe Howe, *Memoirs of the Life and Services of the Right Reverend Alonzo Potter* (Philadelphia: J.B. Lippincott and Company, 1871), p. 260.

47. The working-class woman depended "upon her daily labor for her maintenance," and she was paid a salary of $9 per month. The lady of cultivation was presumably a volunteer. William Welsh, *Correspondence between Bishop Potter and William Welsh* (Philadelphia, 1861), p. 5. For more information about women's work in the diocese of Pennsylvania, *see* William Welsh, *Woman's Mission in the Christian Church* (Philadelphia: King & Baird, 1864); Welsh, *Lay Cooperation in St. Mark's Church, Frankford* (Philadelphia: King and Baird, 1861); Hoskins, *Rise*, p. 39.

48. M.A. DeWolfe Howe, *Memorial of William Welsh* (Reading, PA: Owen Printer, 1878), pp. 23–24; "Sudden Death of Mr. William Welsh," unidentified newspaper clipping from file Gaa 46, Historical Society of Pennsylvania, Philadelphia; Charles Morris, ed., *Makers of Philadelphia* (Philadelphia: L.R. Hamersly, 1894), p. 259.

190 A Different Call

49. Mrs. A.T. Twing, *The Woman's Auxiliary to the Board of Missions* (New York: Church Missions House, n.d.), pp. 1–6, pamphlet in Woman's Auxiliary File, DNYA; idem., "Fourth Triennial Report of the Honorary Secretary," Board of Missions, *Proceedings*, 1895, pp. 316–17; Mrs. William Welsh, "Church Work in Large Cities," *Church Work* 1 (1885):301–4; *Domestic Missionary* 1 (15 November 1869):72.

50. William Welsh, *Lay Cooperation: Women Helpers in the Church* (Philadelphia: J.B. Lippincott and Company, 1872); *Third Annual Report of the Bishop Potter Memorial House* (Philadelphia: J. Moore and Sons, 1870), pp. 3–5, Diocese of Pennsylvania Archives (hereafter cited as DPA), Philadelphia.

51. E.A. Washburn, "Address," *Third Annual Report*, pp. 18, 6, DPA.

52. Ibid., pp. 4–6, 10.

53. The 1870 report listed students from Wisconsin, England, Ohio, New York, Massachusetts, and North Carolina as well as Pennsylvania. Ibid., pp. 3–9; Diocese of Pennsylvania, *Convention Journal*, 1900, pp. 36–38.

54. *Third Annual Report*, pp. 6–7.

55. Diocese of Pennsylvania, *Journal*, 1872, pp. 38–40; *Spirit* 40 (1875):331–33.

56. Diocese of Pennsylvania, *Journal*, 1878, pp. 36–38.

57. Diocese of Pennsylvania, *Journal*, 1879, pp. 65–68; William Welsh's death on February 11, 1879, forced the new board to assume total responsibility for fund raising and curriculum planning. "Sudden Death of Mr. William Welsh," unidentified newspaper clipping from file Gaa 46, Historical Society of Pennsylvania, Philadelphia.

58. Minutes of the Board of Council for the Bishop Potter Memorial House for Deaconesses, 1877–1891; DPA; Diocese of Pennsylvania, *Journal*, 1881, pp. 52–53; 1883, pp. 42–43; 1885, pp. 37–38; Registrar of Pennsylvania to Mr. George Lamb, 28 January 1937, Bishop Potter Memorial House Collection, ECA. A new training school, called the Church Training and Deaconess House of the Diocese of Pennsylvania, was founded in 1891. Elizabeth N. Biddle, who had been an associate sister of the Bishop Potter Memorial House, served on the new school's board. Funds in the Bishop Potter Memorial House account appear to have been transferred to the new school. See chapter 8.

59. Mrs. A.T. Twing, "Legislation on Woman's Work in the Church," *Church Work* 4 (1888):270.

60. Allen DuPont Breck, *The Episcopal Church in Colorado, 1860–1963* (Denver: Big Mountain Press, 1963), pp. 81, 125, 287, 289.

61. Ibid., pp. 125, 141–42; *The Living Church*, 24 February 1917.

62. *The Faribault Republican*, 14 October 1981. Special edition prepared by the Episcopal Churchwomen of the Diocese of Minnesota, pp. 1, 4.

63. Virginia Driving Hawk Sneve, *That They May Have Life* (New York: Seabury Press, 1977), pp. 44–45, 128; Gertrude S. Young, *William Joshua Cleveland, 1845–1910*, n.p. n.d., pp. 9–10, 12, 26.

64. Bishop Wiliam H. Hare wrote of a woman who had come to him for confirmation, inspired to do so by "the beautiful lives of the Mission ladies." *Spirit* 40 (1875):333.

65. Bishop William Bacon Stevens, in his convention address of 1883, used these words to testify to women's qualities of "prudence, quietness, intelligence, faithfulness, and self-sacrifice." Diocese of Pennsylvania, *Journal*, 1883, pp. 42–43.

66. Adequate wages and training for women church workers had a few notable male supporters: William Welsh and Bishop Alonzo Potter of Pennsylvania; Bishops Henry Codman Potter of New York, Abram Newkirk Littlejohn of Long Island, and Richard Hooker Wilmer of Alabama were probably the best known. But they were

men with many concerns, only one of which was the development of support for women workers.

SIX: THE WOMAN'S AUXILIARY TO THE BOARD OF MISSIONS, 1872–1900

1. Mary Abbot Emery to parochial secretaries, mid-Lent, 1872. *The Woman's Association, Auxiliary to the Board of Missions* (New York: American Church Press Co., 1872), Emery Collection, AEC.
2. Board of Missions, *Proceedings,* 1872, pp. 9–10.
3. The 1862 resolution urged that the House of Bishops explore ways more fully to incorporate into the Church "women whose hearts God has moved to devote themselves to works of piety and charity." General Convention, *Journal* 1862, p. 142. The subject of woman's work first appeared in the General Convention of 1850, with Bishop Alonzo Potter's motion to establish a plan whereby the services of "intelligent and pious persons of both sexes" might be better used. The motion died in committee. General Convention, *Journal,* p. 132. Similar resolutions were offered at each succeeding convention, but no action was taken. *See* General Convention *Journal,* 1865, pp. 207–8; 1868, pp. 71, 111, 219; 1871, pp. 148–50, 587.
4. Reminiscences of Viola Emery and Dorothy Lyford, 14 April 1980, Oral History Collection, AEC; Margaret A. Tomes, *Julia Chester Emery* (New York: The Woman's Auxiliary to the National Council, 1924); John A. Emery, "From the Forecastle to the Pulpit: The Story of Fifteen Years of Unusual Preparation for a Ministry and of Forty Years in the one Diocese of California," n.d., Diocese of California Archives, San Francisco; Margaret A. Tomes, "Julia Chester Emery," *Spirit* 87 (1922):332–36.
5. A reorganization in 1877 established a Board of Managers—made up of fifteen bishops, fifteen priests, and fifteen laymen—that determined policy between General Conventions. Emery, *Century,* pp. 184–86, 190–91.
6. Mrs. A.T. Twing, *The Prehistoric Days of the Woman's Auxiliary to the Board of Missions,* 1895, DNYA.
7. Emery hoped to make this group the beginning of the nationwide auxiliary, but the "ladies" were not so persuaded. With a program already focused on meeting the needs of domestic missionaries, they were unwilling to widen their concern to include foreign missions. Rather than criticizing this decision, Emery affirmed their right to decide. [She herself continued as a member of this association and eventually was elected corresponding secretary. *Spirit* 39 (1874):806–7.] Mrs. A.T. Twing, *The Woman's Auxiliary to the Board of Missions: A Record of Its Work and a Guide to Its Methods* (New York: Church Missions Publishing House, n.d.), pp. 22–23, AEC.
8. Ibid., p. 37.
9. *Spirit* 39 (1874):125–29.
10. Twing, *Woman's Auxiliary,* p. 38.
11. *See* issues of *Heathen Woman's Friend,* 1869–1895, and *Women's Missionary Friend,* 1896–1940 (Woman's Foreign Missionary Society of the Methodist Episcopal Church, North); *Helping Hand,* 1872–1914 (Woman's Baptist Foreign Mission Society); *Light and Life for Heathen Women,* 1869–1922 (Woman's Board of Missions, Congregational); and *Woman's Missionary Magazine of the United Presbyterian Church,* 1887–1956.
12. *Spirit* 37 (1872):251.
13. Ibid., p. 716.
14. Ibid., p. 782.

15. Mrs. A.T. Twing, "Legislation on Woman's Work in the American Church," *Church Work* 4 (1888–1889):61; Board of Missions, *Proceedings*, 1900, p. 271.

16. Women had been appointed to serve as matrons or teachers but without the title of missionary. *Spirit* 45 (1880):242; Julia Chester Emery, *Century*, p. 200.

17. *Spirit* 45 (1880):482.

18. In 1874 the Auxiliary began paying $50 per year for insurance on each foreign missionary. Coverage apparently was haphazard, however, for in 1904 Bishop Ingle of Hankow requested that all his missionaries be covered. His request prompted the women to extend the coverage not only to his but to all other hitherto uncovered clergy. "The Foreign Missionaries' Insurance Fund," *Spirit* 69 (1904):55. Julia C. Emery, "Eighth Annual Report of the Woman's Auxiliary to the Board of Missions," *Spirit* 45 (1880):481; Julia C. Emery, "Triennial Report of the Woman's Auxiliary to the Board of Missions, 1886–1889," *Spirit* 54 (1889):446; General Convention, *Journal*, 1889, p. 569.

19. *Whittaker's Church Almanac* (New York: Thomas Whittaker, 1899), pp. 296–307; *Spirit* 42 (1877):52, 178; *Spirit* 54 (1889):416, 428–29.

20. According to Episcopal Church terminology, a missionary bishop is one whose jurisdiction (district) receives substantial financial aid from the national Church. Emery, *Century*, pp. 360–68.

21. J.L. Tucker to M.A. Twing, 5 February 1883, Emery Collection, AEC.

22. Henry B. Whipple to M.A. Twing, 27 July 1898, Emery Collection, AEC.

23. Peter T. Rowe to M.A. Twing, 17 July 1898, Emery Collection, AEC. Elizabeth Biddle of Philadelphia played a similar role of encouragement and support to Bishop William A. Hare of South Dakota. *See* M.A. DeWolfe Howe, *The Life and Labors of Bishop Hare* (New York: Sturgis and Walson Company, 1911), pp. 13, 19, 33–34, 140–42, 149, 158.

24. Board of Missions, *Proceedings*, 1872, p. 9; William Wilkinson, *A History of the General Convention of the Protestant Episcopal Church in the United States Held in Gethsemane Church, Minneapolis in October, 1895* (Minneapolis: William Wilkinson, 1895), pp. 326–44.

25. Ida Whittemore Soule, "Memoir," 1932. Manuscript in the possession of the Reverend George Blackman, Church of Our Saviour, Brookline, Massachusetts.

26. Julia Emery to Charles Emery, 4 May 1876, Emery Collection, AEC.

27. Margaret A. Tomes, "Julia Chester Emery," *Spirit* 87 (1922):80–85, 332–36.

28. Dr. A.T. Twing to Margaret Theresa Emery, 4 May n.y., Emery Collection, AEC. The sisters lived in various boarding houses until 1891, when Helen and their mother Susan Hilton Emery moved to New York. In 1911, Julia, Theresa and Helen moved to a home they built in Scarsdale. Tomes, *Julia*, pp. 76, 114.

29. M.A. Twing to "My dear people," 10 March 1880; M.A. Twing to mother, n.d., mentions calls from Miss Corneila Jay, Mrs. John Jacob Astor, Mrs. Wetmore, Mrs. Sidney Webster, and Miss Stewart Brown. Several undated letters from Charlotte Augusta Astor discuss gifts to various projects. In one, it is reported that the Astors gave Mrs. Twing $400 "with the hope that my own and Mr. Astor's gift may be dispensed under your own personal direction always." Augusta Astor to Mrs. Twing, Thursday n.y., Emery Collection, AEC. *See* "Society of the Royal Law" in chapter 7.

30. In a letter to Julia Emery, 23 October 1883, Mary Abbot Twing indicated that she had chosen the title "honorary secretary" to free herself from responsibility for "boxes, contributions, parish meetings, diocesan organization, etc. with which I want to have no concern." It appears she also sought support for her appointment to this position from many wealthy women in the Society of the Royal Law network. Among her papers is a carefully preserved envelope marked "Nothing that is excellent

can be wrought suddenly." It contained a copy of the resolution naming her as honorary secretary and a list of names and addresses of the following people, most of whom appear frequently in correspondence about the Society: Mrs. H.A. Neely, Portland, Maine; Mrs. John B. Stebbins, Springfield, Massachusetts; Mrs. T.S. Rumney, Germantown, Pennsylvania; Mrs. William Welsh, Miss Mary Coles, Mrs. William Bacon Stevens, and the Misses Biddle, Philadelphia, Pennsylvania; Mrs. B.H. Paddock, Boston, Massachusetts, and Mrs. S.M. Emery (her mother), Newburyport, Massachusetts. Emery Collection, AEC; Emery, *Century,* p. 203.

31. Ibid., pp. 209–12, 233.

32. Emery, "Fifteenth Annual Report of the Woman's Auxiliary to the Board of Missions," Board of Missions, *Proceedingg,* 1886, p. 132.

33. Mrs. A.T. Twing, "Report of the Honorary Secretary of the Woman's Auxiliary to the Board of Missions on the Training and Systematized Service of Women in the Work of the Church," ibid., pp. 157–60.

34. Resolution of the Board of Missions, October 1886, quoted in Emery, *Century,* p. 212.

35. Mrs. Twing had already organized several diocesan educational meetings for churchworkers. They were held in Philadelphia (February 1884, February 1885), New York City (January 1885), and Milwaukee (September 1885). *Church Work* 1 (1886–1887):55–57. The offering from New York and a grant from Charlotte Augusta Astor helped fund the periodical *Church Work,* which Mrs. Twing edited and mailed to women workers. *See* further information in chapter 7. "Prospectus," *Church Work* 1 (1885–1886):2; "Extracts from the Editor's Report as Honorary Secretary of the Woman's Auxiliary to the Board of Missions, October, 1889," final page in bound volume, *Church Work* 4 (1888–1889); Henry Codman Potter to Mrs. Twing, 5 September 1895, Emery Collection.

36. The designated gift or "special" enabled a local auxiliary to control the distribution of its funds, but the national office could only recommend that some auxiliary fund a given project.

37. Soule, "Memoir," pp. 193–95.

38. Frances M. Young, *Thankfulness Unites: The History of the United Thank Offering* (Cincinnati, OH: Forward Movement Publications, 1979), p. 8.

39. The letter signed by "a member of the Auxiliary" appeared in *Spirit* 54 (1889):362.

40. Soule, "Memoir," p. 193.

41. "If a Canon of Deaconesses . . . could be cordially approved and adopted by both Houses, . . . no doubt many women would offer themselves for service, under a rule thus clearly set forth, who now hesitate, uncertain as to what the Church really wishes of them, or in what way she desires them to work for her." Mrs. A.T. Twing, "Legislation on Woman's Work in the American Church," *Church Work* 4 (1888–1889):356.

42. Mrs. A.T. Twing, "Report of the Honorary Secretary," *Spirit* 54 (1889):22; Henry Codman Potter to Mrs. Twing, 18 March 1884, 5 September 1885, 19 August 1886; William Bissell to Mrs. Twing, 12 September 1886; Emery Collection, AEC.

43. *See* chapter 7. General Convention, *Journal,* 1889, pp. 108, 115, 135, 143, 378, 381.

44. Young, *Thankfulness,* pp. 8–9.

45. Board of Missions, *Proceedings,* 1900, pp. 66–75, 171, 175, 182, 191–92, 198. This number includes only those women listed as missionary staff members. There were also women, such as Anna and Fanny M. Perry in Japan, who served without remuneration, and missionary wives whose unpaid contributions were exten-

sive. *The Churchman,* 19 October 1889, p. 451; Wilkinson, *General Convention,* p. 318.

46. Young, *Thankfulness,* pp. 13–19; *A Study of the United Offering,* U.O. Leaflet No. 19, n.d. (c. 1910), United Thank Offering File in PECUSA Publications Collection, AEC.

47. Board of Missions, *Proceedings,* 1900, p. 36.

48. Two figures are listed. The "Report of the Board of Managers" indicates that $104,650 was contributed by the Woman's Auxiliary through the Board's treasury. The "Report of the Woman's Auxiliary" lists $42,444 as money under appropriation and $62,022 as specials passing through the treasury of the Board, for a total of $104,466. Board of Missions, *Proceedings,* pp. 34, 271.

49. Ibid., p. 41.

50. Ibid., p. 271.

51. Almost half of the amount contributed by men, $200,000 of $468,165 was contributed by one man, William H. Vanderbilt. If his contribution is disregarded, the women's share of the total appears even more impressive. Ibid., pp. 240–57.

52. Julia Emery, "Twenty-first Annual Report of the Woman's Auxiliary to the Board of Missions," Board of Missions, *Proceedings,* 1892, pp. 201–2.

53. Ibid., p. 205.

54. Ibid., p. 480. The Board of Missions approved the action, "it being understood that the function of these committees should be advisory."

55. Allen du Pont Breck, *The Episcopal Church in Colorado* (Denver: Big Mountain Press, 1963), p. 79; Emery, *Century,* pp. 265, 384; *Spirit* 57 (1892):476–81; Margaret A. Tomes, *Julia Chester Emery* (New York: The Woman's Auxiliary to the National Council, 1924), p. 62.

56. "Report of the Committee on Missionary Workers," *Spirit* 60 (1895):541; *Spirit* 62 (1897):38; *Spirit* 64 (1899):79–81.

57. "Report of the Committee on Missionary Workers," *Spirit* 64 (1899):658.

58. Tomes, *Julia,* pp. 68–70; Emery, *Century,* p. 236; "Eighteenth Annual Report of the Woman's Auxiliary to the Board of Missions," *Proceedings,* 1889, p. 170.

59. Ann Harding Robinson, *Morning Glories and Evensong: A Century of the Episcopal Churchwomen in Connecticut* (Hartford: Church Missions Publishing Company, 1981), pp. 7–8; H.F. Giraud, "Report of the Committee on Missionary Publications," *Spirit* 60 (1895):540–41; *The Missionary Leaflet,* Series I, 1896; Series II, Series III, published by the Junior Auxiliary Publishing Company, Miss Mary E. Beach, Secretary.

60. Tomes, *Julia,* pp. 68–70.

61. Letitia Townsend, "Church Work Reference Libraries," *Church Work* 3 (1887):261–63; Julia Emery, "Fifteenth Annual Report," Board of Missions, *Proceedings,* 1886, pp. 133–34.

62. Julia Emery, "A Letter to Diocesan and Parochial Officers on Lenten Work," n.d., c. 1895, Emery Collection, AEC.

63. Emery, *Century,* p. 298.

64. Victoria Scott Gary, Mary Lou Johnson, and Elizabeth W. Mundy, *The Order of the Daughters of the King: In Celebration of One Hundred Years of Prayer and Service, 1885–1985* (Atlanta: The Order of the Daughters of the King, 1985), p. 14.

65. Ibid., pp. 1–3.

66. Ibid., pp. 52–67.

67. Ibid., 67–68.

68. Minutes of the Church Periodical Club, 1892–1897, Church Periodical Club Office (hereafter referred to as CPCO), 815 Second Avenue, New York City.

69. Minutes of the Annual Meetings, 17 November 1897, 16 November 1898,

and 15 November 1899, in Minutes of the Church Periodical Club, 1897–1905, CPCO; Julia Emery, "Twenty-ninth Annual Report of the Woman's Auxiliary to the Board of Missions," Board of Missions, *Proceedings*, 1900, p. 263.

70. Special Church Periodical Club Issue of *The Witness*, 18 March 1948.

71. E.M. Edson, "The Girls' Friendly Society," *Church Work* 1 (1885–1886):45.

72. Alida G. Radcliffe, "The Girls' Friendly Society in America," *Church Work* 1 (1885–1886):73.

73. "Notes for Lawyer in Connection with a Reply to the English Solution," Records of the Girls' Friendly Society, RG 134, pp. 3–25, AEC.

74. E.M. Edson, "The First Ten Years of the Girls' Friendly Society for America," *Church Work* 4 (1888–1889):78–83.

75. Mrs. A.T. Twing, "Third Triennial Report of the Honorary Secretary," Board of Missions, *Proceedings*, 1892, p. 260.

SEVEN: DEVELOPING CHURCH WORK AS A
PROFESSION FOR WOMEN, 1870–1889

1. Robert H. Wiebe, *The Search for Order, 1877–1920* (New York: Hill and Wang, 1967), pp. 111–32.

2. "The Form and Manner of Making Deacons," *The Book of Common Prayer*, 1792.

3. Ibid.

4. "Services for the Admission of the Deaconesses," *Church Work* 2 (1886–1887):277.

5. From 1860 through 1885, for example, 678 men were ordained deacons and 591 men were ordained priests; thus, only 87 of the deacons were not subsequently ordained priests over that 25-year period. Of that 87, some probably left the diaconate and others died before being ordained priest. "Comparative Statistics of the Episcopal Church, U.S.A.," *The Episcopal Church Annual* (New York: Morehouse-Barlow, 1976), p. 18. Eighteen sixty through 1885 were the only years during which the number of ordinations of priests and deacons were published.

6. Acts of the Apostles 5:2.

7. 1 Timothy 3:11; *The Ministry of Women: A Report by a Committee Appointed by His Grace the Lord Archbishop of Canterbury* (London: Society for Promoting Christian Knowledge, 1919), p. 4.

8. An early regulation for the distribution of the offertory, for example, provided that bishops receive four shares, presbyters three, deacons two, and deaconesses one. N.a., "On the Revival of Deaconesses in the Early Church," *The Monthly Packet*, November 1878, reprinted in *Church Work* 1 (1885–1886):68.

9. Owing to abuses, two French provincial councils of the fifth century passed canons forbidding the consecration of any new deaconesses. *Ministry of Women*, pp. 5–15.

10. Ethel Panton and Dorothy Batho, *The Order of Deaconesses, Past and Present* (London: Student Christian Movement Press, 1937), p. 22.

11. John Malcolm Forbes Ludlow, *Women's Work in the Church: Historic Notes on Deaconesses and Sisterhoods* (London: Alexander Strahan, 1865), p. 206.

12. Panton and Batho, *Order*, p. 23. American priests were aware of the English actions. In this sermon "What is a Deaconess?" preached at St. George's Church, 24 April 1887, the Reverend William S. Rainsford quoted the above definition and referred to its approval by the English bishops. *Church Work* 2 (1886–1887):249.

13. *Deaconesses in the Church of England* (London: Griffith and Farran, 1880), pp. 18–21.

14. Panton and Batho, *Order*, pp. 23–24; V. Nelle Bellamy, "Participation of Women in the Public Life of the Church from Lambeth Confrence 1867–1978," *The Historical Magazine of the Protestant Episcopal Church* 51 (1982):88; *Ministry of Women*, pp. 21–28.

15. Ayres, *Muhlenberg*, p. 188. In England, also, both Ludlow and Howson asserted that the success of Dr. Fliedner's work inspired Anglicans to attempt similar organizations. Ludlow, *Women's Work*, pp. 201–6; Howson, *Deaconesses*, pp. 70–85. Charlotte Ransford, one of the most influential of the English deaconesses, urged that the Anglican Church follow the Kaiserswerth model of churchwide economic support for deaconess institutions. "Life and Work of a Deaconess in England," *Church Work* 4 (1888–1889):290.

16. Mrs. A.T. Twing, "Report of the Honorary Secretary," Board of Missions, *Proceedings*, 1898, p. 296.

17. Diocese of Long Island, *Convention Journal*, 1871, p. 14.

18. Henry Codman Potter, *The Gates of the East: A Winter in Egypt and Syria* (New York: E.P. Dutton, 1877), pp. 22–29.

19. Mrs. A.T. Twing, "Report of the Honorary Secreaty," Board of Missions, *Proceedings*, 1892, p. 251. *See also* "Deaconesses in the Mission Field," *Spirit* 30 (1865):113–15; William Reed Huntington, "The Deaconess," *Church Work* 4 (1888–1889):12–13.

20. Cecilia Robinson, *The Ministry of Deaconesses* (London: Methuen and Company, 1898); "A Short History of the Appleton Church Home," n.p. n.d., Deaconess Collection, AEC; William Joseph Barnds, *The Episcopal Church in Nebraska* (Omaha: Omaha Printing Company, 1960), p. 140; Henry Wheeler, *Deaconesses Ancient and Modern* (New York: Hunt and Eaton, 1889), pp. 243–48; Diocese of Pennsylvania, *Convention Journal*, 1879, pp. 65–68; "Deaconesses" and "The Work of Christian Women," *The Diocese* [of Massachusetts], October 1875; William Freeman Galpin, *The Huntington Years* (Boonville, NY: Willard Press, 1968), p. 66.

21. Henry Codman Potter, ed., *Sisterhoods and Deaconesses* (New York: E.P. Dutton and Company, 1873), p. 119.

22. Robinson, *Ministry*, pp. 119–21.

23. "History of the Appleton Church Home," AEC.

24. Galpin, *Huntington*, p. 66; Diocese of Central New York, *Convention Journal*, 1877, pp. 153–54; idem., *Convention Journal*, 1880, p. 155.

25. *See* chapter 5. Board of Council for the Bishop Potter Memorial House for Deaconesses, "Minute Book, 1878–1891," 18 June 1877, DPA.

26. *The Form of Admitting Deaconesses to Their Office According to the Use of the Diocese of Long Island*, 1872, GTS.

27. Barbara Kelley, "The Revival of Deaconesses on Long Island," May 1978. Unpublished term paper in possession of the author; John W. Davis, *Dominion in the Sea* (Hempstead, NY: The Georgin Foundation, 1977), pp. 48, 84.

28. Order of Deaconesses of the Diocese of Maryland, "Form of Setting Apart Those to be Admitted to the Order of Deaconess," Potter, *Sisterhoods*, p. 120; Diocese of Long Island, *Form*.

29. Potter, *Sisterhoods*, pp. 123–24.

30. Diocese of Long Island, *Form*.

31. Potter, *Sisterhoods*, p. 135; "Services for the Admission of the Deaconesses," St. George's Church, New York City, 1 May 1887, *Church Work* 2 (1886–1887):276–78.

32. Frances Densmore, "A Missionary Journey of 1893," *Minnesota History*,

vol. 20, pp. 310–13; "Miss Sybil Carter, Deaconess," *The Fairbault Republican,* 14 October 1981, p. 4.

33. Mrs. Martha C. Vivion to Deaconess West, 29 April 1948, Deaconess Collection, AEC.

34. General Convention, *Journal,* 1871, pp. 27, 148–50, 172–74, 208; George Hodges, *Henry Codman Potter, Seventh Bishop of New York* (New York: The Macmillan Company, 1915), pp. 75–79.

35. Sister Mary Hilary, *Ten Decades of Praise* (Racine, WI: DeKovan Foundation, 1965), pp. 21–31.

36. Diocese of Long Island, *Convention Journal,* 1871, p. 114; Robinson, *Ministry,* pp. 119–21.

37. John Wallace Suter, *Life and Letters of William Reed Huntington* (New York: The Century Company, 1925), pp. 97–100, 234–39; Breck, *Episcopal Church,* p. 66.

38. *See* chapter 4. Other members of the committee were the Reverend Joseph H. Smith, Samuel B. Ruggles, and S. Corning Judd.

39. General Convention, *Journal,* 1874, pp. 64–65.

40. The galleries were filled "by an audience of which a large majority were ladies." As the meeting began, delegates felt it was improper to conduct business in the church nave with the high altar prominently behind the speaker's platform. So a curtain was ordered to be constructed across the chancel, but "though the women worked at it all night," by morning it was not quite finished. *New York Times,* 9 October 1874.

41. William Welsh, Letter to the Editor, ibid.

42. *New York Times,* 28 October 1874.

43. General Convention, *Journal,* 1874, pp. 180, 188; *New York Times,* 29 October 1874.

44. General Convention, *Journal,* 1877, pp. 91, 151, 165–66, 170–73, 261–62; 1880, pp. 23, 78–80, 118–20, 188–89, 196–97. In 1883 the Committee on Canons of the House of Deputies finally concluded that "it it is inexpedient, at this time, to adopt any legislation on the subject of organized religious bodies." General Convention, *Journal,* 1883, pp. 13, 20, 22, 63, 184–85.

45. Mrs. A.T. Twing, "Legislation on Women's Work in the American Church," *Church Work* 4 (1888–1889):269–72. By 1889 Mrs. Twing listed twenty religious societies, two for men and eighteen for women, at work in the Episcopal Church. Twing, "Organized Religious Societies Within the Church," *Church Work* 4 (1888–1889):209–12. In a later article, she listed five other groups: the Order of Deaconesses in Nebraska (1874), the Sisterhood of St. John (1867), and the Sisterhood of St. Paul (1877) from the Diocese of Maryland, the Sisterhood of St. Elizabeth in northern New Jersey, and the Sisterhood of the Bishop Potter Memorial House, Philadelphia (1867). Ibid., p. 269.

46. For one such order, the Sisters of Consolation, *see* Joyce L. White, "Putting Together the Puzzle," in Sandra Hughes Boyd, ed., *Cultivating Our Roots* (Cincinnati: The Episcopal Women's History Project, 1984), pp. 41–52.

47. Thomas M. Peters, "Paper," *Papers and Speeches, Tenth Church Congress* (New York: Thomas Whittaker Publisher, 1886), pp. 174–82.

48. William Crosswell Doane and Calbraith B. Perry, "Papers," ibid., pp. 183–93.

49. Ibid., pp. 174, 178, 181, 193.

50. A. St. John Chambre, "Address," ibid., pp. 194–96.

51. Much of information on the Society of the Royal Law is found in handwritten memos and printed pamphlets in the Emery Collection, AEC. *See* particularly "His-

torical Paper Prepared and Read by Mrs. A.T. Twing at the First and Second Conferences held in New York, February 9th and February 27, 1882." *See also* "The Society of the Royal Law," *Church Work* 2 (1886–1887):166–68; Frederic Dan Huntington, "Spiritual Helps and Failures in Keeping the Royal Law," sermon preached at the Church of the Holy Communion, New York City, 11 October 1880, and reprinted in *Church Work* 1 (1885–1886):287–94.

52. Mrs. A.T. Twing, "Services for Churchwomen," *Church Work* 1 (1885–1886):28–32.

53. *The Society of the Royal Law*, pamphlet #1, Church Work Reprints, n.d., Emery Collection, AEC.

54. Among the original members were Mrs. John Jacob Astor, Mrs. H. Aldrich, Mrs. Bayard Cutting, Mrs. Morgan Dix, Mrs. Hamilton Fish, Mrs. John Jay (and her daughter, E.C.), Mrs. J. Pierpont Morgan, Mrs. Alfred Ogden, Mrs. Henry Codman Potter, Mrs. Alonzo Potter, Miss Catharine Wolfe, and Mrs. Cornelius Vanderbilt. Twing, "Historical Paper." Other materials, including "Leaflet No. 1," 1880, are in the Emery papers belonging to Mrs. Dorothy Lyford and Violet Emery, Cambridge, Massachusetts.

55. Mrs. A.T. Twing, "The First Massachusetts Conference of Churchwomen with the Clergy of the Diocese," *Church Work* 4 (1888–1889):82.

56. Mrs. S.I.J. Schereschewsky, "Missionary Work and the Training of Missionary Workers," *Church Work* 4 (1888–1889):96–98.

57. Charlotte S. Ransford, "Church Work, Christian Work, Missionary Work: How and Where Can Training Be Had by Those Who Desire It?" ibid., p. 99.

58. Pelham Williams, "Church Workers and Their Training," ibid., pp. 93–96.

59. Twing, "Historical Paper" and "Churchwomen Aided in Obtaining Church Work or Other Employment," n.d., c. 1885, Emery Collection, AEC.

60. Mrs. A.T. Twing, "Report of the Honorary Secretary," October 1889; quoted in *Church Work* 4 (1888–1889):264.

61. Mrs. A.T. Twing, "Legislation on Woman's Work in the American Church," *Church Work* 4 (1888–1889):356. *See also* H.Y. Satterly, "The Proposed Canon on Sisterhoods and Deaconesses," 4:153–60; "On the Revival of Deaconesses in the English Church," 1:67–70; Lutheran Church Review, "Life and Training of a Deaconess," 1:94–97; William S. Rainsford, "What Is a Deaconess?" 2:249–78; A.N. Littlejohn, "The Office and Duties of a Deaconess," 3:63–68; W.R. Huntington, "Woman's Service of Christ," 3:123–28; "Mildmay Deaconesses and Their Work," 4:101–5; 4:200–4, 234–37, 258–62, and 289–93.

62. I base my contention that Twing organized the campaign on a series of letters from Henry Codman Potter: "I *preached your sermon.* . . . So you see, my dear, you have not thought and written quite in vain," 18 March 1884; "Your plan strikes me as in every way timely and practicable," 5 September 1885; and the above quotation, 19 August 1886. *See also* William Bissell to Mrs. Twing, 12 September 1886.

63. In an impassioned sermon, he urged the passage of the deaconess canon: "Give . . . to women who are willing to consecrate themselves to the great work of the service of man . . . the protection of position, give her the open acknowledgment of the Church, give her the shield of a profession." William S. Rainsford, "What Is a Deaconess?" *Church Work* 2 (1886–1887):252.

64. Henry Anstice, *History of St. George's Church* (New York: Harper and Brothers, 1911), pp. 316, 326, 330–33, 386, 481. Anstice lists eleven women workers for the period between 1883, when Rainsford arrived, and 1887, when Deaconess Forneret began her work. St. George's Church, *Yearbook*, 1902, p. 22. *See also* William S. Rainsford, *The Story of a Varied Life: An Autobiography* (Garden City: Doubleday, Page and Company, 1922).

65. Services for the Admission of the Deaconesses," *Church Work* 2 (1886–1887):277.

66. "The Form and Manner of Making, Ordaining, and Consecrating Bishops, Priests, and Deacons," *The Book of Common Prayer* (New York: Thomas Nelson and Sons, 1896), p. 512.

67. "Services," *Church Work* 2 (1886–1887):276–78.

68. George Wolfe Shinn, *King's Handbook of Notable Episcopal Churches in the United States* (Boston: Moses King Corporation, 1889), pp. 62–63; Suter, *Huntington*, p. 239.

69. W.R. Huntington to Catherine Meredith, 22 April 1887, 10 February 1888, ibid., pp. 266–68. Meredith was a wealthy Philadelphia resident who continued to be involved in Church-related social work through membership in the Christian Social Union. C.S.U. publication *The Monthly Leader*, June 1902, p. 1.

70. Mrs. A.T. Twing, "Woman's Auxiliary," *The Churchman* 19 October 1889, p. 449.

71. General Convention, *Journal*, 1889, pp. 27, 108–9, 134–35, 276, 334, 378.

72. *The Churchman*, 2 November 1889, p. 39.

EIGHT: THE ORDER OF DEACONESSES, 1889–1900

1. Mary Abbot Twing to Stanley, 7 May 1890, Emery Collection, AEC.

2. The original trustees were: Huntington, Gherardi Davis, Frances A.L. Haven, Dan P. Kingsford, Anne L. Langdon, F.C. Moore, Catherine A. Newbold, Blanche Potter, Mary R. Prime, Edward C. Sampson, Catharine Allen Sullivan, and Spencer Trask. Certificate of Incorporation of the New York Training School for Deaconesses, 9 May 1891, New York Training School for Deaconesses Collection (hereafter NYTSFD Collection), DNYA. The women generally remained on the board for longer terms than the men and attended board meetings more regularly. Minutes of the Board of the New York Training School of Deaconesses, ibid.

3. "History of the New York Training School for Deaconesses," untitled typescript, n.a., box #20, NYTSFD Collection, DNYA.

4. Minutes of the Board of the New York Training School for Deaconesses, 7 May 1891, 10 November 1892, 12 May 1894, NYTSFD Collection, DNYA.

5. Charles N. Shepard, "The New York Training School for Deaconesses, 1890–1942," 8 December 1943, NYTSFD Collection, DNYA.

6. New York Training School for Deaconesses, *Yearbook* 1900–1901, 1918, pp. 24–28, NYTSFD Collection, box 9, DNYA.

7. Susan Knapp to Mary, 20 March 1927, Deaconess Collection, AEC.

8. Susan Knapp, student file, NYTSFD records, DNYA; Susan Knapp, "Autobiographical Sketch," n.d., Deaconess History Research Project, Episcopal Divinity School (hereafter as EDS); "History of the New York Training School for Deaconesses," n.a., n.d., typescript in NYTSFD Collection, DNYA.

9. Knapp, "Autobiographical," EDS.

10. Ibid.

11. Unsigned letter to "My dear Bishop," Farnham Castle, Surrey, 11 May 1896, included the list of recommendations from the meeting and indicated that ten bishops, ten deaconesses, and ten wardens had been present. Randall Thomas Davidson Collection, Lambeth Palace Library, London.

12. *See* correspondence between Deaconess Knapp and Cecilia Robinson, Isabella Fileune, and Edith and Randall Thomas Davidson, 1900–1918, Deaconess History Research Project, EDS. For information about the English deaconesses, *see*

Panthon and Batho, *Order*; Cecilia Robinson, *The Ministry of Deaconesses* (London: Methune & Company, 1898), pp. 76–118; and *The Ministry of Women* (London: Society for Promoting Christian Knowledge, 1919), pp. 24–28, 137–44, 182–200.

13. Susan Knapp, "Characteristics Most Necessary for Deaconesses," typescript, n.d., Deaconess Collection, AEC. Minutes of the Board of Trustees of the New York Training School for Deaconesses, 5 November 1903, NYTSFD Collection, DNYA.

14. Ibid., 1 November 1900.

15. Ibid., 2 May 1901, 5 November 1903.

16. Susan Knapp to Silas McBee, 6 September 1904; Church Students' Missionary Association Minutes, ibid.

17. In 1897 the trustees of the Cathedral of St. John the Divine approved a gift of land on the cathedral grounds for the New York Training School for Deaconesses. Three years later the Sisterhood of the Good Shepherd disbanded as a separate order and transferred its financial assets to the New York Training School for Deaconesses, provided that the school assume perpetual care of the four remaining sisters. With these funds a house at 230 East 12th Street was purchased, to be used for housing until the move uptown. In 1905 a neighboring house (226 East 12th St.) was purchased, with a $30,000 donation from Miss Campbell, to enlarge residential space. A bequest from Charles C. Tiffany in memory of his wife, Julia Wheeler Tiffany, provided funds for the construction of the school on the cathedral grounds. The school opened in the new location in December 1910. "History of the New York Training School for Deaconesses," pp. 1–3, NYTSFD Collection; Agreement between the Sisterhood of the Good Shepherd and the New York Training School for Deaconesses, 23 January 1900, Sisterhood of the Good Shepherd Collection, box #80, DNYA.

18. Susan Knapp, "Characteristics Most Necessary for Deaconesses," Deaconess History Research Project, EDS; a long letter from Knapp to "Anna," 24 October 1933, analyzed her experience as dean, ibid.

19. Members of the household of St. Faith's to the Trustees of the New York Training School for Deaconesses, 19 December 1916, Susan Knapp file, Box #17, NYTSFD Collection, DNYA.

20. Mary Clelland West, "Susan Trevor Knapp, A Recollection," ibid. *See also* Vivian H. Johnston to William E. Gardner, n.d., ibid.

21. "The Pan-Anglican Congress" by our special commissioners, *The Church Times*, n.d., clipping in Knapp Collection, Deaconess History Research Project, EDS.

22. Susan T. Knapp, "Deaconesses: Their Qualification and Status," Pan-Anglican Congress, *Official Report* (London: Society for Promoting Christian Knowledge, 1908), vol. 4, pp. 10–11.

23. "The Congress," *The Church Times*, 26 June 1908, clipping in Knapp Collection, Deaconess History Research Project, EDS.

24. Susan T. Knapp, "The Relation of Social Service to Christianity," in *The Church Congress Journal* (New York: Thomas Whitaker, 1913), pp. 26–33.

25. Minutes of the Board of the New York Training School for Deaconesses, volume 2, January 1909, NYTSFD Collection, DNYA.

26. Knapp, "The Relation," p. 31.

27. Howard Caswell Smith to Dean Grosvenor, 1 December 1915; Report of the Committee to Consider the Duties of the Dean of the Training School, May 1916, NYTSFD Collection, DNYA.

28. Howard Caswell Smith, ibid.

29. Report of the Committee to Consider the Duties of the Dean of the Training School, May 1916, NYTSFD Collection, DNYA.

30. "A Letter from Dean Knapp," *New York Training School for Deaconesses Alumnae Bulletin,* January 1917.

31. Gardner was a priest who worked in New York for the General Board of Religious Education. He served for three years as warden, then resigned to become executive secretary of religious education on the newly formed National Council of the Episcopal Church. Dahlgren and Gillespy appear to have become the effective heads of the school (as Knapp had been), calling on the successive wardens appointed by the Board for largely ceremonial duties.

32. Susan Knapp to Romula Dahlgren, 23 March 1932. Knapp had been paying $140 per year to keep the mortgage on Deaconess Wilkie's House and wrote to ask the Deaconess Retirement Fund to take over those payments.

33. James De Wolf Perry, "Address Given at the Memorial Service for Miss Coles," Deaconess History Research Project, EDS; Deaconess Robinson to Susan Knapp, 8 September 1902, ibid.; Mrs. A.T. Twing, "Third Triennial Report of the Honorary Secretary," Board of Missions, *Proceedings,* 1892, p. 251; "Historical Sketch of the Church Training and Deaconess House," Church Training and Deaconess House, *Newsletter,* July 1920, pp. 9–13.

34. Diocese of Pennsylvania, *Convention Journal,* 1891, pp. 58–61. The members of the Board of Council were George C. Thomas, C.C. Harrison, W.M. Merrick, John Ashurst, Jr., and R. Francis Wood. The members of the Board of Managers were: Frances E. Bennett, E.N. Biddle, E.C. McVickar, Esther P. Aertsen, Anne Buchanan, Agnes Irwin, Helen L. Parish, Annie Fassitt, Mrs. Effingham Perot, and Anne N. Sanders.

35. Deaconess Gertrude Stewart, "Epiphany, 1931 to Mark the Church Training and Deaconess School's Fortieth Anniversary," *The Church News of the Diocese of Pennsylvania,* pp. 18–19,. n.d., clipping in the Deaconess Training School file, DPA.

36. *Second Annual Report of the Church Training and Deaconess House of the Diocese of Pennsylvania* (Philadelphia: William F. Fell and Company, 1893), Deaconess Collection, ECA; Diocese of Pennsylvania, *Convention Journal,* 1892, pp. 63–65; 1893, pp. 70–71, 304.

37. Diocese of Pennsylvania, *Journal,* 1891, pp. 58–61.

38. Stewart, "Epiphany," p. 19; *Twenty-sixth Annual Report of the Church Training and Deaconess House in the Diocese of Pennsylvania* (Philadelphia: William F. Fell and Company, 1916), pp. 8–10.

39. Diocese of Pennsylvania, *Convention Journal,* 1893, p. 304.

40. Ibid., 1894, p. 100.

41. Ibid., 1893, p. 70.

42. *Tenth Annual Report of the Church Training and Deaconess House of the Diocese of Pennsylvania* (Philadelphia: William F. Fell and Company, 1901), pp. 30–31.

43. Bethany Institute was chartered in 1890 in Virginia "for educating women in the care of the poor and the sick, the religious training of the young . . . and the work of moral reformation." Though funds were raised for the project, it appears as if only a few women were trained at a local orphanage. Diocese of Virginia, *Convention Journal,* 1890, pp. 27–29; 1894, pp. 21–25; 1905, p. 85; 1907, p. 88; "A Deaconess Training School in Virginia," *The Southern Churchman,* 14 May 1904. The Minnesota Deaconess Home had nine students and in 1899 had already trained three deaconesses. *Spirit* 64 (1899):77.

44. Diocese of California, *Convention Journal,* 1891, p. 77; Louis Childs Sanford, *The Province of the Pacific* (Philadelphia: The Church Historical Society, 1949), pp. 106–7.

45. Ibid., pp. 104–9.

46. William R. Huntington, "The Deaconess," *Church Work* 4 (1888–1889):16.

47. Because of the problems with some deaconesses who wanted to marry, the Deaconess Institute in Rochester raised the minimum age for entrance to thirty and added the requirement that candidates do field work in a parish before being admitted to the order. Deaconess Isabella Fileune to Susan Knapp, 19 September 1900; Susan Knapp, "Deaconesses: Their Qualification and Status," Pan-Anglican Congress, *Official Report* (London: Society for Promoting Christian Knowledge, 1908), vol. 4, section C, pp. 10–14; Susan Knapp to Editor, *The Churchman*, 23 April 1904, p. 502.

48. Susan Knapp to Randall Davidson, 15 November 1899, Davidson Collection, Lambeth.

49. "The Trustees take occasion to declare their continuous loyalty to the Founder of the School, the Reverend William R. Huntington, . . . and that the policy of this school is founded upon cordial obedience to the law of the Church, and further to declare that while the students in this school are educated for their vocation in the mutual understanding that they intend to make the office and work of a Deaconess their permanent career, they are not required or understood to engage, expressly or tacitly, that if they be set apart for that office they will never marry." New York Training School for Deaconesses Board of Trustees Minutes, 4 April 1914, NYTSFD Collection, DNYA; Knapp herself admitted to Davidson that "to him [Huntington] the deaconess who resigns in order to marry is taking an entirely justifiable step." Knapp to Randall Davidson, 1902, Deaconess History Research Project, EDS.

50. Ibid.

51. The canon also added the phrase "or widowed" to the previous qualification that the woman must be unmarried. General Convention, *Journal*, 1901, pp. 98, 105, 106, 140, 144, 274, 302, 304, 308.

52. L.W. Batten to Editor, *The Churchman*, 2 April 1904; W.S. Rainsford to Editor, ibid., 16 April 1904, p. 471; Susan Trevor Knapp to Editor, ibid., 23 April 1904, p. 502.

53. Arthur C.A. Hall to Editor, ibid.

54. Men were admitted to the diaconate at age twenty-one. The canon on deacons included no provisions as to the marital state of the candidate. It did, however, have definite provisions about the examinations required of all candidates. General Convention, *Journal*, 1904, pp. 29, 35, 70, 230, 241, 256; *Constitution and Canons for the Government of the Protestant Episcopal Church in the United States of American, Adopted in General Conventions, 1789–1904*, pp. 24–31, 60–61.

55. Grace Church, New York City, was one exception to this practice. By 1903 the parish employed seven deaconesses (a number Huntington chose to correspond to the seven deacons in *Acts* 6:3 who were appointed to distribute food and alms to the poor). The Grace Church deaconesses lived together in a home designed especially for them. "Dr. Huntington and the Beginnings of St. Faith's House," pamphlet published by St. Faith's House, April 1918, NYTSFD Collection, DNYA. By 1908 St. George's Church, New York City, employed six deaconesses who also lived in community. Anstice, *St. George's Church*, p. 481. George Hodges, *The Administration of an Institutional Church* (New York: Harper and Brothers, 1906), includes extensive information on the parish deaconesses at St. George's Church. There the deaconesses had essentially the same responsibilities as assistant priests—one deaconess even prepared candidates for confirmation (a function generally reserved for priests). *See also* Elizabeth Moulton, *St. George's Church 1906–1912* (New York, 1964), pp. 96–100; Hopkins, *Rise,* pp. 154–56.

56. Twenty-two deaconesses were at work in New York City parishes by 1900.

Diocese of New York, *Convention Journal*, 1900, p. 20; "List of Deaconesses in Active Service," *The Living Church Annual*, 1920, pp. 180–83.

57. Robert A. Woods and Albert J. Kennedy, *Handbook of Settlements* (New York: Charities Publication Committee, 1911), pp. 11, 278.

58. The uniform evolved gradually. The early Grace Church deaconess wore a simple, dark blue gown and, at the throat, a small silver medal inscribed with her name. She had a long, flowing blue cape for outdoor wear. At St. George's Church, the deaconess had a similar garb but of black rather than blue. Both wore starched white collars and cuffs and dark veils. Photographs taken from 1890 through 1920 portray deaconesses wearing dark dresses or suits, conservatively styled, with white collars and cuffs. Veils were always dark, but often they were edged in white around the face. Every deaconess wore around her neck the cross that had been presented to her during the ceremony at which she was set apart. Unidentified newspaper clipping, NYTSFD Collection, Box #6, DNYA. *See* photographs in *Spirit*, 1890–1920.

NINE: WOMEN AS MISSIONARIES, 1900–1920

1. *Ecumenical Missionary Conference*, 1900,, vol. 1, p. 10.

2. Emery, *Century,* pp. 245–61; Young, *Thankfulness,* pp. 18–19; Kenneth Scott Latourette, *A History of Christianity* (New York: Harper and Row, 1975), vol. 2, pp. 1334–45.

3. Frederic Dan Huntington, quoted in Mary Abbot Twing, "Report of the Honorary Secretary," Board of Missions, *Proceedings,* 1898, p. 291.

4. *See* chapter 6 for analysis of the Board of Missions' budget.

5. *Spirit* 66 (1901):729–30, 766–68.

6. *Spirit* 63 (1898):499, 562–63.

7. Ibid., p. 499.

8. Hester Louisa Clark Shortridge served as president of the Woman's Auxiliary in Tennessee from 1888 to 1920, Elizabeth Hart Colt in Connecticut from 1880 to 1905; Sallie Stuart in Virginia from 1890 to 1916, and Mrs. James Newlands in California from 1893 to 1907. Al W. Jenkins, *The History of the Episcopal Churchwomen of the Diocese of Tennessee* (Bradenton, TN: Manatee County Advertising and Press, 1981), pp. 22–23; Robinson, *Morning,* pp. 1–9; untitled clipping from *The Living Church,* Fall 1916, on Sallie Stuart's death, Diocese of Virginia Archives, Richmond; Edward Lambe Parsons, *The Diocese of California: A Quarter Century* (Austin: The Church Historical Society, 1958), p. 165.

9. *Spirit* 66 (1901):774.

10. Frugal though she was, Julia Emery would telegraph to her brothers and sisters the sum of the United Offering as soon as it was tallied at the Triennial Meeting. Violet Emery and Dorothy Lyford, *Reminiscences,* AEC; *see* Emery's yearly reports in Board of Missions, *Proceedings,* 1900–1916.

11. To get these percentages, I tabulated the number of workers reported by each missionary bishop, omitting native workers and nongender-specific titles, e.g., "teachers." I assumed all clergy listed were men and all nurses were women. I did not include missionary wives unless they were listed as paid workers by the bishop. Board of Missions, *Proceedings,* 1900, 1916. Because of the dislocation in the mission field caused by World War I, I used the 1916 reports rather than those of 1919 as more representative of the general trend.

12. Exact salary figures are difficult to find, for they varied from field to field and from year to year. Nowhere, however, have I found any indication women were

paid the same salaries as men. A 1913 table of salaries and allowances listed the following annual salary figures. Foreign field: Single men, $750–$1,100; single women, $450–$900. Domestic field: Single men $150–1,600; single women, $200–$600. Alaska and the Islands: Single men, $300–1,850; single women $300–$900. "Triennial Report of the Board of Missions Made to General Convention, 1913," *Proceedings*, 1913, p. 23. For a comparison of the salaries of missionary women with those of nonchurch employees in one diocese, *see* Bishop Restarick, "Request for Adjustment of Salaries of Women Workers," in the Original Minutes of the Board of Missions, 13 December 1916, D&FMSC RG39–21, AEC.

13. *The Story of the United Offering*, 1907, United Thank Offering Collection, AEC.

14. Julia Emery, "The Thirty-sixth Annual Report of the Woman's Auxiliary to the Board of Missions," *Proceedings*, 1907, p. 393.

15. Julia Emery, "The Thirty-eighth Annual Report of the Woman's Auxiliary to the Board of Missions," *Proceedings*, 1909, p. 288.

16. Board of Missions, *Proceedings*, 1916, pp. 52, 60, 69.

17. Frances Densmore, "A Minnesota Missionary Journey of 1893," *Minnesota History*, vol. 20, p. 310; George C. Tanner, *Fifty Years of Church Work in the Diocese of Minnesota* (Minneapolis, 1909), pp. 406–8, 515–16; Susan E. Salisbury file, D&FMSC, RG 52–68, AEC; Board of Missions, *Proceedings*, 1916, p. 98.

18. Ibid., p. 108.

19. Eliza Thackara file, D&FMSC, RG 52–75, AEC; *Spirit* 84 (1919):848.

20. Board of Missions, *Proceedings*, 1916, pp. 113, 116–17; Elizabeth C. Barber file, RG 52–2, D&FMSC, AEC.

21. Laura R. Callaway, *Report*, September 1902. D&FMSC, RG 52–13, AEC. Susan Trevor Knapp, "The Rural Deaconess," in Henry Y. Satterlee, ed., *The Calling of the Christian and Christ's Sacrament of Fellowship* (Washington, DC: Church Militant Publishing Company, 1903), pp. 79–81; "A Message from the Mountains," *Spirit* 84 (1919):346; Shilda Burns, "Women Mission Workers in this Diocese [western North Carolina]," *The Highland Churchwoman*, 26 September 1984, p. 14; Dottie Hall has interviewed Deaconesses Mary Sandys Hutton and Virginia Cary about their work in Virginia, Episcopal Women's History Project Collection, General Theological Seminary; Miss Proffe, "Before the Skyline Drive," n.d., typescript, reminiscences in the author's possession; Esther Fox Maxey, "Miss Ora and Miss Etta," 1983, typescript in the author's possession.

22. Laura R. Callaway, *Report*, 1 June 1904; D&FMSC, ECA.

23. Board of Missions, *Proceedings*, 1916, pp. 110, 117.

24. Ibid., p. 111; Ida Whittemore Soule, "Memoir," 30 June 1934, manuscript in the possession of the Reverend George Blackman, Church of Our Saviour, Boston, Massachusetts, p. 396. Ida Soule worked with Deaconess Knight during the summer of 1914 and reported that the deaconess had full charge of the local church, even preached, under special license of the bishop, the Sunday-morning sermon.

25. Board of Missions, *Proceedings*, 1916, pp. 75, 77; *New York Daily News*, 2 July 1979.

26. *Whittaker's Church Almanac*, 1899, pp. 293–326.

27. *See* entry for Elizabeth Ann Rogers and Ellen Albertina Polyblank (Sisters Beatrice and Albertina) in James, *Notable American Women*, vol. 3, pp. 188–89.

28. *See* entries for Ruth Benedict and Grace Abbott, ibid., vol. 1, pp. 2, 128, and entry for Miriam Van Waters, in Sicherman and Green, *Notable American Women: The Modern Period*, p. 709.

29. Strong, *Diary*, vol. 4, p. 497.

30. Emery, *Century*, pp. 434–39; Board of Missions, *Proceedings*, 1900,

pp. 233–39. The missionary districts of the Philippines, Puerto Rico, Alaska, Hawaii, and Panama were designated as domestic rather than foreign missions. They are discussed in this section, however, because the work of the women there was very similar to that in foreign missionary jurisdictions.

31. Ibid., p. 190.

32. "Report of the Committee on Missionary Workers," *Spirit* 60 (1895):542.

33. Board of Mission, *Proceedings,* 1916, pp. 41, 176.

34. William C. Sturgis, "Report to the Presiding Bishop and Council and to the Department of Missions and Church Extension," August 1921, RG79–63, D&FMSC, AEC.

35. Board of Missions, *Proceedings,* 1916, p. 184.

36. Sturgis, "Report," p. 35.

37. Miriam U. Chrisman, *"To Bind Together": A Brief History of the Society of the Companions of the Holy Cross* (Adelynrood, MA: The Society of the Companions of the Holy Cross, 1984), p. 21; Susan Knapp, *Diary,* 1915, pp. 40–49, EDS.

38. Mary L. James to Mr. Parson, 31 July 1924, in file entitled "Women in the Church, Place of Women in the Mission Fields, 1924–1925," D&FMSC, AEC.

39. Ibid., p. 180.

40. Edith Hart to the Rt. Reverend L.L. Roots, 10 June 1914, RG 64–202, D&FMSC, AEC.

41. Mrs. A.T. Twing, "A Missionary Journey Around the World," *The Churchman,* 14 January 1893.

42. Board of Missions, *Proceedings,* 1900, p. 83.

43. Irene P. Mann to Dr. Langford, 12 May 1896, D&FMSC, ECA.

44. Dorothea Carlsen to Susan Knapp, 19 September 1915, Deaconess History Research Project, EDS.

45. Board of Missions, *Proceedings,* 1916, p. 5.

46. Ibid., p. 8.

47. Edith Hart to Dr. Wood, 16 January 1918, RG64–202, D&FMSC, AEC.

48. File entitled "Women in the Church, Place of Women in the Mission Files, 1924–1925," D&FMS Collection, AEC.

49. John W. Wood, "The Power House on Higushi Ishi Ban Cho," *Spirit* 84 (1919):339–43.

50. Charles W. Inglehart, *A Century of Protestant Christianity in Japan* (Rutland, VT: Charles E. Tuttle Company, 1959), pp. 125–26.

51. "Minutes of the Triennial Meeting of the Woman's Auxiliary to the Board of Missions," *Spirit* 81 (1916):828–31; 84 (1919):853; Young, *Thankfulness,* pp. 16–27.

52. "The Triennial Conference," *Spirit* 72 (1907):940.

53. "The Evolution of the Triennial," "The Officers' Conference in Cincinnati," *Spirit* 75 (1910):955–60.

54. "The Triennial in Richmond," *Spirit* 72 (1907):940.

55. *Spirit* 75 (1916):830–31.

56. On the committee, Bishop S.E. Lines of Newark, the Reverend Theodore Sedgwick of New York, and Burton Mansfield of Connecticut represented the Board, whereas the Auxiliary was represented by Elisabeth R. Delafield of New York, Lydia Paige Monteagle of California, Matilda Markoe of Pennsylvania, Cornelia Prime Lowell of Massachusetts, Annie Lewis of Missouri, Cornelia Baxter of Minnesota, Lily Reffin Pettigrew of Atlanta, and Jessie Peabody Butler of Chicago. Ibid., p. 830.

57. The women named above also served on the second committee. Ibid.

58. Julia Emery to Stanley Emery, 19 November 1916; Julia Emery to Bishop Lloyd, 7 April 1916, Emery Collection, AEC.

59. Julia Emery to Stanley Emery, 19 November 1916, AEC.

60. "Forty-sixth Annual Report of the Woman's Auxiliary to the Board of Missions, 1916–1917," Board of Missions, *Proceedings*, 1909, p. 289.

61. Julia Emery, "Thirty-eighth Annual Report of the Woman's Auxiliary to the Board of Missions," Board of Missions, *Proceedings*, 1909, p. 289; *Spirit* 81 (1916):828–34.

62. Grace Lindley herself counted willingness to change as one of Julila Emery's chief virtues. "She was the most progressive, not to say radical, one of us all!" wrote Lindley. Grace Lindley, "Miss Emery in Office," *Spirit* 87 (1922):83–84.

63. W.C. Sturgis complained about "the almost complete absence of laymen" at the 1919 Wellesley Conference. W.C. Sturgis, "Wellesley," Ada Loaring Clark, "Sewanee," Claudia Hunter, "Blue Ridge," *Spirit* 84 (1919):611–13; Grace Lindley, "Forty-sixth Annual Report of the Woman's Auxiliary to the Board of Missions," Board of Missions, *Proceedings*, 1917, pp. 245.

64. Emery, *Century*, pp. 297–99.

TEN: THE SOCIAL GOSPEL

1. Mary Kingsbury (Simkhovitch) led a teenage-girls' club at St. Augustine's Episcopal Church while in college; Mary Willcox (Glenn) began her social-service career as a volunteeer at St. Paul's Chapel and Guild House in Baltimore; Eleanor McMain began her career in social work at the Episcopal-sponsored Free Kindergarten Association. Sicherman and Green, *Notable*, p. 649; James, *Notable*, p. 474; Don Frank Fenn, "Mary Willcox Glenn: 1869–1940," Diocese of Maryland Archives (hereafter cited as DMDA), Maryland Historical Society, Baltimore; Mary Simkhovitch, *Neighborhood: My Story of Greenwich House* (New York: W.W. Norton, 1938), pp. 39–42.

2. Allen F. Davis, *Spearheads for Reform* (New York: Oxford University Press, 1967), pp. 14–16, 262; Robert A. Woods and Albert J. Kennedy, *Handbook on Settlements* (New York: Charities Publication Committee, 1910); Florence Winslow, "The Settlement Work of Grace Church," *Charities Review* 8 (November 1898):418–25.

3. *The Church News of the Diocese of Pennsylvania*, October 1930, pp. 16–17; *Church Training and Deaconess House Newsletter*, July 1920, p. 12; *see* St. Martha's House File, DPA.

4. Lavinia Dock to Paul U. Kellogg, c. 1904, Kellogg Collection, K293 100, Social Welfare History Archives, University of Minnesota, Minneapolis, Minnesota.

5. Miriam U. Chrisman, *To Bind Together: A Brief History of the Society of the Companions of the Holy Cross* (Byfield, MA: Printed by the Society, 1984), pp. 1–5. Emily M. Morgan, *Letters to Her Companions*, edited by Vida Scudder (Byfield, MA: The Society of the Companions of the Holy Cross, 1944), pp. 2–20, 187, 210–14; I am grateful to Ruth S. Leonard, Archivist of the Society, for additional information about its activities.

6. For an example of the way one woman used the Companion's Rule to structure her own spiritual life, *see* Ellen Gates Starr's *Religious Journals*, Starr Papers, Sophia Smith Collection, Smith College Library, Northampton, Massachusetts. Starr left the Society in 1921 when she became a Roman Catholic.

7. Morgan, *Letters*, p. 45.

8. Alice M. Lewitan has compiled a list of nine Companions who were members of Episcopal sisterhoods and nineteen deaconesses who were members of the Society prior to 1920. Ruth Leonard compiled a list of eleven foreign missionaries who were

also Companions during the same period. Archives of the Society of the Companions of the Holy Cross, Adelynrood (hereafter cited as SCHA), Byfield, Massachusetts.

9. Ibid., pp. 115, 141–42, Chrisman, *To Bind*, pp. 5–7; Morgan, *Letters*, p. 181.

10. Chrisman, *To Bind*, pp. 16, 63; Morgan, *Letters*, p. 166.

11. Ibid., pp. 41, 56–57, 150–52.

12. Membership lists, SCHCA. Biographies of all the secular workers are found in one of the four volumes of *Notable American Women*; for Glenn, *see* Frank J. Bruno, *Trends in Social Work, 1874–1956* (New York: Columbia University Press, 1957), p. 22; for Florence Teresa, *see* Simpson and Story, *Stars*, pp. 142–44, 177–78, 214–48; Knapp, Colesberry Carlson, Crosby, and Waterman letters are found in D&FMS Records, AEC; Keyser and Lawrance are found in C.A.I.L. Records, DNYA.

13. Chrisman, *To Bind*, pp. 60, 70; Morgan, *Letters*, p. 178.

14. Emily Morgan, Helen Dudley, Vida Scudder, Ellen Starr, and Florence Converse signed the petition. Ibid., p. 102; Chrisman, *To Bind*, pp. 70–72; Albright, *History*, p. 323.

15. Chrisman, *To Bind*, pp. 71–72; SCHC Secretary's Report, 1907, pp. 4–5, as quoted in Marion B. Rollins, "Statements Compiled from Emily Morgan's *Letters*, Secretary's Reports, and News Leaflets Prepared for the Ad Hoc Committee on Public Corporate Stands," n.d., SCHCA.

16. General Convention, *Journal*, 1913, p. 7.

17. Copies of both reports are on file in SCHCA. *See also* Winifred E. Hulbert, "Seventy-five Years of Progress in Social Justice," 26 August 1959, typescript, SCHCA.

18. Chrisman, *To Bind*, p. 74.

19. SCHC Secretary's Report, 1916, pp. 26–27, and SCHC *News Leaflet*, July 1917, p. 5, quoted in Rollins, "Statements," p. 3; Albright, *History*, pp. 323–24; General Convention, *Journal*, 1916, p. 372. Robert Moats Miller, *American Protestantism and Social Issues, 1919–1939* (Westport, CT: Greenwood Press, 1977), pp. 37–38.

20. SCHC *News Leaflet*, April 1918, p. 8, quoted in Rollins, "Statements," p. 4; Addison, *Episcopal*, pp. 308–9.

21. SCHC, Annual Report, 1919, pp. 21f., quoted in Rollins, "Statements," p. 5; Hopkins, *Rise*, p. 244; Chrisman, *To Bind*, pp. 74–80; Morgan, pp. 181–96. During an earlier discussion on the subject of social activism, Morgan had urged moderation with the following poem:

> What a mighty reformation
> > We should witness through the land
> If the masses and the classes
> > Could be made to understand
> That he wins at least one sinner
> > From dishonesty and pelf
> Who will leave alone his neighbor
> > And just practice on himself.

22. *See* Ruth Huntington Sessions, *Sixty-Odd: A Personal History* (Brattleboro, VT: Stephen Dave Press, 1936); Vida Scudder, *On Journey* (New York: E.P. Dutton & Co., 1917); Burton J. Rowles, *The Lady at Box 99: The Story of Miriam Van Waters* (Greenwich: The Seabury Press, 1962); Emily M. Morgan, *A Book of Social Prayers and Devotions* (New York: Presiding Bishop and Council, 1922); Simkhovitch, *Neighborhood*.

23. Even at age 85, Vida Scudder addressed the annual Conference on Christian Social Thinking at the Episcopal Theological School in Cambridge, Massachusetts. *Notable American Women: The Modern Period,* p. 637. Mary Glenn served as national president of the [Episcopal] Church Mission of Help from 1919 until 1937, resigning at age 68. Bruno, *Trends,* p. 22. Mary Van Kleeck ran the Companions' annual conference in 1942 on "The World We Seek as Christians." Mary Van Kleeck Collection, Sophia Smith Collection, Smith College, Northampton, Massachusetts. At age 67, Mary Simkhovitch urged Church members to involve themselves in the campaign for public housing. Mary Kingsbury Simkhovitch, *The Church and Public Housing* (New York: The National Council, 1934).

ELEVEN: DEFINING MEMBERSHIP RIGHTS FOR WOMEN

1. New York Training School for Deaconesses, *Alumnae Bulletin,* February 1919, p. 5, NYTSFD Collection, DNYA; Viola Young to Susan Knapp, 27 September 1918, Deaconess History Research Project, EDS.
2. Carter was a Massachusetts woman who had trained at the Philadelphia School and then returned to Boston to found a training school for volunteer church workers. She became head deaconess at the Philadelphia school in 1913. Agnes Irwin, "Training School for Church Workers," *The Church Militant,* October 1899, pp. 4–7; *Twenty-third Annual Report of the Church Training and Deaconess House in the Diocese of Pennsylvania* (Philadelphia: William F. Fell Company, 1913), p. 18.
3. New York Training School for Deaconesses, *Alumnae Bulletin,* January 1917, pp. 5–8.
4. Ibid., February 1919, p. 6.
5. *Twenty-sixth Annual Report of the Church Training and Deaconess House in the Diocese of Pennsylvania* (Philadelphia: William F. Fell Company, 1916), pp. 23–24; New York Training School for Deaconesses, *Alumnae Bulletin,* October 1913, pp. 9–10.
6. *Spirit* 81 (1916):829.
7. Board of Missions, *Proceedings,* 1917, p. 248.
8. Ibid., 1919, p. 239; *The Living Church,* 18 October 1919, p. 887.
9. *Spirit* 84 (1919):415.
10. Ibid., pp. 414–16.
11. "Summary of Material Received in Answer to Questionnaire No. 1 Sent Out in 1918 to Diocesan Presidents by the Program Committee for the Triennial of 1919," Woman's Auxiliary Collection, Organization and Officers file, AEC.
12. Arthur Selden Lloyd, *Report of the Board of Missions to the General Convention,* 1919, p. 718; summarizing the opinion of the dioceses on putting women on the Board, Miss Delafield reported thirty-nine dioceses approved, ten disapproved, and six were undecided. *Spirit* 84 (1919):344.
13. Hulbert, "Seventy-five years," p. 10.
14. Morgan, *Letters,* p. 178.
15. Chrisman, *To Bind,* p. 75.
16. Chrisman, *To Bind,* p. 76; SCHC Annual Report, 1919, p. 26, quoted in Rollins, "Statements," p. 10.
17. "The Officers' Conference," *Spirit* 84 (191):271–75.
18. General Convention, *Journal,* 1919, p. 265.
19. *The Living Church,* 18 October 1919, p. 887.
20. Those elected were: Eva Corey, Massachusetts; Elizabeth Delafield, New York; Marcelline C. Adams, Pittsburgh; Ada Loaring Clark, Tennessee; Mrs. Herman

Butler, Chicago; Edith Brent, Colorado; Mrs. John Ames, Kansas; and Mrs. Louis Monteagle, California. Ada Loaring Clark, "Triennial Days in Detroit," *Spirit* 84 (1919):785.

21. Canon 60, Section III, i, *Constitution and Canons for the Government of the Protestant Episcopal Church in the United States of America*, 1919, p. 155.

22. "Report of the Department of Missions and Church Extension for the Year Ending December 31, 1920," *Annual Report of the Presiding Bishop and Council for the Year 1920*, p. 11.

23. There is no mention of Mrs. R.W.B. Elliott in the minutes of the Woman's Auxiliary, the reports of the secretary of the Woman's Auxiliary, or articles about the Woman's Auxiliary in *Spirit* in 1919.

24. Even the 1934 decision did not open the Council to general women's membership; it simply provided that four women might be nominated by the Woman's Auxiliary to represent women on the Council. Council members elected by the General Convention or by the Provinces still could only be laymen or clergy. Frances M. Young, *Thankfulness*, p. 36.

25. Diocesan canons regulated voting rights in parishes and at diocesan conventions. But if women were declared eligible to serve as deputies to the General Convention, one would expect that diocesan canons would be adjusted to meet that reality.

26. General Convention, *Journal*, 1916, p. 321.

27. Evelyn L. Gilmore, *Christ Church, Gardiner, Maine: Antecedents and History* (Gardiner, ME: The Reporter Journal Press, 1893, reproduction by *The Kennebec Journal*, Augusta, Maine, 1962), pp. 102, 125; John Richards, *A Continuation of the Story of Christ Church* (Augusta, ME: *The Kennebec Journal*, 1962), pp. 5–17, 25, 54–59; SCHC Annual Report, 1919, p. 26.

28. Petition to the General Convention of the Protestant Episcopal Church in the United States of America, 1919, General Convention Files, Memorials and Petitions, Record Group 9, Box 4, AEC.

29. Ibid.

30. *See* other petitions, ibid.; J.R.H. Moorman, *A History of the Church in England* (London: Adam and Charles Black, 1953), p. 417.

31. Virginia Shadron, "The Laity Rights Movement, 1906–1918," in Thomas and Keller, *Women in New Worlds*, pp. 261–75; The Methodist Episcopal Church officially recognized women as laypeople in 1906, an action that affirmed the latter's full membership rights. Rosemary Skinner Keller, "Creating a Sphere for Women," ibid., p. 250.

32. Memorial from the Diocese of Pittsburgh, 1919 General Convention Memorials and Petitions, Record Group 9, Box 4, AEC.

33. General Convention, *Journal*, 1919, pp. 80, 348, 346.

34. Those appointed were Bishops William Ford Nichols, Charles Edward Woodcock, and Alfred Harding; Presbyters H.H. Powell, William T. Manning, and Z.B.T. Phillips; and Laymen Philip S. Parker, Warren Kearney, and Mortimer Matthews. Ibid., pp. 210, 454.

35. *The Churchman*, 15 November 1919, p. 10. Women were appointed to another joint commission established at the 1919 convention—that regarding deaconesses.

36. Membership in the Provincial Synod, for example, was changed from "Clerical and Lay Deputies" to "four Presbyters" and "four Laymen." *See* Section IV, Canon 51, 1916 Canons, and Section VI, Canon 53, 1919 Canons. An amendment initiated by the House of Bishops and confirmed by the Deputies inserted the word "male" before "communicant" in Canon 60, Section V, regarding the election of a

vice-president of the Council. The amended version read, "The Council may, in its discretion, elect one of its own member or any male communicant of the Church, whether clercial or lay, to be Vice-President of the Council." 1919 Canons, General Convention, *Journal*, p. 447.

37. 1919 Constitution, Article XI.

38. No comprehensive study has been made of diocesan provisions for women to vote, serve on vestries, or serve as members of diocesan conventions. Edwin Augustine White's survey *American Church Law* (New York, 1898) stated that most dioceses required voters to be "baptized males of full age," but in Lexington, Maine, Indiana, and many of the western dioceses, "the franchise is granted to females as well as to males," p. 140. The New York State Religious Corporations Law was amended in 1915 to allow women the right to vote in parish elections but not to serve on vestries. Meeting in November of that year, the Diocese of New York granted the women the vote "whenever so determined by the Parish." Diocese of New York, *Convention Journal*, 1915, p. 72. An article from *The Woman Citizen*, 9 August 1919, announced that the dioceses of Harrisburg, Washington, Rhode Island, Kansas, and Western New York had voted to give women the franchise. In the House of Bishops of 1919, when Bishop Louis Sanford of San Joaquin asked for the right to allow women to sit in his diocesan convention, "the three bishops of North and South Dakota and Nebraska rose consecutively to say that they had found women sitting in convocation in their districts when they went to their jurisdictions, the latter revealing the fact that women had sat in convocation in Nebraska for twenty-nine years." *The Churchman*, 25 October 1919, p. 21. Though women deputies were elected to the diocesan convention in Arkansas in 1895, the convention refused to seat them. Margaret Simms McDonald, *White Already to Harvest: The Episcopal Church in Arkansas, 1838–1971* (Sewanee: University Press, 1975), p. 453. When women deputies were seated in the convention of the Diocese of Pennsylvania in 1958, an article in *The Sunday Bulletin*, 4 May 1958, stated that Philadelphia had thus become the forty-fourth of the eighty-seven dioceses of the Episcopal Church to admit women to its diocesan convention as deputies.

39. General Convention, *Journal*, 1970, p. 127.

40. Memorial concerning a Joint Commission on the Office of Deaconess, 1919 General Convention Memorials and Petitions, Record Group 9, Box 4, AEC.

41. General Convention, *Journal*, 1919, pp. 138–39, 404, 436.

42. Church Pension Fund Records, Episcopal Church Center, New York City.

43. Arthur Selden Lloyd, "The Church's Mission at Home and Abroad," Address to the General Convention, *Spirit* 84 (1919):718.

TWELVE: THE QUESTION OF MINISTRY

1. Estelle Freedman, "Separatism as Strategy: Female Institution Building and American Feminism, 1870–1930," *Feminist Studies* 5 (Fall 1979):512–29.

2. Board of Missions reports do not include tabulations of the numbers of men and women until 1940. To arrive at these percentages, I counted the number of men and women on the published list of domestic and foreign missionaries. I omitted those workers labeled "native" or "retired." Missionary bishops were included in the total. Presiding Bishop and Council, *Annual Report*, 1920, pp. 257–79; National Council, *Annual Report*, 1930, pp. 251–71; idem., *Annual Report*, 1940, p. 253.

3. Frances M. Young, *What Ever Happened to Good Old "Women's Work"?* (New York: The Episcopal Women's History Project, 1986), p. 6.

4. Anne Bass Fulk, *A Short History of the Triennial Meetings of the Women*

of the Episcopal Church (Little Rock, AR: Democrat Printing and Lithographing Company, 1985), pp. 22–23.

5. Ibid., p. 34.

6. The Reverend Sandra Boyd maintains a current list of the women who have been ordained to the diaconate and to the priesthood.

Selected Bibliography

MANUSCRIPT COLLECTIONS

AEC   Archives of the Episcopal Church, Austin, Texas
AESL   Arthur and Elizabeth Schlesinger Library, Radcliffe College
CSJB   Community of St. John Baptist Archives, Mendham, New Jersey
CSM   Community of St. Mary Archives, Peekskill, New York
CUL   Columbia University Library, New York City
EDS   Episcopal Divinity School, Cambridge, Massachusetts
GTS   General Theological Seminary, New York City
DMA   Diocese of Massachusetts Archives, Boston
DMDA   Diocese of Maryland Archives, Baltimore
DPA   Diocese of Pennsylvania Archives, Philadelphia
DNYA   Diocese of New York Archives, New York City
SCHC   Society of the Companions of the Holy Cross Archives, Byfield, Massachusetts
SSC   Sophia Smith Collection, Smith College, Northampton, Massachusetts
SSM   Society of St. Margaret Archives, Boston

Bishop Potter Memorial House Collection, AEC
Church Association for the Interests of Labor Collection, DNYA
Church Training School and Deaconess House Collection, DPA
Community of St. John Baptist Papers, CSJB
Community of St. Mary Papers, CSM
Davidson, Randall Thomas Papers, Lambeth Palace Library, London
Deaconess History Research Project, EDS
Domestic and Foreign Missionary Society Collection, AEC
Emery Collection, AEC
General Convention Papers, AEC
James, Isabella Batchelder Collection, AESL
New York City Mission Society Collection, DNYA
New York Training School for Deaconesses Collection, DNYA

St. Luke's Hospital Papers, DNYA
Sessions, Ruth Huntington Collection, SSC
Simkhovitch, Mary Kingsbury Collection, AESL
Society of the Companions of the Holy Cross Collection, SCHC
Ellen Gates Starr Collection, SSC
Woman's Auxiliary Collection, AEC

PERIODICALS

Church Work, 1885–1889
Hammer and Pen, 1896–1910
New York Training School for Deaconesses, Alumnae Newsletter, 1890–1920
The Churchman, 1850–1920
The Living Church, 1850–1920
St. Mary's Messenger, 1890–1920
The Spirit of Missions, 1850–1920

EPISCOPAL CHURCH RECORDS

Board of Missions, *Proceedings of the Missionary Council of the Domestic and Foreign Missionary Society of the Protestant Episcopal Church in the United States of America*. 1850–1920. Published annually at Church Missions House. AEC.
Convention Journals. Reports from each parish and the proceedings of the diocesan convention are published annually for each diocese. I used particularly those from the dioceses of California, Colorado, Massachusetts, Minnesota, New York, North Carolina, Pennsylvania, Tennessee, Texas, and Virginia. 1850–1920.
General Convention of the Protestant Episcopal Church. *Journal of the General Convention*. Published triennially, 1850–1919.

ORIGINAL SOURCES

An Account of St. Luke's Hospital, 1860. New York: Robert Craighead, 1862.
Annual Reports of the Board of Managers for Christ Church Hospital. Philadelphia, 1850–1910. DPA.
Annual Reports of the Home for Respectable Girls. New York, 1880–1920. CUL.
Ayres, Anne. *Evangelical Sisterhoods*. New York: T. Whittaker, 1867.
———. *The Life and Work of William Augustus Muhlenberg*. New York: Thomas Whittaker, 1889.
———. *Practical Thoughts on Sisterhoods*. New York: T. Whittaker, 1864.
———. *Thoughts on Evangelical Sisterhoods*. New York: T. Whittaker, 1862.
Board of Council for the Bishop Potter Memorial House for Deaconesses, "Minute Book, 1878–1891." DPA.
Chronicle of the Church of the Church of the Holy Communion, 1901. GTS.
The Church Almanac, 1850–1870. New York: The Protestant Episcopal Tract Society.
The Church Home Society, *The Challenge of a Heritage*. Boston: Thomas Todd Company, 1955. DMA.

Community of St. John Baptist. *Diary, 1874–1926*. CSJB.

Community of St. Mary. *Mount Saint Gabriel Series: Historical Papers*. Peekskill: St. Mary's Convent, 1931.

Community of St. Mary. *The Sisterhood of St. Mary, Its Life and Work*. Peekskill: Convent of St. Mary, 1941.

Daggett, Mrs. L.H. *Historical Sketches of Woman's Missionary Societies in America and England*. Boston, 1879.

Deaconesses in the Church of England. London: Griffith and Farren, 1880.

Dix, Morgan. *Harriet Starr Cannon*. New York: Longmans, Green and Company, 1896.

———. *Instructions on the Religious Life Given to the Sisters of Saint Mary*. New York: Community of St. Mary, 1909.

———. *Lectures on the Two Estates: That of the Wedded in the Lord and that of the Single for the Kingdom of Heaven's Sake*. New York: Pott, Young and Cox, 1872.

Douglas, George William. *Essays in Appreciation*. Norwood, MA: The Plimpton Press, 1912.

"Dr. Huntington and the Beginning of St. Faith's House." Pamphlet published by St. Faith's House, April 1918. NYTSFD Collection, DNYA.

Dyer, Herman. *Records of an Active Life*. New York: Thomas Whittaker, 1886.

Ecumenical Missionary Conference. 2 vols. New York: American Tract Society, 1900.

Emery, Dorothy. *The Reminiscences of Dorothy Emery*. 1980. AEC.

Emery, John. "From the Forecastle to the Pulpit: The Story of Fifteen Years of Unusual Preparation for a Ministry and of Forty Years in the One Diocese of California." n.d. Diocese of California Archives, San Francisco.

Emery, Julia. *Alexander Viets Griswold and the Eastern Diocese*. Hartford, CT: Church Missions Publishing Company, n.d.

———. "Annual Report of Woman's Auxiliary to the Board of Missions of the Protestant Episcopal Church in the United States of America," Board of Missions, *Proceedings, 1877–1916*.

———. *A Century of Endeavor, 1821–1921*. New York: The Department of Missions, 1921.

———. *John Henry Hobart*. Hartford, CT: Church Missions Publishing Company, 1921.

———. *The Woman's Auxiliary to the Board of Missions: A Handbook for the Use of Its Members*. New York, 1914. AEC.

Emery, Mary Abbot. "Annual Report of the Woman's Auxiliary to the Board of Missions of the Protestant Episcopal Church in the United States of America," Board of Missions, *Proceedings, 1872–1876*.

Emery, Violet. *The Reminiscences of Violet Emery*. 1980. AEC.

The Form of Admitting Deaconesses to Their Office According to the Use of the Diocese of Long Island, 1872. GTS.

Grace Church [New York]. *Yearbooks, 1880–1920*.

Grafton, Charles C. *A Journey Godward*. Milwaukee: The Young Churchman, 1910.

Hodges, George, and John Reichert. *The Administration of an Institutional Church: A Detailed Account of the Operation of St. George's Parish in the City of New York*. New York: Harper and Brothers, 1906.

Howe, M.A. DeWolfe. *Memoirs of the Life and Services of the Right Reverend Alonzo Potter*. Philadelphia: J.B. Lippincott and Company, 1871.

———. *Memorial of William Welsh*. Reading, PA: Owen Printer, 1878.

History of the St. Luke's School for Nurses. New York, 1938.

"History of the New York Training School for Deaconesses," untitled typescript, n.a. Box #20, NYTSFD Collection, DNYA.

Huntington, Arria S. *Memoir and Letters of Frederic Dan Huntington.* Boston: Houghton Mifflin and Company, 1906.

Klepser, Mary, "History of St. Barnabas House." 1963. File #57, DNYA.

Knapp, Susan T. "Characteristics Most Necessary for Deaconesses," Typescript, n.d. Deaconess Collection, AEC.

———. "Deaconesses: Their Qualification and Status," Pan-Anglican Congress, *Official Report.* London: Society for Promoting Christian Knowledge, 1908.

———. "Diary, 1915–1916." Deaconess History Research Project, EDS.

———. "The Relation of Social Service to Christianity," in *The Church Congress Journal.* New York: Thomas Whittaker, 1913.

The Living Church Annual, 1899–1920.

Ludlow, John Malcolm Forbes. *Women's Work in the Church: Historic Notes on Deaconesses and Sisterhoods.* London: Alexander Strahan, 1865.

The Ministry of Women. London: Society for Promoting Christian Knowledge, 1919.

Minutes of the Board of the New York Training School for Deaconesses, 1891–1920. NYTSFD Collection, DNYA.

Minutes of the Freedmen's Aid Commission of the Domestic and Foreign Missionary Society Executive Committee, 1865–1878. D&FMS Records, AEC.

Minutes of the Episcopal Female Tract Society of Philadelphia. 4 vols., 1849–1921. DPA.

Montgomery, Helen Barrett. *Western Women in Eastern Lands: An Outline of Fifty Years of Women's Work in Foreign Missions.* New York: Macmillan, 1910.

Muhlenberg, William A. *Two Letters on Protestant Sisterhoods.* New York: Hobart Press, 1852.

New York Protestant Episcopal City Mission Society Minutes, 1831–1869. DNYA.

New York Training School for Deaconesses, *Yearbook,* 1892–1919. NYTSFD Collection, DNYA.

Panton, Ethel, and Dorothy Batho. *The Order of Deaconesses, Past and Present.* London: Student Christian Movement Press, 1937.

Rainsford, William S. *A Preacher's Story of His Work.* New York: The Outlook Company, 1904.

———. *The Story of a Varied Life: An Autobiography.* Garden City: Doubleday, Page and Company, 1922.

Register of the Community of St. John Baptist, 1874–1920. CSJB.

The Reports Made to the Convention of the Diocese of Pennsylvania on Organizing the Services of Christian Women and on the Sunday School System. Philadelphia: J.S. McCall, 1863.

Robinson, Cecilia. *The Ministry of Deaconesses.* London: Methune & Company, 1898.

Roche, Scott. *Forty Years of Parish Life and Work, 1883–1923.* New York: Friebele Press, 1930.

St. Barnabas House Register, DNYA.

St. Bartholomew's Episcopal Church [New York City]. *Yearbook.* 1900–1920.

St. George's Episcopal Church [New York City]. *Yearbook.* 1900–1920

St. Thomas' Episcopal Church [New York City]. *Yearbook.* 1900–1920.

Scudder, Vida. *The Church and the Hour.* New York: E.P. Dutton and Company, 1917.

Shepard, Charles N. "The New York Training School for Deaconesses, 1890–1942." 8 December 1943. NYTSFD Collection, DNYA.

Shinn, George Wolfe. *King's Handbook of Notable Episcopal Churches in the United States.* Boston: Moses King Company, 1889.
Simkhovitch, Mary Kingsbury. *The Church and Public Housing.* New York: The National Council, 1934.
———. "The Settlement's Relation to Religion," *Annals of the American Academy of Political Science* 30 (1907):490–95.
Sisterhood of the Good Shepherd. *Annual Reports, 1870–1887.* CUL.
The Society of the Royal Law, pamphlet #1. Church Work Reprints, n.d. Emery Collection, AEC.
Soule, Ida Whittemore. "Memoir." 1932. Typescript in the possession of the Reverend George Blackman, Church of Our Saviour, Boston, Massachusetts.
Starr, Ellen Gates. *Settlements and the Church's Duty.* 1896. Publications of the Church Social Union, #28.
Trinity Church, New York City. *Yearbook,* 1874–1920.
Twing, Mrs. A.T. *Triennial Reports of the Honorary Secretary of the Woman's Auxiliary to the Board of Missions,* 1886–1901. Board of Missions, *Proceedings.*
———. *Twice Around the World.* New York: James Pott & Company, 1898.
———. *The Woman's Auxiliary to the Board of Missions.* New York: Church Missions House, n.d. Pamphlets #1–6, in Woman's Auxiliary File, DNYA.
Welsh, William. *Correspondence between Bishop Potter and William Welsh.* Philadelphia, 1861.
———. *Lay Cooperation in St. Mark's Church, Frankford.* Philadelphia: King and Baird, 1861.
———. *Lay Cooperation: Women Helpers in the Church.* Philadelphia: J.B. Lippincott and Company, 1872.
———. *Woman's Mission in the Christian Church.* Philadelphia: King & Baird, 1864.
Wheeler, Henry. *Deaconesses Ancient and Modern.* New York: Hunt and Eaton, 1889.

SECONDARY SOURCES

Abell, Aron I. *The Urban Impact on American Protestantism, 1865–1900.* Cambridge, MA: Harvard University Press, 1943.
Albright, Raymond W. *A History of the Protestant Episcopal Church.* New York: The Macmillan Company, 1964.
All Saints Sisters of the Poor. *As Possessing All Things.* Catonsville, MD, 1972.
Allchin, A.M. *The Silent Rebellion: Anglican Communities, 1845–1900.* London: Student Christian Movement Press, 1958.
An American Cloister: An Account of the Life and Work of the Order of the Holy Cross. West Park, N.Y.: Holy Cross, 1917.
Anson, Peter. *The Call of the Cloister* London: Society for the Propagation of Christ's Kingdom, 1955.
Anstice, Henry. *History of St. George's Church in the City of New York, 1752–1911.* New York: Harper and Brothers, 1911.
Barnds, William Joseph. *The Episcopal Church in Nebraska.* Omaha: Omaha Printing Company, 1960.
Barry, J.G.H. *From a Convent Tower.* New York: Edwin S. Gorham, 1919.
Beaver, R. Pierce. *All Loves Excelling: American Protestant Women in World Mission.* Grand Rapids: Eerdmans, 1968.

Bellamy, V. Nelle. "Participation of Women in the Public Life of the Church from Lambeth Conference, 1867–1978." *The Historical Magazine of the Protestant Episcopal Church* 51 (1982):81–98.

Berg, Barbara J. *The Remembered Gate: Origins of American Feminism.* New York: Oxford University Press, 1978.

Blair, Karen J. *The Clubwoman as Feminist: True Womanhood Redefined, 1868–1914.* New York: Holmes and Meier Publishers, 1980.

Booty, John E. *The Church in History.* New York: The Seabury Press, 1979.

Boylan, Anne M. "Evangelical Womanhood in the Nineteenth Century: The Role of Women in Sunday Schools." *Feminist Studies* 4 (October 1978):62–80.

Breck, Allen du Pont. *The Episcopal Church in Colorado, 1860–1963.* Denver: Big Mountain Press, 1963.

Brent, Charles H. *A Master Builder: Henry Yates Saterlee, First Bishop of Washington.* New York: Longmans Green & Company, 1916.

Brereton, Virginia Lieson. "Preparing Women for the Lord's Work." In *Women in New Worlds,* edited by Hilah F. Thomas and Rosemary Skinner Keller, pp. 178–99. Nashville: Abingdon, 1981.

Brewer, Clifton Hartwell. *A History of Religious Education in the Episcopal Church to 1835.* New Haven: Yale University Press, 1924.

Burt, Nathaniel. *First Families: The Making of an American Aristocracy.* Boston: Little, Brown and Company, 1970.

Carter, Noreen. "Entering the Sanctuary: The Struggle for Priesthood in Contemporary Episcopalian and Roman Catholic Experience." In *Women of Spirit,* edited by Rosemary Reuther and Eleanor McLaughlin, pp. 356–72. New York: Simon and Schuster, 1979.

Catherine Louise, S.S.M. *The House of My Pilgrimage.* Glenside, PA: Littlepage Press, 1973.

Chitty, Arthur Ben. "Women and Black Education: Three Profiles." *Historical Magazine of the Protestant Episcopal Church* 52 (June 1983):153–65.

Chrisman, Miriam U. *"To Bind Together": A Brief History of the Society of the Companions of the Holy Cross.* Byfield, MA: The Society of the Companions of the Holy Cross, 1984.

Cleveland, Grace Elizabeth. *Mother Eva Mary, C.T.* Milwaukee, WI: Morehouse Publishing Company, 1929.

Costin, Lela B. *Two Sisters for Social Justice: A Biography of Grace and Edith Abbott.* Urbana: University of Illinois Press, 1983.

Cott, Nancy. *The Bonds of Womanhood: "Woman's Sphere" in New England, 1780–1835.* New Haven: Yale University Press, 1977.

Cross, Robert D. *The Church and the City, 1865–1910.* Indianapolis: Bobbs-Merrill Company, 1967.

Davis, John H. *St. Mary's Cathedral.* Memphis: Chapter of St. Mary's Cathedral, 1958.

Davis, John W. *Dominion in the Sea.* Hempstead, NY: The Georgin Foundation, 1977.

DeMille, George. *The Catholic Movement in the American Episcopal Church.* Philadelphia: The Church Historical Society, 1941.

———. *A History of the Diocese of Albany, 1704–1923.* Philadelphia: The Church Historical Society, 1946.

Densmore, Frances. "A Missionary Journey of 1893." *Minnesota History,* vol. 20, pp. 310–13.

Dock, Lavinia L., and Isabel M. Stewart. *A Short History of Nursing.* New York: G.P. Putnam's Sons, 1938.

Douglas, Ann. *The Feminization of American Culture.* New York: Knopf, 1977.

Dunn, Mary Maples. "Saints and Sisters: Congregational and Quaker Women in the Early Colonial Period." In *Women in American Religion,* edited by Janet Wilson James. Philadelphia: University of Pennsylvania Press, 1980.

Edelblute, Lucius A. *The History of the Church of the Holy Apostles.* New York: Printed by author, 1949.

Entrikin, Isabelle Webb. *Sarah Josepha Hale and Godey's Lady's Book.* Philadelphia: University of Pennsylvania, 1946.

Falls, Helen Emery. "Baptist Women in Missions Support in the Nineteenth Century." *Baptist History and Heritage* 12 (January 1977):26–36.

Fishburn, Janet. *The Fatherhood of God and the Victorian Family.* Philadelphia: Fortress Press, 1981.

Flexner, Eleanor. *Century of Struggle: The Woman's Rights Movement in the United States.* 1959. Reprint. New York: Atheneum, 1973.

Frederick, Peter J. "Vida Dutton Scudder: The Professor as Social Activist." *New England Quarterly,* September 1970.

Freedman, Estelle. "Separatism as Strategy: Female Institution Building and American Feminism, 1870–1930." *Feminist Studies* 5 (Fall 1979):512–29.

Galpin, William Freeman. *The Huntington Years.* Boonville, NY: Willard Press, 1968.

Gilmore, Evelyn L. *Christ Church, Gardiner, Maine: Antecedents and History.* Augusta: The Kennebec Journal, 1962.

Griffen, Clyde C. "Rich Laymen and Early Social Christianity." *Church History* 36 (1967):45–65.

Handy, Robert T., ed. *The Social Gospel in America.* New York: Oxford University Press, 1966.

Harris, Barbara J. *Beyond Her Sphere: Women and the Professions in American History.* Westport, CT: Greenwood Press, 1978.

Hewitt, Emily, and Suzanne Hiatt. *Women Priests: Yes or No?* New York: Seabury, 1973.

Hill, Patricia R. *The World Their Household: The American Woman's Foreign Mission Movement and Cultural Transformation, 1870–1920.* Ann Arbor: University of Michigan Press, 1985.

Hodges, George. *Henry Codman Potter, Seventh Bishop of New York.* New York: The Macmillan Company, 1915.

Holifield, E. Brooks. *The Gentlemen Theologians: American Theology in Southern Culture, 1795–1860.* Durham: Duke University Press, 1978.

Hoover, Theressa. *With Unveiled Face: Centennial Reflections on Women and Men in the Community of the Church.* New York: Women's Division, General Board of Global Ministries, The United Methodist Church, 1983.

Hopkins, Charles H. *The Rise of the Social Gospel in American Protestantism.* New Haven: Yale University Press, 1940.

Huyck, Heather. "To Celebrate a Whole Priesthood: The History of Women's Ordination in the Episcopal Church." Ph.D. diss., University of Minnesota, 1981.

Johnston, Mary Elizabeth. *Across a Stage: The Extra Clap.* Oberlin: Oberlin College, 1982.

Jones, Jacqueline. *Soldiers of Light and Love: Northern Teachers and Georgia Blacks, 1865–1873.* Chapel Hill: The University of North Carolina Press, 1980.

Kelley, Barbara. "The Revival of Deaconesses on Long Island," May 1978. Unpublished term paper in possession of the author.

Kenneally, James J. "Eve, Mary, and the Historians: American Catholicism and

220 *A Different Call*

Women." In *Women in American Religion*, edited by Janet Wilson James, pp. 191–206. Philadelphia: University of Pennsylvania Press, 1980.

Kerber, Linda. *Women of the Republic: Intellect and Ideology in Revolutionary America*. Chapel Hill: The University of North Carolina Press, 1980.

Keyser, Harriette A. *Bishop Potter: The People's Friend*. New York: Thomas Whittaker, 1910.

Kolmer, A.S.C., Sister Elizabeth. "Catholic Women Religious and Women's History: A Survey of the Literature." In *Women in American Religion*, edited by Janet Wilson James, pp. 127–40. Philadelphia: University of Pennsylvania Press, 1980.

La Fontaine, Charles V. "Sisters in Peril: A Challenge to Protestant Episcopal-Roman Catholic Concord, 1909–1918." *New York History*, vol. 58, pp. 440–69.

Lerner, Gerda. "The Political Activities of Antislavery Women." In *The Majority Finds Its Past: Placing Women in History*. New York, 1979.

Lindsley, James Elliott. *This Planted Vine: A Narrative History of the Episcopal Diocese of New York*. New York: Harper and Row, 1984.

Lubove, Roy. *The Professional Altruist: The Emergence of Social Work as a Career, 1880–1930*. Cambridge: Harvard University Press, 1965.

Lutz, Alma. *Crusade for Freedom: Women in the Antislavery Movement*. Boston: Beacon Press, 1968.

McBeth, Harry Leon. "The Role of Women in Southern Baptist History." *Baptist History and Heritage* 12 (January 1977):3–25.

McLeod, Hugh. *Class and Religion in the Late Victorian City*. Hamden, CT: Archon Books, 1974.

Malone, Henry Thompson. *The Episcopal Church in Georgia, 1733–1957*. Atlanta: The Protestant Episcopal Church, 1960.

Manross, W.W. *History of the American Episcopal Church*. New York, 1950.

May, Henry F. *Protestant Churches and Industrial America*. New York: Octagon Books, 1963.

Melder, Keith. *Beginnings of Sisterhood: The American Woman's Rights Movement, 1800–1850*. New York: Schocken Books, 1977.

———. "Ladies Bountiful: Organized Women's Benevolence in Early 19th Century America." *New York History* 3 (July 1967):231–53.

Melville, Annabelle M. *Elizabeth Bayley Seton, 1774–1821*. New York, 1951.

Miller, James Arthur. *Apostle of China: Samuel Isaac Joseph Schereschewsky, 1831–1906*. New York: Morehouse Publishing Company, 1937.

Miller, Robert Moats. *American Protestantism and Social Issues, 1919–1939*. Westport, CT: Greenwood Press. Reprint of University of North Carolina Press edition, 1958.

Miller, Spencer, and Joseph F. Fletcher. *The Church and Industry*. New York, 1930.

Morgan, Emily M. *Letters to Her Companions*. Edited by Vida Scudder. South Byfield, MA: The Society of the Companions of the Holy Cross, 1944.

Morgan, William Manning. *Trinity Protestant Episcopal Church, Galveston, Texas, 1841–1953*. Galveston: The Anson Jones Press, 1954.

Moulton, Elizabeth. *St. George's Church, 1906–1912*. New York, 1964.

Oates, Mary J. "Organized Voluntarism: The Catholic Sisters in Massachusetts, 1870–1940." In *Women in American Religion*, edited by Janet Wilson James, pp. 141–71. Philadelphia: University of Pennsylvania Press, 1980.

Perkins, J. Newton. *History of the Parish of the Incarnation, 1852–1912*. Poughkeepsie: Frank B. Howard Press, 1912.

Peters, John Punnett, ed. *Annals of St. Michael's, 1807–1907*. New York: G.P. Putnam's Sons, 1907.

The Poor Clares of Reparation and Adoration. *Religious Commmunities in the American Episcopal Church and in the Anglican Church in Canada.* West Park, NY: Holy Cross Press, 1945.

Porter, H. Boone, Jr. *Sister Anne: Pioneer in Women's Work.* New York: The National Council, 1960.

Potter, Henry Codman. *Sisterhoods and Deaconesses at Home and Abroad.* New York: E.P. Dutton & Company, 1873.

Prelinger, Catherine M., and Rosemary S. Keller. "The Function of Female Bonding." In *Women in New Worlds,* edited by Rosemary Skinner Keller, Louise L. Queen, and Hilah F. Thomas, vol. 2, pp. 318–38. Nashville, TN: Abington Press, 1981.

Roberts, George B. "Christ Church Hospital." *Historical Magazine of the Protestant Episcopal Church* 45 (1976):89–102.

Rothman, Sheila M. *Woman's Proper Place: A History of Changing Ideals and Practices, 1870 to Present.* New York: Basic Books, 1978.

Rowell, T. Geoffrey. *The Vision Glorious.* New York: Oxford University Press, 1983.

Rowles, Burton J. *The Lady at Box 99: The Story of Miriam Van Waters.* Greenwich: The Seabury Press, 1962.

Ruether, Rosemary, and Eleanor McLaughlin. *Women of Spirit: Female Leadership in the Jewish and Christian Traditions.* New York: Simon and Schuster, 1979.

Ryan, Mary P. *Cradle of the Middle Class: The Family in Oneida County, New York, 1790–1865.* New York: Cambridge University Press, 1981.

Sartori, Shirley. "Conflict and Institutional Change: The Ordination of Women in the Episcopal Church." Ph.D. diss., State University of New York at Albany, 1978.

Sellew, Gladys, and Sister M. Ethelreda Ebel, O.S.F. *A History of Nursing.* St. Louis: C.V. Mosby Company, 1955.

Sesssions, Ruth Huntington. *Sixty Odd: A Personal History.* Brattleboro, VT: Stephen Dave Press, 1936.

Silliman, Charles A. *The Episcopal Church in Delaware.* Diocese of Delaware, 1982.

Simpson, James B., and Edward M. Storey. *Stars in His Crown: A Centennial History of the Community of St. John Baptist.* Sea Bright, NJ: Ploughshare Press, 1976.

Skardon, Alvin. *Church Leader in the Cities: William Augustus Muhlenberg.* Philadelphia: University of Pennsylvania Press, 1971.

Sklar, Kathryn Kish. *Catharine Beecher.* New Haven: Yale University Press, 1973.

Smith-Rosenberg, Carroll. "The Female World of Love and Ritual: Relations between Women in Nineteenth Century America." In *Women's Experience in America,* edited by Esther Katz and Anita Rapone. New Brunswick: Transaction Books, 1980.

Sneve, Virginia Driving Hawk. *That They May Have Life.* New York: Seabury Press, 1977.

Sockman, Ralph W. *The Revival of the Conventual Life in the Church of England in the Nineteenth Century.* New York: W.D. Gray Press, 1917.

Stewart, William Rhinelander. *Grace Church and Old New York.* New York: E.P. Dutton and Company, 1924.

Straw, Thelma. "An Analysis of the American Religious Sisterhoods." Master's thesis, Middle Tennessee State College, 1983.

Suter, John Wallace, ed. *Life and Letters of William Reed Huntington.* New York: The Century Company, 1925.

Thomas, Albert Sidney. *A Historical Account of the Protestant Episcopal Church in South Carolina, 1820–1957.* Columbia: The R.L. Bryan Company, 1957.

Tomes, Margaret A. *Julia Chester Emery.* New York: The Woman's Auxiliary to the National Council, 1924.

Verdesi, Elizabeth Howell. *In But Still Out: Women in the Church.* Philadelphia: The Westminster Press, 1976.

Welter, Barbara. "The Cult of True Womanhood." *American Quarterly* 18 (Summer 1966):151–74.

———. "The Feminization of American Religion: 1800–1860." In *Dimity Convictions.* Athens: Ohio University Press, 1976.

———. "She Hath Done What She Could: Protestant Women's Missionary Careers in Nineteenth-Century America." *American Quarterly* 30 (1978):624–38.

White, Joyce. "Putting Together the Puzzle." In *Cultivating Our Roots,* edited by Sandra Hughes Boyd. Cincinnati: The Episcopal Women's History Project, 1984.

White, Ronald C., Jr., and C. Howard Hopkins. *The Social Gospel.* Philadelphia: Temple University Press, 1966.

Wiebe, Robert H. *The Search for Order, 1877–1920.* New York: Hill and Wang, 1967.

Williams, Thomas J. "The Beginnings of Anglican Sisterhoods." *Historical Magazine of the Protestant Episcopal Church* 16 (1947):350–72.

Wilson, James Grant, ed. *The Centennial History of the Protestant Episcopal Church in the Diocese of New York, 1785–1885.* New York: D. Appleton and Company, 1886.

Woodham-Smith, Cecil. *Florence Nightingale.* New York: McGraw-Hill, 1951.

Young, Frances M. *Thankfulness Unites: The History of the United Thank Offering.* Cincinnati, OH: Forward Movement Publications, 1979.

Young, Gertrude S. *William Joshua Cleveland, 1845–1910.*

Index